Media, culture and the environment

A volume in the series
Communications, Media and Culture
George F. Custen, series editor

Series board
Larry Gross, University of Pennsylvania
Ellen Seiter, University of California, San Diego
Virginia Wright Wexman, University of Illinois, Chicago

Media, culture and the environment

Alison Anderson
University of Plymouth

Rutgers University Press
New Brunswick, New Jersey

First published in Great Britain 1997
by UCL Press
UCL Press Ltd
1 Gunpowder Square
London EC4A 3DE
The name of University College London (UCL) is a registered trade mark
used by UCL Press with the consent of the owner.

First published in the United States 1997
by Rutgers University Press
New Brunswick, New Jersey

Library of Congress Cataloging-in-Publication Data

Anderson, Alison, 1965–
    Media, culture and the environment / Alison Anderson
    p.   cm. -- (Communications, media and culture)
    Includes bibliographical references and index
    ISBN 0-8135-2394-X (alk. paper). -- ISBN 0-8135-2395-8 (pbk.:
alk. paper)
    1. Environmental risk assessment. 2. Natural disasters -
Environmental aspects. 3. Oil spills --Environmental aspects.
4. Mass media -- Political aspects. 5. Communication in human
geography. 6. Lobbying. 7. Pressure groups. I. Title. II. Series.
GE145.A53   1997
363.7 -- dc21   96-39287
                                                                    CIP

Printed and bound in Great Britain.

Contents

CONTENTS

Acknowledgements

A number of people have contributed in various ways to this book. I would particularly like to thank Alan Hutchison whose enthusiasm for sociology inspired me to study the subject further, and Justin Vaughan (now at Open University Press) for seeing the project through its initial stages.

Philip Schlesinger, Jacquie Burgess, John Corner and Peter Golding have in different ways played a role in shaping the contents of this book, which originally began life as a PhD thesis. I am grateful to my supervisor, Philip Schlesinger, for his critical comments on earlier drafts of work in progress. I would also like to thank two reviewers of the manuscript who made some valuable suggestions. My colleagues Lyn Bryant, Tim May (now at Durham University), Tony Spybey (now at Staffordshire University) and Malcolm Williams provided much appreciated encouragement and advice. Also I would like to thank the University of Plymouth for providing me with a semester's partial sabbatical to write up some of the material, and to my editor Caroline Wintersgill and staff at UCL Press.

I would particularly like to thank my partner, Peter, for his support throughout the writing process. He gave up a generous amount of his time to read final drafts of the book, while at the same time studying for a demanding part-time course. I would also like to thank my parents, along with Andy, Jenny and Mike, for their constant support and encouragement.

Finally, last but not least, thanks are due to the interviewees, many of whom gave up a considerable amount of their time, and the staff of the British Newspaper Library for their assistance in accessing archive material.

Interviews conducted between 1993–4 formed a part of the ESRC project, 'Mass media and global environmental learning' (L320253059). All reasonable steps have been taken to trace the copyright holders but if there are any omissions please contact the publishers.

I would like to thank the following for their kind permission to use copyright material:

Sage Publications for Figure 1.1, p. 24, 'A typology of media effects', reprinted from D. McQuail 1991, *Mass communication theory*, London: Sage, p. 258; and Table 2.1, p. 50, 'Four types of news bias', reprinted from D. McQuail 1992, *Media performance*, London: Sage, p.193.

Open University Press for Table 2.2, p. 57, 'A comparison of newspapers, television and radio formats' in R. V. Ericson, P. M. Baranek, J. B. Chan 1991, *Representing order*, Buckingham: Open University Press, p.22.

Blackwell Publishers for Table 3.1, p. 78, 'New and old social movements' in L. Martell 1994, *Ecology and society*, Cambridge: Polity, p.112; and Figures 6.1, p. 184, 'Estimates of possible sea-level rises' and 6.2, p. 185, 'Distribution of New Zealand consumption of ozone depleting substances' in A. Bell 1991, *The language of news media*, Oxford: Blackwell, p. 244 & p. 241.

Robert Worcester for Table 3.2, p. 93, 'Actions taken to protect the environment', R. Worcester 1994, 'Societal values, behaviour and attitudes in relation to the human dimensions of global environmental change', August, XVith IPSA World Conference, Berlin.

Solo Syndication for Figures 5.1 & 5.2, *Mail on Sunday*, 28 August 1988.

Greenpeace for Figure 3.2, p. 90, 'Nuclear free seas', copyright Greenpeace/Morgan.

The Detroit News for Figure 6.4, p. 194, cartoon by Larry Wright, *Detroit News*, 8 April, 1979.

Addison-Wesley Longman for Figure 6.3, p. 193, 'Circuit of communication' from D. Punter (ed.) 1986, *Introduction to contemporary cultural studies*, Essex: Longman, p.284.

Introduction

Over recent decades the environment has become a key area of international debate. At various points in time different environmental issues have come to the fore of public and political attention. In this book I argue that to some extent this reflects the activities of issue sponsors such as politicians, scientists and environmental pressure groups, as well as news media agendas. We currently face a number of pressing problems concerning the global environment, yet this is an area that involves making complex choices about a number of interconnecting issues that are often characterized by a great deal of scientific uncertainty. In my view the study of risk and the environment deserves to occupy a central place within media and cultural studies since the news media play a crucial role in framing this contested terrain. As I will explain, the speeding up of time and shrinking of space through modern communication systems has contributed to major transformations in the way we view nature. This book is based upon a critical examination of the news-making literature, and my own research conducted with claims-makers and reporters covering environmental affairs from the late 1980s to the mid 1990s.

Environmental issues

There are a number of global environmental issues that I think warrant serious attention from media sociologists as well as others in related disciplines. Of all the current environmental issues we face, perhaps global warming gives the greatest cause for concern since predicted rises in sea levels, as a result of the warming of the earth's atmosphere, could potentially have devastating effects for low-lying areas of the world. The so-called "greenhouse effect" is thought to be mainly caused by emissions of carbon dioxide (CO_2) from the burning of fossil fuels such as coal and oil, and from vehicles. In addition to this the burning of the world's forests heightens the problem since this releases large quantities of CO_2 into the atmosphere and, at the same time, less carbon dioxide is removed if there is less photosynthesis occurring. Greenhouse gases also include: methane; nitrous oxide; ozone; CFCs (chlorofluorocarbon gases released into the air from, among other things, aerosol cans) and water vapour. The build up of carbon dioxide gases is thought to act like the glass of a greenhouse, allowing the sun's rays to penetrate but not letting them escape, thus resulting in the warming of the earth's atmosphere.

The depletion of the ozone layer has also been the subject of considerable debate since Joe Farman's discovery of a "hole" in the early 1980s. In particular, concerns have been raised about the believed link between the rise in skin cancers, cataracts of the eye, a weakening of immune systems, and the greater amounts of ultraviolet radiation from the sun reaching the earth. The production of CFCs is thought to be the major cause of the thinning of the ozone layer and a number of steps have already been taken to phase out their use.

Air pollution is another major area of concern. Exhaust emissions, together with a cocktail of industrial pollutants released into the air, are believed to pose acute problems in countries such as Poland, the Czech Republic, former East Germany and Mexico. The inhabitants of Mexico City, for example, are said to be exposed to the equivalent of smoking 40 cigarettes a day. In addition to smogs, acid rain is believed to have serious consequences. Acid rain derives from the burning of fossil fuels from power stations, factories and motor vehicles. It can have far-reaching effects upon other countries damaging buildings and forests, and affecting water quality in lakes and rivers.

Alongside this, nuclear issues remain a key area of international concern. Major nuclear disasters such as Three Mile Island (in the USA, 1979) and Chernobyl (in the Ukraine, 1986) have undoubtedly contributed to a lack of public trust in the authorities. More recently, the news that France had decided to resume nuclear testing in the South Pacific sparked off widespread condemnation in September 1995.

Another set of issues surround the whole question of waste disposal and spillages at sea. In the summer of 1995 plans by Shell/Royal Dutch, the multinational petrol giant, to sink the Brent Spar oil platform in the Atlantic, sparked off a major controversy. A series of oil spillages since the late 1960s undoubtedly played a part in bringing issues concerning the pollution of the sea to the fore. These include: the *Torrey Canyon* (1967), the *Amoco Cadiz* (1978), the *Exxon Valdez* (1989) and the *Sea Empress* (1996). Photographs of wildlife enmeshed in oil make for vivid images of the trail of destruction often left behind.

Conservation and animal welfare issues are also important areas to consider. Broadly, this concerns the impact of modern industry and technology on land use, wildlife habitats and attitudes towards animals; although conservation and animal welfare principles may often conflict. The destruction of tropical forests and the extinction of animal and plant species are major areas of concern. Also, the treatment of animals as simply another resource to "exploit" is attracting significant criticism in some parts of the world.

Last, but by no means least, there are a range of issues surrounding food production, population and wider questions relating to the distribution of the world's resources. In the rich Northern hemisphere, concerns are periodically voiced about intensive agriculture and the use of pesticides and nitrates. At particular points in time major anxieties have surfaced in Europe and the USA concerning, for example, salmonella in eggs and, more recently, bovine spongyform encephalopathy (BSE). At the same time, less developed countries suffer from acute problems of famine, overpopulation and disease. Furthermore, highly dangerous toxic wastes are often dumped upon these countries, which are highly economically dependent upon advanced industrial societies.

Ecology and social theory

This book grew out of a personal interest in the role of the news media in the cultural politics of the environment. In this book I interweave two distinct areas of research, namely those studies that focus upon the "environment" and those that seek to address the production, transmission and negotiation of news discourse. It will be of interest not just to those studying sociology or media/cultural studies, but to students of human geography and environmental studies. Social theorists of the environment have concentrated almost exclusively upon the social and economic spheres and have tended to neglect the cultural sphere (Beck et al. 1994). It is within the increasingly pervasive cultural arena (incorporating media, education and science) that ideologies compete for ascendancy. In this book, then, I seek to take a new departure through underscoring the role of the news media.

Studies of representations of the environment in human geography have tended to concentrate upon what may be loosely termed "high culture": the representation of landscapes and the city in literature and art (for example, Renne-Short 1991, Simmons 1993). Until recently, however, geographers and environmental scientists have paid relatively little attention to the mass media. Burgess, for example, noted that: "Just in terms of the sheer numbers of people who consume different media products in everyday life, the general inattention given to the media by geographers is surprising" (1990a: 140). This tendency to compartmentalize these particular facets of social life has, I argue, limited our understanding of the complex ways in which perceptions of the environment are produced and consumed. Moreover, I think it has important implications for other areas of social life where rigid disciplinary boundaries conceal the ways in which social, environmental and political factors interconnect.

The environment has for some considerable time occupied a position on the margins of sociological debate (Newby 1991). By and large sociologists have tended to treat socio-economic structures and processes as though they are divorced from the natural world. The environment is more often associated with the natural than the social sciences. In my view this goes some way towards explaining sociology's silence on these issues, and its failure to engage critically with the debates. However, this way of thinking is deeply rooted in the historical development of the discipline and the movement away from attempts to model the study of human behaviour upon the natural sciences. Perhaps one of the most convincing explanations is that this general reluctance stems from a desire to break away from biological determinism (Martell 1994).

The central focus of the founders of the discipline of sociology was the social organization of industrial capitalism. Their analysis of the social order tended to be based upon certain taken for granted assumptions about the relationship between society and nature (Macnaghten & Urry 1995). The social and the natural were seen as distinct spheres governed by different temporal mechanisms. Nature was abstracted and separated from society. Throughout the history of

Western thought there have been competing models of the relationship between humans and nature. Some have depicted nature as a state of chaos. The seventeenth century philosopher Thomas Hobbes viewed the natural human condition prior to the emergence of civilized society as nasty, brutish and short. By contrast, his contemporary John Locke thought that nature was a state of humanitarian bliss; "natural laws" must form the basis of a just society (ibid.). Thus, to some extent, "nature", or our relationship with the physical environment, is socially constructed. "Nature" is culturally and historically constructed since our perceptions are inextricably bound up with particular models of society that are dominant at any one period in time.

However, this view of nature as socially and culturally constructed is a relatively recent development. At the beginning of the twentieth century the division between the "natural" sciences and the "social" sciences reflected the thinking of the time that saw them as two distinct areas of study. Clearly the rigid boundaries that divide social science disciplines further compartmentalized our understanding of the social world. Yet in recent years a growing body of literature has emerged that sees ecological debates as central to developments in social and political theory (for example, Beck 1992, Dickens 1992, Martell 1994, Redclift & Benton 1994, Yearley 1991). Martell (1994), for example, calls for sociologists to pay greater attention to the effects of social activity on non-humans and the natural environment. His perspective constitutes a radical break with traditional approaches for he develops a position that acknowledges the objective character of environmental problems, while also recognizing that the environment is mediated by social processes. As I explain later, I think a realist approach to these issues moves the debate forward.

Environmentalism and the news media

The needless exploitation of the natural world has been going on for centuries, yet at certain points in time particular issues come to be defined as mainstays of public concern – rainforests; live animal exports; animal experimentation for cosmetics; the pollution of the sea. These issues tend to have particular "carrying capacities"; they become icons or symbols for a wider range of concerns that people can easily identify with. Campaigns surrounding such issues become a sort of symbolic gesture of responsibility. Often they are promoted by popular folk heroes including pop music idols or film stars such as Sting (rainforests), Bob Geldof (development issues) or Bridgette Bardot (live animal exports). Modern systems of communication demand that campaigns must be 'media friendly', attuned to the news values of vast profit-making organizations.

The furore over the Brent Spar oil rig in June 1995 provides a useful example. During the summer of 1995 Greenpeace protests against the intended sinking of the Brent Spar oil platform in the Atlantic by Shell/Royal Dutch, the multinational petrol giant, sparked off a major controversy. Greenpeace action against plans to sink the platform into the sea became a major media stunt. Europe-wide boycotts of Shell petrol garages were encouraged as Greenpeace, together with the German Green Party, mobilized citizen protest. While the German, Dutch and several Scandinavian governments supported Green-peace's case, the British Prime Minister found himself culturally isolated in strongly defending Shell's stance.

In an about-turn on 20 June 1995 Shell bowed to international pres-sure and announced that they had: "decided to abandon deepwater disposal and seek from the UK a licence for onshore disposal". This had all the ingredients of an archetypal morality play; David pitted against Goliath. Yet the dumping of toxic waste is going on around the world all the time without generating very much media interest. What made the Brent Spar case special was a skilful public relations campaign mounted by Greenpeace together with a set of concerns that resonated with deeply held cultural beliefs concerning the ethics of polluting the sea.

Though Shell reversed their decision to dump the platform at sea they continued to maintain that deep-sea disposal was the "best prac-tical option". As we will see in Chapter 4, this dramatic about-turn attracted considerable attention from the news media. However, Shell's announcement was followed in September by an admission from Greenpeace that their estimate concerning the amount of oil on the platform had been inaccurate. Following this some commentators argued that broadcasters had been too ready to accept video news releases supplied by the pressure group, and had failed to report the affair in an "objective" manner (see Pearce 1996). In some cases, Greenpeace's acknowledgement of their inaccurate estimates was taken as an apology for the whole of their case.

In my view, some news editors did not apply sufficient critical judgement to the news releases supplied by the pressure group. Yet Greenpeace was very much constrained by the news media in terms of the way the issues were framed. As we will see in Chapter 4, environmental reporting tends to thrive on dramatic "events" involving "goodies" and "baddies". I think it is too simplistic to view the Brent Spar affair as simply a case of moral outrage versus hard science. Both cases involved value-judgements about the desirability of various courses of action. The decision whether to dispose of the oil platform at sea or on land involves social, ethical and aesthetic considerations, as well as scientific, technical and economic factors.

Clearly different criteria were being used to weigh up whether the oil platform should be disposed at sea. I think Shell failed to recognize the extent of public feeling (particularly in Germany) about the disposal of waste at sea, and neglected the broader cultural context in which environmental risks are framed. Several commentators, notably the German sociologist, Ulrich Beck, have highlighted an increased consciousness of risk in contemporary society. As I explain in Chapter 4, socio-cultural processes impact upon how societies select and deal with risks. Research suggests that lay perceptions of risk tend to incorporate intuitive judgements about the relative trustworthiness of institutions regarding risk-management (see Cutter 1993). Furthermore, Shell's bureaucratic culture meant public relations output tended to be slow and largely reactive. The company's approach also displayed a lack of openness and willingness to engage in wide consultation.

There are some striking parallels between the Brent Spar battle and the Greenpeace campaign concerning dying seals, discussed in detail in Chapter 5. Here again, Greenpeace enjoyed a considerable amount of media attention. During the summer of 1988 it was discovered that a major virus was affecting large numbers of common seals off the coast of Denmark, Sweden and the UK. Greenpeace was quick to seize upon this and define it as a political issue. The outbreak of disease received widespread coverage from tabloid newspapers in the UK. One newspaper, the *Daily Mail*, turned the story into a long-running "Save our seals" campaign. Clearly images of innocent, wide-eyed seals were powerfully symbolic of an environment under threat.

Unlike the Dutch virologists, who generally refused to offer any speculations about the cause of the virus until their findings were published, Greenpeace was willing to offer speculations to the press. Greenpeace maintained that the evidence suggested pollution was a factor in the seal deaths. Much of the coverage in the tabloid press supported this view, despite there being a great amount of scientific uncertainty as to the precise cause of the virus. The Dutch scientists' suspicious attitude towards the media, particularly tabloid newspapers, meant that Greenpeace was able to act as a principal "gate-keeper" in the early "definition" period. As with the Brent Spar affair, some commentators accused the news media of bias.

In drawing upon these two high profile campaigns I do not wish to imply that they are necessarily representative of environmental reporting in general. It seems to me, however, that they do enrich our understanding of the relationship between news processes, claims-making and the wider cultural context. In particular, they illustrate the role of modern systems of communication in the transformation of meanings concerning the natural environment.

Cultural, spatial and temporal contexts

In this section I want briefly to draw out some broader themes within social and communications theory illustrated by the Brent Spar affair and the campaign over dying seals. Over recent years we can identify three major "turns" in academic discourse with an increasing emphasis upon the cultural, the spatial and the temporal. First of all I want to consider the movement towards focusing upon the cultural sphere. I will then go on to explore ways in which this relates to debates about space and time.

Culture

Over the last few decades there has been a significant revival of interest in "culture". The term, "culture", is rather a vague term and difficult to define. As Taylor & Whittier note: "although culture has become a core concept in the field of sociology, its definition and impact remain the subject of considerable controversy" (1995: 163). Culture has variously been defined as incorporating values and norms, ideology, subjective states, ritual and discourse. Since the late 1980s a major "cultural turn" has radically influenced the whole spectrum of social science disciplines in the UK (see, for example, Gray & McGuigan 1993, Hall & Neitz 1993).

8

Both the Brent Spar battle and the "Save our seals" campaign illustrate the ways in which environmental initiatives often tune into deeply held cultural beliefs. In the chapters that follow I argue that particular issues that attract attention tend to be mediagenic, and often possess a powerful symbolic resonance. In the case study of the seal virus I suggest the image of the dying seal became an icon not only for the pollution of the oceans but, more broadly, for an environment in crisis. Also, in Chapter 6, I underscore the importance of local culture in framing public understandings of environmental issues. Local knowledge is often drawn upon by lay audiences in making sense of environmental issues. Though the news media undoubtedly play a significant role in shaping attitudes and behaviour, audience research suggests we may take on different subjectivities in interpreting media texts. Our responses may be contradictory, including a range of competing subjectivities (see for example, Morley 1986, Billig 1991). Also, our readings of media texts are framed by our pre-existing attitudes and social class background, ethnicity and gender.

I think the recent controversy concerning the Brent Spar highlights the increased pressure for industry to take consumer habits and ethics, values and responsibility very seriously. In Chapter 3 I argue that a new-style politics is emerging that operates outside the formal structures of power. The new consciousness-raising movements that arose in the 1980s are characterized by an emphasis upon lifestyle politics, and the absence of a fixed leadership or hierarchical structure.

Finally, I think these cases of environmental reporting raise important questions about the relationship of journalists to their news sources, such as government, industry, scientists or environmental groups. In this book I develop a culturalist position that views news production as the outcome not merely of ownership and control of the media, or of journalistic routines and rituals, but also of the relationship between the news media, news sources and the wider institutional arena. Put simply, there are a number of potential news sources competing with one another to secure favourable media access. These news sources possess differing amounts of economic power and "cultural capital" that influence their perceived legitimacy. By "cultural capital" I mean the differing cultural competences, skills and assets possessed by news sources. A large body of research has established that official sources, such as government departments, tend to enjoy privileged access to the news media in a number of institutional fields (see Anderson 1993b). Official sources are here defined as news sources that operate as organs of the state. Non-official sources include pressure groups or vox pops who are not a part of the institutional structures of the state. As we will see in Chapter 2, categorizing news sources as "official" or "non-official" is often problematic as some organizations straddle the two. Nevertheless, the influence on UK journalism resulting from a "green" speech by the former British Prime Minister, Mrs Thatcher, in September 1988, illustrates the close links between the political domain and structures of news-gathering. However in writing this book I was particularly interested to explore the relationship between environmental non-governmental organizations and the news media. As non-official sources, they are generally seen as facing many more difficulties in attracting sustained media attention. Traditionally, little attention has been devoted to this area in news production research so the subject matter of this book is timely.

The analysis of source–media relations brings to the fore a number of key questions that connect with issues of ideology and power. Ideology and structures of power are a major preoccupation of cultural studies. This draws upon the European culturalist tradition in critical theory and is particularly associated with the work of Stuart Hall and John Thompson. This tradition owes much to the influence of the French Marxist philosopher, Louis Althusser. In a famous article Althusser (1971) argued that "ideological state apparatuses" including the media, the education system, religion and the family, reproduce the dominant ideology in capitalist society. Culturalists, however, have tended to reject an overly deterministic notion of ideological persuasion. Gramsci's concept of "hegemony" has been particularly influential in attempting to explain the role of ideology in modern culture. According to Hall (1977: 332),

> . . . "hegemony" exists when a ruling class (or, rather, an alliance of ruling class fractions, a "historical bloc"), is able not only to coerce a subordinate class to conform to its interests, but exerts a "total social authority" over those classes and the social formation as a whole. "Hegemony" is in operation when the dominant class fractions not only dominate but *direct* – lead: when they not only possess the power to coerce but actively organise so as to command and win the assent of the subordinated classes to their continuing sway. "Hegemony" thus depends on a combination of force and consent. [original emphasis]

Consent, therefore, is gained through some accommodation of oppositional practices so that dominant social groups maintain their social, cultural and political power. Gramsci's more subtle theorization solves some of the difficulties with Althusser's rather mechanical view of the operation of ideological state apparatuses.

The fact that many environmental groups have become key players in the policy-making process reflects the increasing institutionalization of environmental demands. This is one means by which those in power may seek to contain environmental concerns within established boundaries. Also, I think it is important not to judge the success of a campaign simply by the amount of media coverage generated; this may serve to accommodate issues and fail to result in any change of policy.

Space, place and temporality

Greenpeace's sophisticated media strategy during the Brent Spar affair was based around dramatic news footage, beamed via satellite to television stations around Europe. Globalization has opened up the possibility of gazing at several different environments. These images may be directly consumed or mediated through communications technology. One increasingly important way in which people develop a sense of place and identity is through the local, national and global media (see Burgess 1985, Massey 1993). The shrinking of space in globalized society has produced a greater awareness of the interconnectivity of places and of the intricate links between issues (see Gregory 1994, Gregory et al. 1994). Greenpeace managed skilfully to communicate their message across borders to people in a variety of cultural contexts.

Although Shell failed to meet this challenge, there is a growing environmental promotion industry that is concerned with managing our consumption of the environment. According to Alex Wilson (1992: 12),

Our experience of the natural world – whether touring the Canadian Rockies, watching an animal show on TV, or working in our own gardens – is always mediated. It is always shaped by rhetorical constructs like photography, industry, advertising, and aesthetics, as well as by institutions like religion, tourism, and education.

11

In his seminal book, *The culture of nature*, Wilson analyzes the way in which the North American landscape is represented through ideological constructs. He is right to observe that "nature" is bound up with "culture" (see also Sopher 1995). Since the late 1970s corporate initiatives promoting industry as environmentally responsible have grown. Undoubtedly, these mask an attempt to contain environmentalism through adopting green credentials. This has introduced what Wilson describes as an: "environment of promotion and speech about nature, its management, its protection, its fragility, its sacredness, its marketability" (1992: 86).

Increasingly, particular cultural symbols are manipulated to exploit our experience of the "natural world". The growth industry of "nature tourism" is based around spectacles like the Taj Mahal in India, or theme parks such as Disneyland. In a seminal study entitled *Consuming places*, John Urry looks at the way in which we visually consume places through tourism and travel, changing perceptions of the natural and built environment. Urry rightly argues that few social theories have adequately explained the nature of place because they have failed to engage with the complex interrelationships between time, space, nature and consumption. Much of the problem, he suggests, stems from an unsatisfactory specification of the relations between society, and time and space. Time, for example, is often discussed in relation to social change as though temporality only takes on significance when large-scale transition occurs.

Global communication systems make possible a shrinking of time as well as space. During the Brent Spar battle Greenpeace supplied video news releases to news organizations in a form that accorded with their tight timescales and demands for newsworthy material. As societies become more complex and develop higher levels of communications systems they are able to achieve a greater transcendence of time and space through telephones, television, VCRs and the internet. Often this is referred to as "time–space distanciation" (see Giddens 1991). Time and space have become, in the words of the Marxist geographer David Harvey,"compressed". As Harvey (1989) suggests, this may be seen in terms of the capitalist age; in particular the mechanisms governing the accumulation and circulation of capital.

The campaigns surrounding the Brent Spar and the dying seals illustrate the differing timescales employed by scientists, news organizations and environmental groups. Many environmental issues are extremely complex and involve long-drawn-out processes. By contrast, as we shall see in Chapter 4, news organizations revolve around very tight daily schedules. In particular, news bulletins tend to be very short, and summarizing complex material without distortion can pose a major problem. In some cases a major conflict may arise between scientists' lengthy research cycles and the 24-hour cycle that dominates news organizations. Moreover, complex risk assessments possess little intrinsic newsworthiness when contrasted with dramatic footage of Greenpeace stunts, or photographs of seals.

Social constructionism

I have spent some time discussing these shifts in thinking since they underpin the argument I develop in this book. Although I have treated culture, spatiality and temporality separately they are all interlinked in various ways. Environmental discourse is influenced by a combination of spatial, temporal and cultural factors. News sources and the news media, it will become apparent, operate in specific cultural, spatial and temporal contexts. In many respects, then, I suggest that news media representations of the environment are socially and culturally constructed. However, I take issue with extreme forms of social constructionism which assert that we cannot make any assumptions about an objective "reality". This suggests that one account of reality is of no more intrinsic value than another. In the case of the Brent Spar or the seals campaign, the charge that some of the claims presented were inaccurate, or served an ideological function, would make no sense.

Constructionism is a relatively new development within the social sciences; it arose in response to some sociologists' concerns about traditional objectivist thinking and has attracted much controversy. We cannot easily generalize about social constructionism because it represents a very loose collection of theoretical approaches. There is a great deal of disagreement over how "constructionism" is defined. Broadly speaking, constructionists reject the realist argument that social phenomena have a "real" independent existence, and emphasize the subjective factors involved in defining problems. In response to major critiques of this position, Best (1989) distinguishes between what he calls "strict constructionists" and a considerably watered down version of social constructionism that is adopted by "contextual constructionists". While "strict constructionists" take the view that researchers cannot make any assumptions about an objective reality, "contextual constructionists" concede that the analysis of claims-making processes inevitably involves making some judgements about objective conditions.

Most of us would concede that there are few problems in establishing the objective "reality" of a tree or a tiger unless we wish to question every assumption we make in the course of everyday life. However, making judgements about the reality of, say, global warming is clearly much more complex since there are many contending viewpoints and vested interests involved. Moreover, journalistic accounts are inevitably selective since they are influenced by, among other things, news values, news formats, editorial and advertising pressure, news sources and personal commitments. Also much reporting of environmental affairs involves simplifying complex scientific and technical information. However, although I believe total objectivity is very difficult to achieve, I argue we should not abandon the concept altogether. Notions of bias and partisanship imply deviation from an objective norm, or from the "truth" of the situation. Objectivity should not be confused with neutrality or value-freedom. An objective account may not necessarily be neutral as it may come down on one particular side rather than another.

Perceptions of reality clearly differ over time and in different cultures. What is considered to be "polluting" in one society may radically differ from another society's beliefs. For example, the nomadic Hima people will not allow women near cattle because they believe women will contaminate them and cause them to die (Douglas & Wildavsky 1982). Also, views of the AIDS virus have varied across time and in different cultures. Of course objectivity is not a static concept; scientific hypotheses are continually open to refinement or refutation. But although I believe values inevitably enter into any description of the social world, that does not rule out the possibility of objectivity. I argue that rather than viewing objectivity in absolute terms it is better to view it in terms of a continuum of degrees of detachment. Yet I think it is also crucial to remember that notions of objectivity and balance are used by media practitioners to legitimate their professional conduct. Their claims and the assumptions on which they are based, like the claims of any other institutional actors, must be laid open to critical scrutiny.

Structure of the book

Chapter 1 considers the role of the news media in environmental pressure politics and centres the environment as a contested discursive terrain. Claims-making about the "environment" is analyzed in relation to social problem claims about crime and deviance, race, and gender. This opens up a wider debate concerning the social organization of the newsroom and Chapter 2 explores the powerful ideologies of objectivity and impartiality. Are media practitioners really impartial and independent? Is objectivity possible?

Chapter 3 examines the current environmental lobby in the context of the rise of new consciousness-raising movements. The discussion includes an evaluation of major explanations for the rise of environmentalism. Chapter 4 looks at how risk and the environment are framed in the news media. How do journalists and broadcasters decide which stories they consider most newsworthy? Is there an underlying consensus about what makes the headlines? And what role do news sources play? Chapter 5 focuses in more detail on the relationship between news sources and the media. It draws upon a case study of claims-making activities surrounding the seal virus already mentioned. Chapter 6 discusses how audiences make sense of mediated messages concerning risk and the environment. Key approaches to the audience are examined, and the notion of the "active" audience is critically assessed. The final chapter concludes by drawing together the themes of the book to restate the role of culture and the mass media in the elaboration of contemporary social problems.

Further reading

Chapter summaries and lists of suggested further reading can be found at the end of each chapter.

Structure of the book

Further reading

Chapter 1

Pressure politics and the news media

Introduction

We live in a society in which mass communication is becoming an increasingly pervasive part of our lives. Everywhere one looks it is hard to escape from the images relayed by the media. With the development of new media technologies such as video, satellite, cable and the internet, the boundaries between nations are to some extent blurring. These new technologies have also profoundly changed political behaviour and the nature of political negotiation. In fact one theorist claims that the mass media: are "so deeply embedded in the [political] system that without them political activity in all its contemporary forms could hardly carry on at all" (Seymour-Ure 1974: 62). Election campaigns in advanced industrial societies, for example, have become highly managed media spectacles. Party image has in many respects come to be perceived as more important than policy content. Personalities have become as important as issues. Party "spin doctors" hold powerful positions.

In the Introduction to this book I argued that global systems of communication have to some degree compressed time and space. In other words movement and communication across space is more fluid. It is now possible, for example, for millions of viewers around the world to view the same live instantaneous broadcast. However, I would not want to exaggerate the extent to which boundaries have dissolved. Time–space compression is experienced differently by various social groupings and it affects places in different ways. Here Doreen Massey's notion of "power-geometry" is useful (Massey 1993). Massey uses the term "power-geometry" to describe how individuals and social groups have different degrees of power and control

17

in relation to communication flows and movements. Politicians and journalists in the wealthy Northern hemisphere, for example, typically have much greater opportunity to turn power to their own advantage compared to poor labourers in the Southern hemisphere. Of course the media form only a part of the processes of globalization, but nevertheless they play a central role in lubricating consumerist ideologies.

Media theory

The media, then, are at the heart of processes of political negotiation. In my view they provide us with the frames with which to assimilate and structure information about a whole range of social problems and issues. Judgements concerning the newsworthiness of items reinforce dominant power relations and perceptions of order (see Ch. 2). Those stories that are selected are likely to resonate with existing stocks of social and cultural "knowledge". And at the same time the news media play a part in shaping future cultural referants (Negrine 1989). Far from the political system being external to the news media, it is deeply bound up with it through a complex web of influences.

Any consideration of the role of the news media in pressure politics hinges upon the issue of media effects. Before moving on to consider how concern over particular social issues is mobilized, I want to look briefly at how mass communications theorists have conceptualized the role of the media in relation to audience effects. The history of media research can be broadly divided into three main periods: the effects tradition, the uses and gratifications paradigm, and critical theory (see McQuail 1991).

The effects tradition

The first major period was between roughly 1900 and 1940. The earliest theories of media effects viewed the audience as highly susceptible to manipulation and propaganda. The European "mass society" tradition was highly critical of moves towards mass education and the development of the press. The theory was not based upon empirical research but anecdotal evidence of the increasing influence of the media in people's lives. Although mass society theory has greatly influenced modern European social and political thought, it was based

18

upon a simplistic view of the audience. Typically people were seen as a homogeneous mass of damp sponges, uniformly soaking up messages from the media. It failed to account for the sheer diversity of interpretations that could be drawn by different subsections of the population.

Modern communications theory can also be traced back to another major influence; that of the "hypodermic model", which became popular in the USA following the emigration of members of the Frankfurt School during the early part of the twentieth century. Again this theory was not grounded in empirical research and it treated the audience as though it was in a social and historical vacuum. The audience was conceived of as essentially passive; the media simply injected messages into the audience like a syringe and individuals responded in a predictable way.

Uses and gratifications

Both mass society theory and the hypodermic model were challenged during the 1940s by the rise of a new commercially oriented approach to the media in the USA. This became known as the "uses and gratifications" approach and dates from approximately 1940 to 1960. In contrast to earlier theories, it was based upon empirical research into the ways in which people use the media. The audience were rightly viewed as active receptors who were selective about the information they received from the media. For example, Katz and Lazarsfeld's (1955) "Two-step flow" model implied that the effects of the media on the audience were limited, while the social and cultural contexts in which communication took place were of great importance. Rather than viewing the audience as a mass of atomized individuals, they recognized that individuals were members of social groups and that responses to the media are mediated through these networks. Thus media were seen as having an indirect rather than a direct influence. However, this paradigm was based upon a liberal pluralist conception of the media in society and overemphasized individual autonomy. The liberal-pluralist position makes a number of basic assumptions. First, it assumes that having a diverse range of newspapers and broadcasting outlets ensures that different points of view can be given adequate representation. However, in my view, the assumption that all interests can be adequately represented has long since ceased to stand up to critical scrutiny. Second, the theory suggests that we have a free press that is not controlled by the state.

Private ownership of newspapers is seen as guaranteeing editorial independence. Third, it maintains that consumers have ultimate sovereignty since they can always switch to another channel or purchase a different newspaper. If a particular point of view is not represented in the press this is seen as reflecting the fact that it does not have enough support among the public. Finally, I think it overplays the extent to which public opinion is formed through a rational process.

In recent years this traditional perspective has come under increasing attack. In particular, it failed to recognize the ideological character of the informational role of the media; that a number of social and political groups are competing with one another to influence media agendas, and some versions of reality privilege the interests of one section of society over another.

Critical theory

Finally, the third major phase of mass communications research dates from the 1960s to the present day. A number of critical approaches to the North American effects tradition have been developed by British and European scholars. These perspectives can be broadly located within the Marxist school of thought although they encompass a very wide range of thinking. Rather than being concerned with the question of effects, up until present times critical research was largely preoccupied with the processes of production and content and with the concept of ideology (Fejes 1984). The critical school of thought attacked the idea that the media have minimal influence. Theorists such as Stuart Hall (1977) and Stanley Cohen (1972) built their models around the premiss that the media play a central role in the reinforcement of ruling-class ideology, although there was disagreement as to the precise nature of the ideological role of the media and their relationship with the wider social structure. Three main strands have emerged within the critical theory of mass communications; the political economy perspective, the structuralist approach and cultural theory (Curran et al. 1982). However, there are a number of different variants on these approaches, and a significant degree of convergence.

First, the political economy perspective suggests that the workings of the media need to be understood in the context of their economic determination. This strand of theory focuses upon ownership and control of the media, and the impact of commercial imperatives. Researchers such as Murdock & Golding (1977) argue that the media produce a false consciousness that legitimates the position and interests of those who own and control the media. Thus studies within this tradition place more emphasis upon the economic structure of the media and production processes, than on ideological content (for example, Garnham 1986, Halloran et al. 1970, Murdock & Golding 1974). The complexity of the exact mechanisms through which economic factors shape media messages is acknowledged. However, this strand of media theory has tended to be primarily concerned with macro structural influences. Until relatively recently, little work has been carried out into micro-relations, such as the relationship between journalists and their sources. As Curran et al. (1982: 20) observe,

> . . . the macro-level at which the "political economy" analysis is conducted leaves some micro-aspects of this relationship unexplored. In particular, questions concerning the interaction between media professionals and their "sources" in political and state institutions appear to be crucial for understanding the production process in the media.

Structuralism forms the second major strand of media theory. This collection of diverse approaches is primarily concerned with forms of media representation and signification, through the analysis of media texts such as newspaper articles, television programmes or photographs (Curran et al. 1982). The concept of ideology is central to structuralism and many studies in this tradition have applied Althusser's concept of ideology to the study of semiotics (cf. Althusser 1965). This approach was most notably associated with Stuart Hall and colleagues, at the Birmingham Centre for Contemporary Cultural Studies, during the 1970s. Clearly, it was a move forward from the idea that media texts mirror reality, but there were tensions between the fusion of the economic determinacy of Marxist theory and linguistic theory concerning the structure of texts. Cultural theory developed, in part, as a response to structuralism's deterministic assumptions and its failure to consider socio-cultural factors.

Finally, in contrast to the above approaches, culturalist studies of the media tend to be more preoccupied with "lived traditions and practices", and with micro-level aspects of news production processes. As its label suggests, the concept of "culture" occupies a key place within this paradigm. This strand of theory views media institutions and cultural practices as bound up in a complex web of interrelationships.

Cultural theorists (for example, Corner 1986, Hoggart 1957, Johnson 1986, Williams 1974) rightly view social phenomena as being determined by much more complex factors than purely the economic infrastructure (cf. Curran et al. 1977). They distinguish between "public" and "private" types of cultural production and consumption and suggest that a variety of different "readings" can be made of texts. For example, Morley (1983: 117) maintains:

> To understand the potential meanings of a given message we need a cultural map of the audience to whom that message is addressed – a map showing the various cultural repertoires and symbolic resources available to differently placed sub-groups within that audience. Such a map will help to show how the social meanings of a message are produced through the interactions of the codes embedded in the text with the codes inhabited by the different sections of the audience.

In a classic study, entitled *Policing the crisis*, Hall et al. (1978) sought to blend a culturalist approach with structuralism. This interesting account of the moral panic over "mugging" explores the mechanisms through which the state attempts to manage the ongoing crises of legitimacy and economic difficulties associated with advanced industrial society. Central to Hall et al.'s approach is the concept of class-biased ideology, or "hegemony". The notion of "hegemony" (associated particularly with the theoretical work of Gramsci) suggests that the news media present us with a very narrow view of the world which upholds the interests of the dominant class. According to this perspective, although differing points of view are given some expression, "establishment" opinions are invested with greater significance. This is seen as an inevitable feature of the news production process rather than resulting from a direct conspiracy between the media and the state. Rather than ideology being forced upon the populace, this view suggests that control is achieved more subtly through gaining the voluntary consent of the subordinate classes.

There is abundant evidence to suggest that journalists are socialized into their own particular newsroom culture where many judgements are taken as "common sense" and rarely questioned. Moreover, as we shall see later on, institutional voices tend to enjoy advantaged access to the media. In contrast, relatively powerless members of the public, or representatives of anti-establishment political organizations, tend

22

to have a much more difficult task in securing favourable coverage on their own terms (Golding & Middleton 1982).

Marxist challenges to the liberal-pluralist concept of power partly led researchers to review the role of the media and to recognize the importance of studying media institutions and the actual processes involved in the production of news (for example, Tunstall 1971, Murdock 1982, Schlesinger 1987). This sort of analysis, which locates the media within the wider context of the political structure, without assuming determinism, is one of the most promising recent developments. Recent approaches have increasingly recognized that the process of manufacturing consensus is complex, and there has been a degree of convergence between liberal-pluralist and Marxist thought (cf. Schlesinger 1990).

Conceptualizing the role of the media

The problem of determining media effects

Despite decades of empirical investigation into media effects little consensus among researchers has been reached about the long-term impact of, for example, television violence on real-life aggression or political campaigns on voting behaviour. McQuail (1991: 251) observes: "The entire study of mass communication is based on the premise that there are effects from the media, yet it seems to be the issue on which there is least certainty and least agreement." In some ways this is relatively surprising since media effects are often taken for granted at a common sense level. However, one of the major problems is that it is difficult, if not impossible, to isolate the role of the media from other major social influences such as the education system, the peer group or religion. I think it is all the more complicated with deeply contested issues that may invoke powerful emotional responses. Also, it makes little sense to generalize about "media effects" when research suggests there are important variations between and within the media.

Much depends upon how "effects" are defined (McQuail 1991). Effects may be short term or long term. They may be temporary or relatively permanent. Effects can be measured in terms of direct behaviour change among individuals. Or media can be said to have affected individuals more subtly through acting as a catalyst. Effects

23

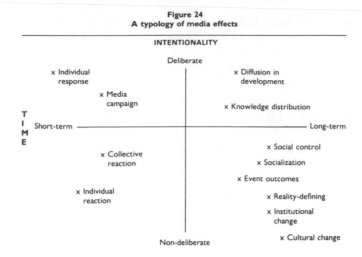

Figure 24
A typology of media effects

INTENTIONALITY

Deliberate

x Individual
response

x Diffusion in
development

x Media
campaign

x Knowledge distribution

T
I   Short-term ———————————————————————— Long-term
M
E

x Social control

x Collective
reaction

x Socialization

x Event outcomes

x Individual
reaction

x Reality-defining

x Institutional
change

Non-deliberate

x Cultural change

Figure 1.1   A typology of media effects. *Source*: McQuail 1991: 258.

may be intended as part of a planned campaign or they may be unintended, resulting from inbuilt biases within the news-making process. Media may reinforce existing attitudes or contribute to new knowledge or opinion. Finally, media may play a part in producing collective hysteria following, for example, food scares over salmonella in eggs or BSE (see Figure 1.1).

Perhaps one of the most striking ways in which the news media exert an individual and collective influence is through "agenda-setting" (see for example Allen & Weber 1983, Benton & Frazier 1976, Gormley 1975). The term "agenda-setting" was first used by McCombs & Shaw (1972) to refer to the process by which issue hierarchies are mediated to the public through election campaigns. From this perspective the news media may not tell us *what* to think, but they present us with a range of issues to think *about*. On any typical week day there is a remarkable amount of consensus among the news media concerning prominent lead items. A number of studies have sought to compare the agenda-setting effects of television with newspapers (for example, Eyal 1981, McClure & Patterson 1976, McCombs 1977).

Early agenda-setting studies tended to assert that there was a simple causal relationship between media agendas and public agendas (see Shaw & McCombs 1977). However, recent studies suggest that the hypothesis needs to be developed in order to take account of the complex interaction between social variables. Because the model is based upon the assumption that the frequency with which an item is mentioned is a reliable indicator of its position in terms of media priorities, it tells us little about the actual content of the messages (Fejes 1984). Furthermore, in focusing upon media agendas, agenda-setting studies have tended to ignore the whole process through which social issues are taken up by the media. As Fejes (1984: 229) observes,

> If agenda-setting is one demonstrable effect of the media, then the next logical question should be what is the process by which the media's agenda is formulated in the first place. This raises issues of the organizational structure of the media, the role of professionalism, the larger structure of control of the media such as ownership, and the media's relationship to other social and political institutions, all of which mainstream research on agenda-setting ignores.

A few studies have, however, attempted to go beyond the traditional agenda-setting approach that assumes a causal link between the media agenda and the public agenda. Lang & Lang (1981) developed the concept of "agenda-building". Drawing upon an analysis of Watergate, the authors focus upon the issue of how social problems originate on the media agenda and how they are subsequently transformed into political issues. They suggest that there is no simple connection between media coverage and public attention; in order for a social problem to become a public issue people must be able to relate it to the wider political context. Also, issues have to compete for space with other objects of media interest. The Langs rightly suggest, then, that the role of the media is primarily to forge links between social issues and the political domain in order for a topic of media or public interest to be transformed into a political issue. The process by which this occurs is a complex one and many different factors are involved. I think a further strength of this approach is that it views the media as sites of competition between news sources and suggests that they pursue distinct strategies towards gaining media attention.

Social problems and the media

Public and political concerns for social issues tend to be cyclical. These agendas do not mirror objective conditions (see Ch. 2). Just because an issue becomes less prominent it does not necessarily mean that the problem has become less severe, or that it has been solved. It may be that it is competing with other issues that are considered more "sexy" or compelling (see Ch. 4). In some cases, power holders in society may be successful in diverting attention away from an issue that threatens their interests. Mass communication research focuses upon the amount of attention media devote to "social problems", and analyzes how they are represented. Much early attention was devoted to investigating the role of television in fostering real-life aggression. As a result of extensive research, mostly conducted in the USA, a variety of political initiatives were instigated and "violence" became "the" dominant interest within the empirical sociology of the media (see Howitt 1982).

Since the 1960s there has been a growing interest in how counter-cultural groups, viewed as representing minority interests or in some way deviant in relation to mainstream society, use the media and in turn are used by the media (McQuail 1992). In particular, the civil rights and women's movements have singled out media for critical attention. The media are frequently viewed as negatively (and some-times positively) influencing awareness of issues concerning crime and deviance, women, and ethnic minorities. George Gerbner's cultivation model suggests that cumulative exposure to particular media messages is likely to encourage the audience to develop a consonant worldview, though the process is considerably more complex than simple cause and effect. He argues:

> Cultivation is what a culture does. That is not simple causation, though culture is the basic medium in which humans live and learn. . . . Cultivation is not the sole (or even frequent) determinant of specific actions, although it may tip a delicate balance, mark the mainstream of common consciousness, and signal a sea-change in the cultural environment. Strictly speaking, cultivation means the specific independent (though not isolated) contribution that a particularly consistent and compelling symbolic stream makes to the complex process of socialization and enculturation. (Gerbner 1990: 249)

This theory has been empirically tested for a range of issues including violence, and racial or sex-role stereotyping (see Signorielli & Morgan 1990). There is a good deal of evidence to suggest that media contribute in various ways to shaping particular cultural climates. Let us briefly consider each of these areas in turn. Since the central preoccupation of this book is with environmental issues, this brief discussion is not intended to form a representative overview of the topics concerned (for a fuller discussion of these issues see Cumberbatch & Howitt 1989, Curran & Gurevitch 1996, Dines & Humez 1995, McQuail 1992).

Deviance and the news media

A very high proportion of all news coverage is taken up with issues of crime and deviance. Frequently riots and juvenile delinquency are said to be stimulated by media reporting; although this is extremely difficult to verify. A large amount of interest has been generated in the representation of deviant subcultures in the news media (for example, Cohen 1972). Such studies demonstrate that the reporting of crime and deviance is highly symbolic and stage-managed. Evidence suggests the news media tend to focus upon violent and sexual crime disproportionate to their occurrence in "real" life (for example, Ericson et al. 1987, 1989, 1991, Goode & Ben-Yehuda 1994, Schlesinger & Tumber 1994). Also, Gerbner's research suggests that those viewers who are heavy consumers of television are much more likely to view society as a basically violent environment. There are, of course, many different explanations that could be offered for this apparent association (see Sparks 1995). It could be, for example, that those who are already predisposed towards viewing society as violent, for example the elderly, are more likely to stay indoors and view large amounts of television. Also, self-reported heavy viewing may not necessarily imply large exposure to content (see Ch. 6). Finally, as Sparks (1995) argues, given the problems involved in assessing media effects, the strength of the cultivation effect is overplayed. Although we must treat the cultivation analysts' claims with caution, we cannot ignore the large body of evidence that suggests the news media play an important role in framing issues.

Women and the news media

Media influence concerning sex-role attitudes has also dominated much recent cultural analysis. The countercultures of the 1960s promoted a greater awareness of issues that bring women together as a disadvantaged group within society. A considerable number of studies have focused upon ways in which women, and to a lesser extent women's rights, are featured in the media (see, for example, Dominick

& Rauch 1971, Fowler 1991, Gunter 1986, Morgan 1982, Thornborrow 1994). Across a range of genres, women tend to be stereotyped in a very limited range of occupational roles. Also, sex stereotyping occurs with the sorts of personality characteristics typically associated with men and women (Gunter 1986). The cultural symbolism employed by the news media has provoked particular criticism. We cannot lay all the blame here since sexism existed long before the mass media were established. However, here again cultivation analysis suggests that there appear to be some significant associations between sex-role attitudes and levels of exposure to the media.

Ethnicity and the news media

Many of the same issues are raised when we look at the relationship of ethnic minorities to mainstream media. Research suggests the news media play a crucial role in the representation of ethnic minorities (see, for example, van Dijk 1988, 1991, Gross 1984, Hall et al. 1978, Hartmann & Husband 1974, Burgess 1985). Much interest has centred around the role of the media in stimulating moral panics around such issues as "mugging". Studies suggest relatively few members of ethnic minority communities believe the media adequately represent their interests (see Howitt 1982). While the majority of ethnic minorities want the mainstream news media to give them sympathetic coverage, some radical groups eschew it and develop their own alternative channels of communication (McQuail 1992). However, undoubtedly there has been a movement towards greater consciousness concerning racial inequality in society as a whole. The extent to which ethnic minorities are dependent upon the media varies according to many factors. Perhaps one of the most important is the extent to which the minority group is culturally distinct or isolated in the "host" society (McQuail 1992).

Cultivation analysis and the environment

With some reservations, then, I think the cultivation approach offers a useful way of analyzing how deviance, race and gender are represented in the media. But how well does it aid our understanding of environmental affairs? As Shanahan (1993) argues, cultivation theory applies rather differently to environmental issues. Instead, we may observe a process of cultivation occurring as a result of what is missing, or relegated to "soft" news. Shanahan (1993: 187) suggests that "cultivation may be possible because of a *lack* of images, or even as a result of having one's attention directed somewhere else" [original emphasis]. Thus what is left off the agenda becomes just as important an object of study as what becomes prioritized. Yet when Shanahan sampled US university student attitudes over time, and related this specifically to news media usage (as opposed to television in general), he found only a weak relationship between heavy exposure and levels of environmental concern. This points to the conclusion that a range of non-media factors must also be taken into account.

Public arenas and issue entrepreneurs

Issue-attention cycles

Why do some issues come to be perceived as "social problems" at a given point in time? From a constructionist point of view a social problem may be said to exist when a significant number of people define it as such, and are sufficiently concerned to do something about it or call for action (Goode & Ben-Yehuda 1994). Levels of public anxiety do not "necessarily" bear much resemblance to the "objective" seriousness of a problem. Public concern about social problems may be measured in a number of different ways through, for example, opinion surveys, participation in protest action, or the letters-to-the-editor pages of newspapers. As Goode & Ben-Yehuda (1994) point out, we cannot generalize about what prompts a major sea-change in levels of public anxiety since this tends to be issue-specific. The careers of social problems, however, are closely associated with political and ideological factors. Various organizations often stand to gain from promoting particular issues as "social problems".

To a large extent success in defining a social issue as a problem is a reflection of the level of resources (time, staff, members, money, media access) an organization commands (McCarthy & Zald 1982, Anderson 1991, Goode & Ben-Yehuda 1994). A major investigation into resource-poor radical interest groups in Boston, and their strategies towards the press, was undertaken by Goldenberg in the early 1970s (Goldenberg 1975). This research suggested that resource-poor organizations tended to experience much greater difficulty in securing access to the news media compared with official sources. The perceived credibility of the organization was found to constitute a major factor, linked to the group's size, finance, geographical location, public relations skills and expertise. However, as Goode & Ben-Yehuda point out, in some cases a social problem is suddenly "discovered" as a result of sensational claims from a charismatic figure in the public domain, who may have had little in the way of resource backing. In some cases the news media may seek out individuals from within a loose movement and invest them with celebrity status, as was the case in the anti-Vietnam War student movement during the 1960s (see Gitlin 1980). That said, the ability of a given news source to gain access to the news media on a long-term basis is closely associated with resource backing.

The relative prominence of a social issue is not in any way a simple reflection of levels of public concern; it is heavily influenced by the activities of issue sponsors such as politicians, or successful interest or pressure groups. Evidence suggests that interest in social issues such as crime, race, gender or ecology goes through a cyclical process of fervent concern and increasing boredom. Downs (1972, 1973) conceptualizes this in terms of an "issue-attention cycle". He argues:

> I believe there is a systematic "issue-attention" cycle in American domestic affairs. This cycle causes certain individual problems to leap into sudden prominence, remain there for a short time, and then gradually fade from public attention – though still largely unresolved. (Downs 1973: 59)

Thus, for a number of reasons, interest in American social issues is transient. Downs argues that there are five main stages in the cycle: (1) the "pre-problem" stage; (2) "alarmed discovery and euphoric enthusiasm"; (3) "realizing the cost of significant progress"; (4) "gradual decline of intense public interest" and (5) the "post-problem" stage. In general, Downs suggests that an issue is likely to fade from media interest if its dramatic/entertainment value decreases, if it no longer affects everyone or if it is not in the interests of the power holders in society and will involve a major upheaval or costs. However, he predicts that environmental issues are unlikely quickly to enter the "post-problem" stage and fade from media attention because of the peculiar nature of environmental issues. That is, environmental problems tend to be more visible and threatening than other social issues; most environmental problems can be solved through technological means; environmentalism encompasses a wide range of causes and overrides political barriers; a small group in society (industry) can be blamed and companies can profit from environmental products/services.

Downs (1973: 69) maintains: "In my opinion it [the environment] has certain characteristics that will protect it from the rapid decline in public interest that has characterized many other recent social issues."

Although interest in environmental issues is subject to fluctuations, if one looks at "broad trends" in public opinion then it appears that Downs was right: concern about the environment has not declined. An underlying latent interest remains, despite periods when economic self-interest takes priority. As McCormick (1989: 65) observes,

> Rather than enter a decline, environmentalism gradually became tempered by a less emotional and more carefully considered response to the problems of the environment. It shifted from euphoria to reason and temporarily became lodged in stage three, where, instead of discouragement in the face of the costs of action (which were often high, but perhaps no higher than the potential costs of inaction), the environment became a central public policy issue.

In my view one difficulty with Downs's analysis is that he tends to assume environmental issues can be lumped together within one category. However, different sorts of environmental issues receive different treatment in the media. While some issues remain simmering and from time to time spark off media attention, others rapidly disappear from attention (see Ch. 2).

Another major weakness of Downs's theory is he fails to take into account the role that news sources play in maintaining interest in social issues. In my view the character and survival of issues on the political agenda is not solely determined by gatekeepers within media organizations; the activities of non-governmental organizations (NGOs) and official bodies play a crucial role in managing the news (Gandy 1980, Lowe & Goyder 1983, Miller 1993, Solesbury 1976). As McCormick (1989: 65–6) argues:

> Downs' model fails to take account of the integration of popular issues with the political fabric of societies. Time and again, such social movements achieve some or all of their intended goals by transforming society; this happened with the civil rights and women's movements, it happened with anti-war movements, and it has happened with environmentalism. By no means have the goals of all of these movements yet been achieved, but in

31

most cases the social reformers successfully scaled the walls and entered the citadel of public policy.

Downs's approach tends to focus rather narrowly upon a limited number of fora, or arenas of influence, namely: the mass media and public agendas. However, we should not ignore other important fora in the elaboration of social problems. In particular, we should not underestimate the role of political institutions, the wider political culture, NGOs and the scientific community in defining the important issues of the day. In an increasingly risk-conscious society, the "expert" tends to dominate in the process of public policy decision-making (Beck 1992). Social actors compete with one another in each of these public arenas in order to make their demands more visible. Moreover, none of these public arenas are discrete units; they encompass a wide range of platforms employing different strategies and aimed at diverse audiences.

Claims-making arenas

The "environment", then, is one of a number of competing issues within the public policy arena. It competes for attention with a range of other issues or problems such as "crime", "economic affairs", "poverty", "unemployment", "health", "race" and "gender". Inevitably politicians, media practitioners and the public are selective in choosing which issues they prioritize. Moreover, those issues that come to gain the highest place on such agendas are not necessarily the most serious or important as measured against objective indicators (see Ch. 2). With the exception of dramatic events like natural disasters or major terrorist incidents, social issues do not ordinarily draw attention to themselves. They rely heavily upon the activities of issue-entrepreneurs or claimsmakers to project them into the public domain. Pressure groups play a vital role in attempting to keep issues on the boil through lobbying government and targeting the news media.

Perhaps one of the best starting places to analyze the role of the media within the wider policy-making framework is Hilgartner & Bosk's (1988) "public arenas model". This model provides a useful account of different spheres that are involved, to varying degrees, in the definition and legitimation of social problems. They include the following fora:

- Mass media arenas (such as television, newspapers, radio and

32

magazines).
- Government arenas (including the executive and legislative branches of government, political parties and the civil service).
- Research community (including natural scientists and social scientists).
- Educational arenas (including schools, colleges and universities).
- Courts and public inquiries.
- Industry.
- Non-governmental organizations (including pressure groups and public bodies).

Hilgartner & Bosk analyze the dynamic environment in which symbols compete for attention and are manipulated in various ways. As they observe, "The fates of potential problems are governed not only by their objective natures but by a highly selective process in which they compete with one another for public attention and societal resources" (1988: 57).

Different arenas have different "carrying capacities" that constrain the number of problems that can receive widespread attention at any one time. In other words they have different organizational procedures, mechanisms and channels that govern information flows and impact on policy-making in different ways. Also, they have their own frames of reference and offer differing levels of access depending upon the organization and issue in question. As a general rule issues only succeed in commanding widespread attention once they have permeated political institutions (Solesbury 1976). Particular assumptions about the ordering of social values are mediated by the journalist from news sources to the audience. These sources play a key role in sifting, selecting and presenting potential news material. However, all sources do not enjoy the same level of access to the news media (Gandy 1982, Goldenberg 1975, Golding & Middleton 1982, Hall et al. 1978, Schlesinger 1990).

Different types of organization tend to place special emphasis on targeting particular arenas. Friends of the Earth, for example, has acquired a reputation for political lobbying and campaigning through using educational arenas, including the research community, in addition of course to targeting the media. Likewise, quasi-official interest groups such as Britain's National Trust tend to place a great deal of importance on using educational and governmental arenas. However, they do not see themselves as a campaigning organization and therefore have a very different relationship with the media than, say,

Friends of the Earth or Greenpeace. Campaigning organizations tend to be much more proactive in their relations with the media because they are concerned with bringing about political change. However one major weakness with Hilgartner & Bosk's analysis concerns their tendency to treat different categories as homogeneous. The media, for example, are viewed as forming one arena (see Cracknell 1993). I would contend that the media comprise a range of arenas governed by their own temporal and social characteristics, audience profiles and ideological positionings. Sunday newspapers, for example, can deal with issues at more length than daily newspapers since they have more time to research their material – though even here there are important differences between the broadsheets and the popular press.

There are a variety of different ways in which one can analyze the role of the news media in pressure politics. Two major approaches have been adopted within the empirical study of pressure politics; the internalist and the externalist approach (Schlesinger 1990). Those who adopt an internalist approach derive their analysis of news sources from interviews with media practitioners, from textual analysis, or a combination of both. An externalist account, on the other hand, involves a detailed examination of the process through which news sources seek to exert influence upon the media from the perspectives of sources themselves. For example this may involve interviews with representatives of pressure groups, government departments or industry, in addition to interviews with journalists and analysis of media texts and official documentation. In some cases it may take the form of reconstructing the role of various issue-entrepreneurs in the news-management of particular cases. I shall restrict my discussion here to a consideration firstly of discourse-analytic approaches and, secondly of source-centred perspectives.

News discourse

Since the mid 1970s discourse analysis has become an increasingly popular form of interdisciplinary qualitative mass communications research. It is used in a wide variety of disciplines including anthropology, sociology, social psychology and linguistics. A discourse-analytic approach has informed recent work in a variety of subject areas such as race (for example, van Dijk 1988, 1991, Burgess 1985), deviance (for example, Ericson et al. 1987, 1989, 1991), gender (for example, Fowler 1991, Thornborrow 1994) and, of course, environmental issues (for example, Bell 1991, Fowler 1991). Discourse analysis focuses upon the way in which meanings are constructed in media texts through language and imagery. There are various different branches of thought that are associated with developments in different disciplines. Thus "critical linguistics" is associated with linguistic theory, "semiotics" with European structuralism and "discursive rhetoric" with social psychology. Over recent years there has been an increasing convergence of semiotic approaches and discourse analysis (Bell 1991). Semiotics is a theoretical approach concerned with the meanings produced by the signs embedded within media texts.

Several theorists have noted how competition is played out between social actors over "symbolic packages" that are framed around particular overarching themes (see, for example, Gamson & Modigliani 1989, Eder 1996). Journalists and news sources are involved in a continual struggle over "'signs" (Ericson et al. 1989, Gans 1980). News sources battle to privilege their version of reality over others. They trade on stocks of cultural mythology through the use of particular codes of expression and ways of reasoning. A number of studies in the North American constructionist tradition suggest media arenas are prime sites where this symbolic contest is played out (Gamson 1992, Gamson & Modigliani 1989, Gamson & Wolfsfeld 1993, Johnston & Klandermans 1995, Kielbowicz & Scherer 1986).

Environmental pressure groups such as Greenpeace have become increasingly adept at providing the media with pre-packaged material that accords with journalists' taken for granted assumptions about what constitutes "news". Nick Gallie, a former publicity director for Greenpeace, once observed:

> Greenpeace has always been inherently fascinating and newsworthy as far as the media are concerned. It presented them with totally pre-packaged, simplistic but very powerful images of confrontation that were very new and exciting. TV journalists saw it as fascinating and bizarre that people were willing to stand in front of whaling harpoons or under a barrel of nuclear waste being dumped at sea. These activities were seen as heroic and they were an absolute gift for the media. They were packaged in such a way that the media – newspapers as well as TV – could swallow them without having to chew. (cited in Porritt & Winner 1988: 94)

The above discussion suggests that the social construction of news must be situated within a wider theory of culture and society. As Szerszynski observes, we need to look at why particular framings of the interrelationship between society and nature resonate with pre-existing belief-systems and attitudes: "If the spread of environmentalism cannot simply be attributed to the presence of environmental reporting in the mass media, but to the interplay between such reporting and existing attitudes, it is the dynamics of such cultural symbols which must be studied" (1991: 18).

A final example concerns the reporting of the 1988 seal virus in the UK national daily press. During the late 1980s large numbers of common seals were found sick and dying from a mystery virus along the coast of Britain. Pictures of dying seals provided the media with a highly visual metaphor for pollution, and the state of the environment more generally. Seals, splashed on the front pages of mid-market newspapers, became icons. Press coverage of the seal virus largely centred on the visual appeal of the animals and news reports and features often used large close-up photographs of seal pups. The story of a mysterious, spreading virus had cultural resonances with fears of the great unknown and fed upon anxieties about risks to human health, anthropomorphism and a moral appeal epitomized by innocent, wide-eyed seals. Also the conflict between orthodox and adversarial science provided the story with a confrontational frame (see Ch. 5).

As Gamson & Modigliani suggest, some symbols have greater potency than others. To a large extent this depends upon how far they connect with widely held values and cultural themes. It also depends upon how well attuned the issue-entrepreneur is to the operational routines of the news media.

In sum, packages succeed in media discourse through a combination of cultural resonances, sponsor activities, and a successful fit with media norms and practices. Public opinion influences this process indirectly through journalists' beliefs, sometimes inaccurate, about what the audience is thinking. (Gamson & Modigliani 1989: 9)

Two particularly well constructed accounts of the role of language in the reporting of environmental affairs are Allan Bell's *The language of news media* (1991), and Roger Fowler's *Language in the news* (1991). These studies combine an analysis of news production with a detailed examination of the way in which language is used to frame particular social issues. The type of language that is used varies depending upon the particular genre in question. Within the news media we may differentiate, for example, between news stories, editorials and features. Also, newspapers or news programmes tend to have their own particular linguistic styles and ideological conventions. These rest upon particular taken-for-granted assumptions about the make-up of the audience. Furthermore, the complexity of many environmental issues often means that the news media routinely turn to official "expert" discourse in order to explain cause and effect relationships (Corner & Richardson 1993).

In my view, the analysis of media discourse can tell us a great deal about the ideological construction of news. For example, it can reveal the ideologically based perspectives of journalists through unveiling the ways in which particular categories are given prominence and the ways in which news reports are structured (van Dijk 1988). However, like any methodological approach, discourse analysis suffers from a number of drawbacks. Unless detailed examination of media texts is combined with audience reception analysis we cannot make any inferences about the ways in which members of the audience may interpret messages (Livingstone 1990). Also, although inferences can be made about narratives of the same type, thus extending the implications of a particular case study, we cannot generalize beyond this to other forms of narrative. Finally, however revealing such analyses of media content may be, they do not tell us anything about how agendas are formulated in the first place. As Gandy (1982: 210) argues: "To focus solely on the content of the media is to 'assume' complete hegemonic control, and is to ignore the fact that ideology changes in response to objective historical conditions." Recently, however, there has been growing recognition of the need to supplement a media-based assessment of source activity with observational analysis, or interviews with source representatives themselves, in order fully to assess their success or failure in influencing agendas.

Source strategies

News sources play a crucial role in the news-making process yet we still know relatively little about their operational strategies and organizational constraints. Most of the research in this field has concentrated upon media organizations rather than source organizations and their perspectives. Indeed, Schlesinger (1990: 62) observes:

> Once one begins to analyse the tactics and strategies pursued by sources seeking media attention, to ask about their perceptions of other, competing, actors in the fields over which they are trying to exert influence, to enquire about the financial resources at their disposal and the organizational contexts in which they operate, to ask about their goals and notions of effectiveness, one rapidly discovers how ignorant we are about such matters – and this despite the undoubted importance of the contribution that production studies have made to the field.

Environmental NGOs adopt a multitude of roles depending upon the type of organization they represent, the political context and the character of the issues they want to expose. Campaigning organizations are set apart from other groups by their direct involvement in pressure politics; they aim to bring pressure on government in order to bring about political change.

The evolution of the environmental lobby must be located within the wider context of the movement towards increased professionalism and political activism among pressure groups in general. Since the 1960s there has been a significant increase in organized lobbying in the UK with the emergence of several single-issue pressure groups such as the Child Poverty Action Group (CPAG), Shelter, Friends of the Earth and Greenpeace. According to Des Wilson (1984: 16), the single-issue protest groups of the 1960s were: "seen to be pioneering fresh approaches, in particular by combining detailed negotiation with Whitehall and Westminster with exploitation of the media to force politicians and civil servants to take them seriously".

Perhaps one of the best well known is the Child Poverty Action Group (CPAG), which was established in the mid 1960s. As the organization was unable to make its demands heard through the policy-making community it was forced, under its second director, Frank Field, to develop a high profile media strategy. According to McCarthy (1986: 136),

. . . the necessity for CPAG to publish *Poverty and the Labour Government* and to conduct a high-profile media campaign in the early weeks of a General Election run-in, only confirms the group's failure to influence Labour in office and its own exclusion from the official policy community. The "Poor get Poorer" campaign provides a classic illustration of a cause group having to resort to a dramatic media campaign to compensate, in part, for its own inability to achieve regular and effective consultation.

Similarly the UK housing charity "Shelter", which was formed in 1966, adopted a proactive approach to the news media. Its director, Des Wilson, a former journalist with experience of running public relations campaigns, realized the importance of using the media to win public and governmental support. The launch of the charity was accompanied by a major newspaper advertising campaign that was aided by the publicity surrounding the now famous television play, *Cathy come home*, broadcast at around the same time (Seyd 1976). However campaigners found the fact that homelessness was already defined as "political" worked against them, in comparison to the "environment" which was more open in political and ideological terms.

During the 1980s environmental pressure groups used increasingly complex visual symbols to attract attention. For example, the Campaign for Nuclear Disarmament (CND) used the encirclement of nuclear bases as a symbol of peaceful resistance; Greenpeace used their own ship, the *Gondwana*, from which to launch a whaling campaign in the Antarctica; and Friends of the Earth dressed up as aerosol cans to draw attention to the dangers of chlorofluorocarbons (CFCs) destroying the ozone layer (Seymour-Ure 1991). These stunts fitted in with the news values of journalists because they were considered novel and dramatic.

In addition to the sources of competition I have already identified, pressure groups find themselves competing to some degree with other organizations who are campaigning around the same issues. So, for example, Friends of the Earth find themselves in competition with Greenpeace at a number of different levels; for members, for media attention, for political sponsorship. At the same time pressure groups may also cooperate with one another over specific issues and develop coalitions or broad alliances. For example, the National Association for the Care and Resettlement of Offenders (NACRO) adopted a coordinating role among campaigning organizations in the late 1980s opposed to a Private Member's Bill calling for hanging to be re-introduced (see Schlesinger & Tumber 1994). Indeed, it is not uncommon to find that staff have worked for other organizations in the same policy community, or that they serve on one another's councils or committees.

Staging campaigns

Campaigns designed to increase public awareness form a vital part of pressure group activity. Campaigns may be short or long term, designed to educate the general public and/or to influence an elite. As Alderman (1984: 119) observes: "Any form of public campaigning depends crucially on the reaction of the media." The visibility of a group in the mass media, and the way in which issues are framed, will influence the attitudes of the public and policy-makers. For this reason, pressure groups have to develop fine-tuned media strategies if they are to be successful in developing a wide support-base. Gitlin (1980: 3) argues:

> Mass media define the public significance of movement events or, by blanking them out, actively deprive them of larger significance. Media images also become implicated in a movement's self-image . . . . The forms of coverage accrete into systematic framing, and this framing, much amplified, helps determine the movement's fate.

Over recent years a number of studies have considered the ways in which campaigning organizations develop strategies towards the media (for example, Anderson 1991, 1993a, Eyerman & Jamison 1991, Gamson 1990, Kielbowicz & Scherer 1986, Mormont & Dasnoy 1995, Schlesinger 1990, Solesbury 1976). In contrast to earlier organizations, modern groups tend to adopt more radical campaigning techniques and place considerable importance upon generating proactive approaches to the news media. Books such as Des Wilson and Leighton Andrews (1993) *Campaigning* provide practical advice on various skills such as putting together a publicity plan, writing a press release, producing a campaign newspaper, or organizing a press conference. The nature of a campaign is likely to differ according to the targeted audience and the intended outcome.

Over the last few decades many pressure groups have become more professional in campaign tactics and in using the news media. This partly reflects the fact that many pressure groups have experienced a considerable rise in membership and funds in a relatively short amount of time. Also particular case histories such as the success story of the CPAG are now well documented, allowing campaigners to reflect upon past experiences (see, for example, Whiteley & Winyard 1987, Wilson 1984, Wilson & Andrews 1993). Cracknell (1993) makes the useful distinction between "focused" and "diffuse" pressure. He rightly observes that media exposure can be particularly effective when the issue concerns a clear-cut decision. In other contexts, generalizing an issue can produce more widespread interest from policy-makers because it can be harnessed to policy principles, and makes more demands of their skills.

However, I think it is important to recognize that over a period of time targets change. Many pressure groups concentrate upon attracting media publicity during the early stages and later move on to focus more of their energies on parliamentary activities. Deciding upon an appropriate strategy involves weighing up the climate of public and political awareness, the attitudes of the decision-makers in power, and the age and experience of the group. Access becomes a major factor and here, too, important shifts over time occur (Thomas 1983). For example, in the UK over the last decade Friends of the Earth and Greenpeace have gained greater credibility and enjoyed increased access to the political machinery. One cannot simply judge the success of a movement through the amount of media coverage it enjoys (Cracknell 1993). In particular, behind-the-scenes lobbying (extensively practised by groups such as Friends of the Earth) can be extremely effective if the support of influential contacts is gained. On occasions prominent political figures become "information conduits", significantly increasing the chances of ideologies gaining wide circulation in the news media.

Parliamentary arenas

In addition to campaigning through the media, lobbying is absolutely fundamental to bringing about political change. Lobbying through keeping local councillors and MPs informed about campaigns helps boost the profile of pressure groups. Influence can also be exerted through drafting legislation or standing on parliamentary committees. The assistance of MPs, as sponsors or paid consultants, can enhance the credibility of pressure groups. Also, wealthy groups can considerably benefit from the services of a commercial lobbyist who

41

monitors developments in parliament and builds up networks of contacts.

In a seminal article Solesbury (1976) identifies three major processes that issues must go through if they are to become established on the political agenda: they must command attention, they must claim legitimacy, and finally, they must invoke action. As Solesbury points out, satisfying one condition does not necessarily mean that the others are met. Although particular environmental issues may attract widespread attention government responses may be suppressed in various ways. Just because an issue has become defined as "legitimate" it does not guarantee that it will be resolved. Under the British system once issues have passed through this stage they tend to become part of the relatively secret domain of the inner workings of the executive branch of government. There the issue may receive token support, or it may become defined in another way that weakens its political force.

The British system of government, in particular, is characterized by closure and consensuality. Moreover, the news media tend to lose interest once an issue has become sucked into the bureaucratic process. Issues that initially gained media prominence become less newsworthy and are often forgotten about until the outcome is known through, for example, a report being published.

Under the US system of government the growth of citizen groups has played a key role in pressing policy-makers to change the mechanisms by which the demands of a whole network of interest groups are negotiated (see Berry 1993). The traditional sub-government political structures are no longer capable of dealing effectively with interest disputes concerning a very large number of citizen groups, committees and the various agencies of the executive branch of government. As a result, Congress and the executive branch have worked towards creating a more coherent, centralized approach to policymaking. As Berry (1993: 34) observes;

> Policymaking is now best described as taking place within issue networks rather than in subgovernments. An issue network is a set of organizations that share expertise in a policy area and interact with each other over time as relevant issues are debated. . . . the coalitions within networks, often involving scores of groups, define the divisions over issues and drive the policymaking process forward.

This form of interest-group politics in the USA has brought about, in broad terms, a more open and democratic policy-making process. The combination of flagging party discipline and highly effective committees make for a conducive lobbying environment in Congress. As Berry (1993) points out, one consequence of this is that in the field of nuclear politics, the Nuclear Regulatory Commission is now forced to pay attention to its critics such as the Union of Concerned Scientists. Also, further evidence of the increased participation of campaigning organizations may be seen in the attention of environmental groups in negotiations over the free trade agreement with Mexico. Indeed, in some policy disputes the environmental lobby presents a more united front than that of business, since conflicts of interests between actors are less fierce.

One final example concerns the German political system, which I explore in further detail in Chapter 3. This system is based upon proportional representation where each voter possesses two votes; one for candidates in the constituency and one for the party lists, though the latter vote holds the most sway. Seats are allocated to those parties which have won a minimum of 5 per cent of the national vote, or three directly elected seats through the constituency vote. Under this system the West German Green Party, Die Grunen, was able to gain significant representation. In the federal elections of 1983 the party entered the Bundestag, having gained 5.6 per cent of the vote. By January 1987 Die Grunen had captured 8.3 per cent of the vote, although by 1994 this had fallen to 7.3 per cent of the vote (Colomer 1996).

Finally, there are the less prominent manifestations of green politics; grassroots political activity. Green politics is now a firm part of postindustrial, affluent society (Dobson 1995). As we shall see in Chapter 3, although I am sceptical of the idea that the new consciousness-raising movements may be seen as forming a completely radical break with the past, some highly significant changes have occurred. In particular, at least in some European countries, a high degree of political activity is taking place outside of formal political institutions. At the same time, pressure politics are increasingly played out in the context of a global communications industry dominated by a handful of extremely powerful media moguls.

Summary

I began this chapter by noting that the media form an increasingly pervasive aspect of our lives. Having reviewed major traditions within mass communications theory, I argued that early accounts of the role of the news media in pressure politics tended to be based upon a simplistic model of media effects. Contemporary developments suggest that the news media are deeply embedded in a complex web of structures within the policy-making sphere. Although the news media play a crucial role in framing social issues we cannot simply judge the success of a pressure group by the amount of media attention it enjoys. The process of influence is much more complex than this. Just as there is a danger in overlooking the role of the news media, there is the danger of exaggerating it. The role of the news media must therefore be considered in relation to broader questions concerning the politics of pressure.

Suggested further reading

The best general introductory reader on the media is J. Curran & M. Gurevitch (eds), *Mass media and society* (London: Edward Arnold, 1996 (2nd edition).

Two good introductions to pressure politics and the media are M. Moran, *Politics and society in Britain* (London: Macmillan, 1989) and C. Ryan, *Prime-time activism: media strategies for grassroots organising* (Boston: South End Press, 1991). For a comprehensive account of the social constructionist perspective on media and the environment see chapter 3 in J. A. Hannigan, *Environmental sociology* (London: Routledge, 1995).

Two useful practical guides to campaigning including detailed case studies are M. Davies, *The politics of pressure* (London: BBC, 1985) and D. Wilson & L. Andrews, *Campaigning* (London: Hawksmere, 1993).

Chapter 2

News production

News is a product of transactions between journalists and their sources. The primary source of reality for news is not what is displayed or what happens in the real world. The reality of news is embedded in the nature and type of social and cultural relations that develop between journalists and their sources. (Ericson et al. 1989: 377)

Introduction

In Chapter 1, I examined how issues compete for attention in the news media. I argued that different public arenas have differing "carrying capacities". Moreover, I suggested that the news media comprise a range of arenas with their own particular ideological positionings, audience profiles, and temporal and social characteristics. Within these arenas, news stories are selected according to explicit and implicit criteria. This chapter explores the question of ideology, objectivity and impartiality. Are media practitioners really impartial and independent? Is objectivity ever possible? Media practitioners' discourse on the reporting of environmental affairs is analyzed in conjunction with a discussion of the news-making literature.

News production perspectives

Liberal-pluralism
The concept of objectivity is deeply embedded within journalists' professional culture. It is often invoked as a means of legitimating

their role, and forms the basis of their claims to independence. From a liberal-pluralist perspective, the media are viewed as the "Fourth Estate"; alongside the executive, the legislature and the judiciary. This approach suggests the media should reflect the public interest and not be aligned to government or powerful social groups. According to this view the media operate relatively independently and are not, in any major sense, mouthpieces of the state. This conception of society suggests that a range of different interest groups compete for power. Though it is acknowledged that these groups compete on unequal grounds, no one interest is seen as enjoying consistent monopoly. Furthermore, pluralists emphasize that people tend to be selective in their exposure to the mass media, and in their perception and retention of media messages.

The differences between this overly optimistic conception of society and conflict-centred Marxist perspectives have often been over-drawn. These models are not so divorced as is often assumed; they are both guided by similar assumptions about the power of the media in society (Schlesinger 1990). Broadly speaking, the key differences between the two approaches centre on their views of the relationship between the media, political agencies and the state; the degree to which the media operate independently in the production of news; and the consumption of media texts (see Negrine 1989). In contrast to the pluralist model, Marxists suggest the media perform a key ideological role in reproducing the dominant values that underpin the capitalist system. However, some political economists acknowledge that the reproduction of ruling class interests does not occur in any simplistic manner; dominant groups are themselves split into various competing factions (Murdock & Golding 1977).

Typically, media practitioners in liberal democracies view their role in terms of a pluralist conception of society. The concept of objectivity is enshrined in professional codes governing the news media, requiring news stories to be factually accurate reflections of "reality". The ubiquity of this principle reflects a combination of historical, professional and commercial factors, and is closely associated with the early development of the US press (McQuail 1992). Objectivity may be seen as both an approach and a form of practice in processing news (McQuail 1991). A fundamental differentiation is made between news that is grounded upon fact, which is viewed as objective, and opinion-based material that is seen as involving subjective value-judgements

46

(Lichtenberg 1996). However, many of the analytical difficulties in this debate stem from a confusion of key concepts such as objectivity, impartiality and neutrality. As I argue later, facts themselves have evaluative dimensions. Also we may distinguish between objectivity and impartiality. While objectivity implies reflecting the "truth", impartiality suggests competing points of view are given fair and adequate representation. Thus an objective account of reality may not necessarily be neutral as it may favour one set of interests over another.

Objectivity

The question of the degree to which objectivity is possible, or even desirable, forms a central debate within the news studies literature (Lichtenberg 1996). A number of news production studies suggest that total objectivity is unattainable (for example, Carey 1989, Fishman 1980, Gans 1980, Schlesinger 1987). Some of those who reject objectivity as an attainable standard argue that media practitioners, like any other professional group, have their own values and ideologies influenced by cultural factors and working practices. These values, it is claimed, inevitably impinge upon the decisions they make regarding what is considered "news" and "truth" since they are, after all, human beings. Others suggest objectivity is not a worthwhile ideal since it only serves to legitimate structures that favour the interests of the powerful (for example, Gans 1980; Schudson 1978; Sigal 1973, Tuchman 1972). More recently, this has been taken further by postmodernists who argue that there is no such thing as an "objective reality". For postmodernists there can be no universal truths; all knowledge is socially constructed and open to differing interpretations (Lichtenberg 1996). This highly relativist approach implies one account of reality possesses no more intrinsic value than another (see, for example, Glasser 1988). A rather different line of argument is advanced by Allan (1995a: 130) who claims:

> Given that the very notion of "news bias" implies that, by definition, the existence of an "unbiased" news account is possible, this recourse to the concept of "objectivity" is not advantageous in either conceptual or strategic terms.

All of these claims can be seen to rest, as Lichtenberg (1996) force-fully argues, upon a number of often contradictory assumptions. The concept of "bias" itself implies deviation from an objective norm. In other words, the accusation that the news is distorted or biased makes the assumption that a more detached account of events is indeed possible:

> In so far as objectivity is impossible there can be no sense in the claim – certainly none in the rebuke – that the media are ideological or partial, for these concepts imply the possibility of a contrast. Conversely, in so far as we agree that the media serve an ideological function or bias our vision, we implicitly accept the view that other, better, more objective ways are possible. (Lichtenberg 1996: 230)

Furthermore, the claim that objectivity is not desirable (since journalists use it to shield their own interests) conflicts with the charge that the news is not objective. In other words, it makes no sense to complain about a lack of objectivity if it is considered undesirable (Lichtenberg 1996, McQuail 1992). Finally, objectivity itself could be viewed as an ideology (ibid. 1992).

The claim that the news media should protect us from certain anxiety-provoking aspects of "reality", provides a further sense in which "objectivity" may be considered undesirable. Some argue, for example, that the news media have a responsibility to protect the public from shocking images of death and destruction. Television is often singled out for special attention since the combination of strong visual images with words makes it appear a particularly authoritative window on the world. In my view the news media falsify the reality of, say, war or famine, if the real horror and anguish is not conveyed. That is not to say that such reporting can ever be completely objective as it is influenced by all manner of individual, social and cultural judgements.

The notion of objectivity is therefore much more complex than at first it might appear. In my view part of the confusion surrounds the ambiguous use of several key terms such as neutrality, impartiality and truth. Commentators frequently accuse the news media of being partial, but what exactly do they mean? Before we focus upon the concept of bias we must first consider the principle of impartiality.

Impartiality

Like the notion of objectivity, impartiality is often viewed as a key feature of the press in a liberal-democratic state where it is contended a plurality of interests can make their voices heard. It is a cultural standard, and like objectivity, it performs particular ideological functions. Impartiality may be defined in different ways but it usually refers to the representation of different views and interests without taking sides. Thus impartiality is closely associated with balance and neutrality. Impartiality has developed a particularly strong affinity with public service news broadcasting – according to Schlesinger, for example, it forms the "lynchpin of the BBC's ideology" (1987: 163). The formula of presenting two opposing viewpoints – often an official statement balanced against a response from a non-official source – is popular. Frequently, this takes the form of allegation and counter allegation/response, where it is assumed that the truth lies somewhere in the middle (Ericson et al. 1991). However, as Gamson argues, conflicts involving a range of different claimsmakers do not fit this model very well:

> The tendency to single out one alternative to juxtapose with the official package is built into media norms about proper story form. . . . Multi-party conflicts and ambivalent packages do not lend themselves well to this dramatic form. One can meet the demands of form as well as the norm of balance by contrasting what officials say with one major protagonist. Hence, certain package sponsors become, for a given issue, the media-designated opposition. (Gamson 1988: 169)

Moreover, problems may arise in deciding whose views are to be balanced against a statement from an official source. If a statement from a minority radical organization is selected this may convey the impression that they adequately represent the opposing view. At times, such a ploy may be used deliberately in order to marginalize opposition. For example, balancing a statement from the British Field Sports Society (BFSS) with a statement from the Hunt Saboteurs Association (HSA) rather than from more moderate groups with wider support, such as the League Against Cruel Sports (LACS). Balancing an official view with an opposition perspective may give the outward appearance of impartiality yet it subtly influences the debate. As mentioned in the introduction, official sources are institutionalized sources of information.

49

However, there are clearly many difficulties with categorizing sources as "official" or "non-official" (Schlesinger & Tumber 1994). Some organizations, for example the National Trust, receive government funding and yet retain a certain amount of autonomy.

Objectivity and impartiality are commonly juxtaposed against the concept of "bias". The notion of "bias", as we shall see, is also conceptually problematic.

Bias

So far I have suggested that there are various conceptual confusions over the use of the terms "objectivity" and "impartiality". Bias, or the absence of neutrality, can also be used in a variety of senses. Table 2.1 illustrates the different forms that bias may take; bias may be intended or unintended, open or concealed. Two major types of intended bias are partisanship (for example, an opinion column or editorial) that is openly slanted; and propaganda (for example, public relations literature uncritically reproduced by news media) where vested interests are concealed.

One of the most common charges is that news possesses a "political bias". Both right-wing and left-wing politicians accuse the news media of political partisanship (see Eldridge 1993). Some popular accounts of the media go so far as to suggest that the news is deliberately biased in furthering the interests of a particular class. Though one cannot rule out the possibility of a conspiracy, I think several factors tend to work against this. First, the upper classes in capitalist society tend to be fractured by competing elements and divisions. Second, a news culture grounded upon the notion that the media have a public watchdog role. And finally, the sheer speed with which news is created and disseminated leaves little room for conspiratorial interference (Cottle 1993a).

In the past the environment was often viewed as an area that cut across traditional political barriers. Thus Lowe and Morrison were

Table 2.1   Four types of news bias.

| | Concepts of objectivity | |
	Open	Hidden
Intended	Partisanship	Propaganda
Unintended	Unwitting bias (selectivity)	Ideology

Source: McQuail 1992: 193.

50

able to write in the early 1980s: "the mass media have fostered rather than undermined environmental protest, and will continue to do so as long as the environment is taken to be a politically neutral area relating to the quality of life rather than its organization" (1984: 88). As I argued in Chapter 1, the reporting of the environment has become increasingly politicized over recent years. Also, there has been a growing realization that the environment is inter-linked with social, political and economic concerns. The reporting of environmental affairs, therefore, has become perceived as politically more sensitive in the way in which issues are framed.

One of the most influential studies of television news to be published in Britain was the Glasgow University Media Group's *Bad news* in 1976, followed a few years later by *More bad news* and *Really bad news*. The Glasgow University Media Group argued that British television news was consistently unfavourable towards the views of trade unions and workers. These studies stimulated a number of critiques that suggested some of their claims were based upon factual inaccuracies (see Harrison 1985). These critiques were in turn challenged on the grounds of factual errors (Philo 1987). Indeed, Schlesinger (1987: xxxviii) refers to this whole affair as having all the ingredients of a soap opera, with claim followed by counter-claim, followed by counter-claim. This illustrates the complexity surrounding issues of bias; in particular it highlights the need to recognize that facts have evaluative dimensions. Different interpretations of facts may be influenced by conflicting ideological positions.

The extent to which different theorists believe impartiality and objectivity are attainable, or desirable, depends upon their underlying assumptions about the nature of knowledge and truth. In what follows I want to briefly explore the influence of two major traditions in philosophical thought.

Realism and idealism

The above discussion on objectivity and impartiality interconnnects with a wider philosophical debate in the social sciences between realists and idealists (see Blaikie 1993, Lichtenberg 1996, Williams & May 1996). Whether we think objectivity in news reporting is possible or not depends upon whether we believe there is an external reality, independent of our own perspective (for a discussion of realist approaches in human geography see Cloke et al. 1991). Realists, such as Dickens (1992), argue there is an objective reality "out there", independent of our beliefs or values. The task for the realist, then, is to seek to uncover that external reality through analyzing social processes and structures. On the other hand idealists, such as Winch (1990), argue all knowledge is socially constructed, thus we cannot avoid viewing the world "out there" through our own perspectives. An idealist ontology, for example, suggests the environment has reality only in so far as we perceive it to exist. Meaning is critical for idealists since they believe that the contribution of social science is to comprehend how individuals construct meanings in everyday life. Idealists thus reject the view that objectivity is possible. As Eder (1995: 9) observes,

> Facts are socially constructed within the limits of culture. What we perceive and experience as facts is dependent upon culturally organized and shared symbols that give meaning to them. Culture organizes man's relationship to nature, including his way of conceptualizing it: this consequently implies that facts are dependent upon culture.

However, while values inevitably impinge upon the way in which both researchers and media practitioners view the world, the problem with extreme versions of idealism is they ignore the existence of certain objective "facts" where there is a majority consensus (see Williams & May 1996). I would argue that although our views are inevitably shaped by cultural, social and political judgements, we cannot totally abandon the notion of objectivity. For example, there is a large amount of evidence to suggest that smoking is a major contributory factor in lung cancer. Although this "fact" may be disputed by some, notably the tobacco industry who have obvious interests in taking this stand, most people would agree with this contention. Variations in the interpretation of this "fact" may be influenced by particular cultural and social factors that change over time. For example, an individual's perspective may be influenced by the extent to which smoking is deeply embedded within their culture, or whether or not their parents or members of their peer group smoke. Our acceptance of this "fact" at any particular moment in time will be grounded upon a complex set of beliefs about other "facts" that are unlikely to all change simultaneously (ibid.). From a realist perspective, it is possible to arrive at an understanding of external reality (the weight of evidence suggests that smoking is a contributory factor in lung cancer), despite various cultural and social biases. As Lichtenberg observes, cultural differences are not generally insurmountable in the reaching a consensus about fundamental "facts".

All "facts", to a greater or lesser extent, contain to an evaluative dimension. Lichtenberg (1996) provides the example of 10 million gallons of oil spilling into Prince William Sound from the tanker the *Exxon Valdez* in March 1989. Although the scale and effects of the oil spill may be disputed, the vast majority of individuals would take it as fact that the event occurred. Similarly, most people would accept that in June 1995 the multinational oil company, Shell, attempted to dump the Brent Spar oil rig at sea. It is clearly much more difficult to come to a consensus about causes and effects, than about the occurrence of particular events. This is particularly so when the issues are complex and involve a large amount of public concern (McQuail 1992). Moreover, the inclusion or exclusion of particular facts in news reports can skew stories in particular ways.

One of the difficulties with environmental "facts" is they are often very complex and fiercely contested by different parties representing various interests. For example, the Greenpeace claim that deep-sea dumping is more harmful to the environment than disposal on land depends upon complicated scientific cost–benefit calculations and predictions about the future. By the very nature of scientific enquiry, evidence about environmental degradation often remains inconclusive for a long span of time. Moreover, these complexities require journalists to transform technical jargon into laypersons' language; this itself may involve processes of interpretation and selection.

At another level, the news media always present a partial version of reality since news production is based around judgements as to what constitutes a newsworthy story. As Schlesinger (1987: 164–5) observes,

> The "reality" it portrays is always in at least one sense fundamentally biased, simply in virtue of the inescapable decision to designate an issue or event newsworthy, and then to construct an account of it in a specific framework of interpretation. News must be assessed as a cultural product which embodies journalistic, social, and political values. It cannot be, and certainly is not, a neutral, impartial or totally objective perception of the real world."

I would contend that, rather than viewing objectivity in absolute terms, it is better to think of it in terms of a continuum of degrees of representing reality. It is more useful to think of factual statements in terms of correctness and incorrectness than as "true" or "false" (Ericson et al. 1991). Objectivity should not be confused with total accuracy or with value-freedom. The important question is surely, "biased in relation to what?" (Harrison 1985). What are the criteria by which we judge a piece of news and to what degree does it meet the requirements of impartiality and objectivity? Journalistic rules of procedure for producing "objective" news provide some kind of a benchmark by which to judge the degree to which a piece is accurate.

Biases and constraints

In the following part of the chapter I discuss some of the major constraints in the production of environmental news, drawing upon interviews I conducted with journalists and broadcasters covering the environment beat in the British national press, and television news and current affairs. Here I focus upon three major questions: How do issues of objectivity, impartiality and neutrality impact upon different genres? To what extent do environment correspondents display personal commitments towards the environment? And how far is environmental news constrained by secrecy and information management?

News organization and news culture
Categorizing the environment
Issue-categorization may act to constrain or open up the ways in which environmental issues are framed. The ways in which the news media frame a given item depend, to some extent, upon how it is categorized according to preconceived ideas and divisions of labour within the news organization. Writing in the mid 1980s, Lowe & Morrison claimed that what made the "environment" distinctive, compared to other categories of news, was the absence of any broad cultural consensus about how the topic area was defined:

The difference in the reporting of say industrial affairs or race is that, in these other areas, there operates a pre-existing cultural definition of the subject matter so that the parameters of debate are already laid down and the encoding of news circumscribes oppositional elements. (Lowe & Morrison 1984: 79)

Moreover the authors argued the reporting of environmental affairs inevitably draws upon potent cultural symbols concerning heritage and the countryside, tapping into strong public sentiment regarding such issues. Thus, they claimed, the non-partisan reporting of environmental stories could "potentially" stimulate a subversive critique of industrialism. Clearly, the all-encompassing nature of the "environment" rendered it very difficult to accommodate within established news categories. However, it is questionable as to how far the environment is still represented as a politically neutral subject area. Environmentalism, or more specifically political ecology, has become what Klaus Eder (1996) labels a new "masterframe" in popular discourse (see Ch. 3). In other words, as environmentalism has become increasingly institutionalized it has been transformed into a political ideology in competition with liberalism, socialism and conservatism.

During the late 1980s "green" was frequently used as a key signalling term that was used in the reporting of all manner of issues from health to women's issues (Anderson 1993a). For example, a Greenpeace press officer suggested women's magazines played a major role in stimulating environmental awareness during the late 1980s:

The women's press, and that's the women's press in the wider sense, from the sort of general lifestyle magazines right through to the feminist magazines, were one of the sort of front runners in taking up environmental issues and the whole ozone debate really brought it home to peoples' attention. And that was really because the lifestyle magazines were running articles on the hole in the ozone layer. And now what you find is it is very difficult to open them up and find, you know, nothing connected with the environment. (Interview, 17 July 1989)

Although the environment became more established as a news beat area, it was largely defined as excluding development issues (Hannigan 1995, Lacey & Longman 1993). Moreover, there is a strong cyclical element to the reporting of such issues. This is often closely tied to the perceived importance in terms of the political agenda.

News formats

As I suggested in Chapter 1, the mass media are complexly differentiated according to style and genre, patterns of ownership and control, news values, and the types of audiences they reach. Issues of objectivity, neutrality and impartiality impact differently upon different media. News production is influenced by various types of constraints ranging from advertising pressure, editorial policy and ownership, to stylistic conventions, news cultures and the limitations of time and space. Also, there are the subtle and not so subtle forms of news-management and censorship of material that has a right to exist in the public domain.

Media formats fundamentally shape the ways in which news is presented. There is a sense in which the format is of greater significance than the content since, at the most basic level, there has to be a "fit" in terms of the requirements of the medium (Ericson et al. 1991). Television, for example, is a highly visual medium. Images are as important as words; a good picture story therefore tends to be highly rated. On the other hand, radio involves no visual engagement but sound is crucial so format considerations are very different (Altheide 1985). In comparison with television and radio, newspapers are structured around space and, to varying degrees, offer a greater capacity to deal with issues at length (see Table 2.2).

The table usefully illustrates some of the major differences and similarities between television, radio and newspapers formats. As Ericson et al. observe, newspapers are weak in providing contextual information since they rely upon still photographic images and writing does not accurately convey the nuances of speech, or tell us anything about the environment in which it is set. In contrast, television news relies upon actuality footage that makes it a dynamic medium. One of the reasons why television is widely viewed as being more realistic and fair than, say newspapers or radio, is it has the capacity to convey all manner of contextual details from an individual's demeanour to the physical environment in which they are placed. However, as Ericson et al. (1991) argue, television reporting is highly mediated and relies upon imagination and interpretation at every level of the communication chain; from source, to journalist, to audience. As Fowler remarks, " There is no ideologically neutral way of holding the camera" (1991: 26). These considerations will be discussed at greater length in Chapter 4, when I examine news values and the construction of the environment.

56

Table 2.2   A comparison of newspapers, television, and radio news formats.

Newspaper	Television	Radio
Visual	Visual and audio	Audio
Weak validation of context	Strong validation of context	Some validation of context
Least redundancy/simplification	Considerable redundancy/simplification	Most redundancy/simplification
Considerable imaginative work	Least imaginative work	Most imaginative work
Narrative/symbolic/abstraction	Most dramatization/entertaining/concrete	Considerable abstraction/dramatization/entertaining/concrete
Least personalization	Most personalization	Considerable personalization
Structure with space	Structure with time	Structure with time
Least immediacy/past tense	Considerable immediacy/present tense	Most immediacy/present tense
Largest number of items	Intermediate number of items	Least number of items
Longest items	Intermediate length of items	Shortest items
Linear/sequential	Mosaic/episodic	Mosaic/episodic
Static	Dynamic/continuous	Dynamic/continuous
Consistent/permanent/a record	Ephemeral/evanescent	Ephemeral/evanescent
Self-pacing	Imposes own pace	Imposes own pace
Individual/primary activity	More social/secondary activity	Most social/secondary activity

Source: Ericson et al. 1991: 22.

The role of the "expert" in an increasingly risk-conscious society has come under greater scrutiny in recent years. In any one case there are usually several contending voices, each claiming to have expert knowledge and providing conflicting accounts of the extent of risk posed by the problem. The journalist plays a key role in disentangling these claims and simplifying complex ideas for the "lay" public. Media formats vary in their ability to convey the complexities of news stories. Generally newspapers offer a greater capacity for dealing with weighty issues and specialist knowledge than television or radio: "Whether in features or in complex continuing stories, newspapers are more capable of introducing experts and their specialist knowledge than is television or radio news" (Ericson et al 1991: 24). Studies indicate that many environmental pressure groups regard the national broadsheet press as one of their major targets (Lowe & Goyder 1983, Anderson 1993a). A former director of Media Natura claimed:

> ... the real importance of getting stuff into newspapers is to influence politicians because they have people who actually cut them up. And if you want to get a subject on television there's no point going to talk to TV researchers and people like that because television is an extremely mobile world ... The best way to influence television content wise is to get something in a national newspaper because they all start off every morning ... and they're presented with the cuttings from the newspapers and they then proceed to ring up the conservation groups. That's how they do their research basically. They'd deny it but that's what they actually do! (Interview, 24 January 1990)

From an environmental organization's point of view, in practical terms securing national press coverage may often be regarded as more beneficial than inclusion in a short television clip. With newspapers such organizations tend to be less at the mercy of producers' schedules, there is usually little travelling involved, and there tends to be greater space.

While one can go back over and re-read information in newspapers, with television one has to take in specialist knowledge in a very short space of time. Television news tends to be structured around soundbites. Often members of the audience retain general images but the actual details of what has been said are lost. Clearly, there is much less space in television news bulletins to deal with weighty issues compared with other media formats. On average the main evening news broadcasts contain fewer words than one page of a broadsheet newspaper (Ericson et al. 1991). The problem is even greater with radio since the listener has to make sense of information without the aid of visual images. However, radio scores highly in terms of immediacy for there are relatively few hold-ups in the transmission of up-to-the-minute news.

Divergences within the news media

There are important differences within, as well as across, the news media. For example, news stories can be covered in much greater depth in television documentaries compared to news bulletins. Likewise, Sunday newspapers tend to offer much greater space for investigative journalism than daily newspapers, and are not so constrained by time. However, some newspapers contain very little news content, such as the Sunday editions of many British and US popular newspapers (Bell 1991).

There are also general differences in market orientation within the news media. This particularly applies to the press. Popular, mid-market and "quality" newspapers have their own particular market niches. Within these niches individual newspapers have their own "modes of address" by which they maintain a dialogue with their readership (Fowler 1991). Thus, popular newspapers tend to appeal to the reader through the use of frequent dialogic and rhetorical devices so that he/she is encouraged to become directly engaged with the subject matter (ibid.). Topics are treated in an entertaining fashion and the frequent use of colloquialisms enhances the sense of familiarity that is built up between the reader and the newspaper.

To some extent, the reporting of environmental affairs in the press reflects the general identity of the newspaper including its political orientations. Thus a former environment correspondent for *The Times* suggested:

> The *Times* is a paper for the establishment so I tend to do White-hall things. The *Telegraph* is a paper for the petit-bourgeoisie so Charlie tends to do countryside things; the *Guardian* is a paper of the left so Paul does nuclear energy and whales. (Interview, 22 February 1991)

Television news channels also have their own stylistic and ideological conventions through which they attempt to develop a strong sense of identity, though this may be less explicit. Some news formats lend themselves to what Cottle (1993b) describes as "moral partizanship". For example the popular British breakfast news show, TV AM, favours a populist approach. Cottle describes how a presenter on TV AM adopts a tone of moral indignation when discussing the effects of pollution on baby seals. This contrasts with the authoritative, neutral style characterizing BBC and, to a lesser extent, ITN evening news pro-grammes. Cottle (1993b: 129) maintains:

> Delivered in the familiar, at times chatty, idiom of common-sense reasoning and feelings, environmental items can often eschew those professional claims to objectivity and impartiality, deliberately appealing to emotive responses and adopting a position of moral partizanship.

Also, newspapers tend to be more evaluative than television, hence there is greater scope for moral partisanship (Ericson et al., 1991). Popular newspapers frequently engage in moralistic overtures, where they take a blatantly partisan line. For example the *Daily Mirror*'s front page headline on (21 June 1995) Shell's decision to halt the deep-sea dumping of the Brent Spar, hailed it as a victory for the newspaper and the people of Britain: "SHELL–VED Daily Mirror victory as petrol giant halts rig sinking".

But there are lots of subtle ways in which television and radio are able to "window dress" facts through the use of emotional overtones. For example, the use of background music in both radio and tele-vision, and the association of words with images in television.

A further area of divergence concerns the influence of advertising on the news media. There are considerable variations in the propor-tion of advertising in relation to editorial content. Some sectors of the news media depend heavily upon advertising revenue, while others receive their funding through other means. However, advertising does not just impact upon the news media in terms of revenue, it exerts a more subtle influence upon the whole way in which news is packaged (Ericson et al. 1991). Thus newspapers are often divided up into different sections according to marketing considerations, and an emphasis upon entertainment and titillating news is designed to appeal to potential consumers.

The extent to which the individual journalist experiences autonomy in covering such issues as ecology, deviance, race or gender is influ-enced by a number of internal and external pressures associated with news culture. As we have already seen, the way in which the topic is defined by the news organization is of crucial importance. In addition to organizational and economic pressures, social and cultural con-straints play a key role. It is to these I now turn.

Individual values and autonomy

Advocacy and moral partisanship

As I noted earlier, values inevitably impact upon how one interprets "facts". Although journalists frequently appeal to notions of neutrality and value-freedom, they are socialized into a particular news culture, based upon taken-for-granted assumptions about what constitutes "news" (see Ch. 4). These judgements are inevitably shaped both by news culture and individual values. As Gans (1980: 213) argues,

> Like other professionals, journalists practice an expertise that is not and cannot be purely professional . . . Even if they conceive of themselves as outsiders, journalists, both as professionals and as laypersons, react to the news with the same attitudes and values as some, if not all, members of their audience.

If we are to probe beneath the surface of news production we need to briefly consider the individual backgrounds and attitudes of media practitioners. Environment correspondents generally do not have a "hard" science background; most are arts or humanities graduates (see Ch. 4). In interviews, many environment correspondents claim to have a high level of personal interest in environmental affairs. However very few state they are paid-up members of environmental pressure groups, since they tend to view this as compromising their position of neutrality. Most national news organizations do not permit specialist correspondents who report on environmental affairs to belong to environmental campaigning organizations. When questioned about whether he belonged to any environmental organization the response of a former environment correspondent for the *Observer* is typical of many correspondents in this field:

> No because if I did it would sacrifice my independence. How could I possibly? Nor am I a member of any political party or any trade association apart from the National Union of Journalists. I've been invited to join groups on to many boards of environmental groups. I won't do it. (Interview, 28 July 1993)

At the same time, many environmental correspondents express a great degree of personal interest in environmental matters. For example, when I asked a former environment correspondent for a UK national daily newspaper about his commitment to environmental issues, he replied:

> I do care about it a lot. I'm still a fairly keen birdwatcher . . . I'm a fly fisherman. I take a great delight in chalk streams . . . Yes, I've got a great interest in it and I'm seized with the problems. I mean I think very bad things are coming to this little planet of ours . . . the link problems of environmental degradation and poverty and population explosion and climate change, it seems to me, are more or less insolvable. We're just not going to stop putting the carbon dioxide into the air, I can't see how. I can't see the political mechanism that can stop it. (Interview, 22 February 1991)

This response was typical of many other environment correspondents in the broadsheet press. Broadcasters, too, expressed a large amount of personal concern about the environment though they were at pains to stress the importance of balanced coverage. For example, a correspondent for BBC News, claimed:

> I'm very interested in environmental stories at the moment. I think it's the most important area facing mankind. Some of these issues are of particular importance and so this is why I think it's so important that they should be reported accurately and fairly and prominently. (Interview, 5 December 1989)

Another BBC correspondent expressed concerns about major issues affecting less developed countries:

> There are some environmental groups who miss a big opportunity, who really miss the story and in concentrating upon the parts they miss the whole. By which I mean the Earth Summit was alleged to be about saving the planet. Last chance to save the planet. And yet it seemed to do very little for the 40,000 under fives who die every day and have done for years and will do for years from easily preventable diseases and starvation. Now it seems to me that unless the environment starts from there and finishes from there then it is missing the point. (Interview, 5 February 1993)

The news media frequently run campaigns around issues that are perceived to be of popular interest. The question of whether or not journalists should engage in "advocacy" or "moral partisanship" is the subject of much debate. Environment correspondents are typically faced with two major problems that pertain to how the "environment" is defined. The first problem is the tendency for certain types of environmental items to be labelled "soft" news stories. These sorts of news stories tend to be ritually packaged in a lightweight manner and often carry an upbeat ending. The second problem is to do with the difficulty of reporting on environmental issues while at the same time being seen to remain unpartisan. Previous studies have categorized journalists in three main ways – as neutral observer, as participant or as advocate (Kielbowicz & Scherer 1986). When questioned in interviews, the majority of reporters either portray themselves as neutral or as participants – though in practice the distinction is not very clear. Typically, few journalists claim they view themselves as advocates for environmentalism (Gans 1980, Anderson 1993a). Indeed, many go to great lengths to distance themselves from what they regard as a morally partisan approach. For example, a broadcaster at ITN claimed:

> I try very hard not to have a personal interest in my own stories because . . . I mean more than almost any area the environment has the ability to seduce you into being a believer and I think as a journalist, especially on TV, it's extremely dangerous. (Interview, 17 January 1990)

Similarly, a BBC correspondent maintained: "I am a journalist and it is my job simply to try to tell people more about their world to help to expand their understanding of it. The conclusions they draw have to be their conclusions." (Interview, 5 December 1989)

A rather different perspective is provided by a BBC correspondent whose response indicates that moral judgements clearly come into play:

> You have to reflect both sides where there are two sides. It's not our job to make people's minds up on things like that. Although, equally, I do not think it is our job to be neutral over, if you want, fascism or apartheid. I mean these tend not to crop up in environmental coverage, but I would not carry neutrality and objectivity to the state of saying I am going to be even handed about

something which I consider to be morally repugnant. (Interview, 5 February 1993)

In their study of environmental reporting in the Canadian press, Einsiedel and Coughlan (1993) also found a general consensus among reporters concerning the emphasis they placed upon detachment. However, these responses should not be taken at face value. Story selection through the application of news values implicitly prioritizes some issues over others which involves value-judgements. Decisions at virtually every level of the news-making process involve weighing up and interpreting "facts".

Two of the six journalists interviewed by Einsiedel and Coughlan concurred that they might be viewed as adopting an advocacy role. For example, one reporter, stated:

> There is something about the beat that would reinforce the characteristic of "advocacy" because of the knowledge one gains from covering the beat. But I certainly don't see myself as an advocate for environmental groups. In fact, I'm constantly under considerable pressure from the more radical groups in this province to be more sympathetic. (ibid.: 138)

A former environment correspondent for the *Observer* maintained:

> If one goes into this kind of job with a fixed view of particular issues and you try and bend people to your view you're not being a journalist, you ought to be a campaigner with Friends of the Earth or something like that. . . . As people learn facts and truths things will change, but then you know one's own views have to be open to change as other information comes in. Having been in the field for the best part of 25 years I have a fair idea of what some of the issues are, what I feel about some of the issues. . . . But I've got to be open to having my mind completely changed by some new bit of evidence on any one of those issues at any time, whereas a campaigner usually isn't. (Interview, 28 July 1993)

The danger of getting too close to the subject matter is similar to the process that anthropologists or sociologists term "going native", when the individual loses supposed detachment from the community he/she is seeking to understand or represent. In war time, for example, journalists living among soldiers may themselves become desensitized towards war and take things for granted that ordinarily they may have questioned (Morrison & Tumber 1988).

There are a number of pressures upon reporters to stress detachment. Much of their authoritative status is seen as depending upon an ability not to take sides. On occasions journalists have been known to be taken off their beat because they were judged to be getting too "close" to the subject material (Einsiedel & Coughlan 1993). However, some journalists openly see it as their duty to inform the public through adopting an advocacy role; rejecting the myth that complete detachment is possible (Friedman 1991, LaMay 1991, Ryan 1991).

In addition to these problems, the same story may be interpreted very differently by news organizations in other cultures. For example, a correspondent for Channel Four News claimed:

> Particularly in Russia it's a great problem because our stuff often gets shown in Russia whether legally or not on Russian television networks and they tend to, perhaps in translation, interpret things very differently. What I would see as a balanced story here may not be seen as a balanced story on their side. . . . So I think the combination of editing, translation and perception will make an enormous difference. . . . It is a very, very severe problem. Our documentary on nuclear waste dumps in the middle of Russia was not shown by a number of American TV stations because they said it was too political. I think they meant it was too sympathetic to the Russians. (Interview, 19 February 1993)

Despite some media practitioners' claims to value-neutrality, the above discussion has shown how political and moral judgements inevitably play some part in shaping the news.

Autonomy

News items may be covered by general reporters or specialist correspondents, depending upon the subject area and the media format. For example environmental issues are more likely to be covered by general reporters in local compared to national newspapers. The notion that specialist reporters possess a large degree of editorial freedom is, like the myth of detachment, deeply ingrained within journalists' mythology. Tunstall (1971) has shown that specialists in general believe that they have a large degree of autonomy. The environment and science correspondents I interviewed generally claimed to enjoy a peculiar amount of freedom in reporting environmental matters. A typical response was that of an environment correspondent for the former middle-market newspaper, *Today*. When questioned about whether he possessed a great deal of freedom he replied:

> Yes I do. It's basically us telling the editor what the stories are and there are times when he just doesn't think the subject is for us but we're putting the stuff before him. It's very rare that people are coming to us and saying do this, do that. He has the veto but we select. (Interview, 3 November 1989)

Similarly, a former environment correspondent for the *Times* responded:

> Complete freedom. I've never had anybody trying to interfere with my freedom, editorially, or suggest that, you know, it might be an idea if we didn't do this or it might be an idea if we didn't do that. (Interview, 22 February 1991)

However, when the same correspondent was questioned two years later the individual expressed a rather different view shortly after the newspaper axed the position. The correspondent claimed: "The new editor was personally uncomfortable with me writing stories that were critical of the nuclear establishment" (Interview, 28 July 1993).

Tunstall (1971) has established that specialists are constrained by a number of factors including organizational, editorial and advertising pressures. Indeed, evidence suggests that tabloid newspapers experience a considerable amount of editorial interference over political "hot potatoes" such as nuclear power. One middle-market environment correspondent claimed that in the past he had experienced editorial pressure not to cover issues related to nuclear power. However the amount of freedom enjoyed by environment correspondents varies to some degree between and within the news media depending, for example, on news organization practices and political ideology.

Pressures of space and competing news stories also act as major constraint but again this varies depending upon news formats. A former environment correspondent for the *Times* claimed:

I am competing for very limited space with about 15 other specialist writers, a political staff of about ten, about 15 foreign correspondents, agencies from all over the world and agencies
from all over Britain, and *The Times* Home Department gets
about 250 a day in and we use about 30. So I am just simply not
going to cover a story that has got no chance of getting in the
paper . . . I would have said that whether or not it will get in the
paper is a key determinant, whether it's important enough to
force its way in. (Interview, 22 February 1991)

Although specialist correspondents assemble news stories, typically they have little control over final length, headlines or whether
the item is spiked (Burgess & Harrison 1993). Sub-editors, for example, can easily distort what is said through re-ordering paragraphs or
framing the story with a misleading headline. Also, more subtle forms
of self-censorship are at work when a journalist takes a decision not to
cover a story because of what he/she perceives as the likely editorial
response.

Source–media relations

In the previous chapter I noted that news sources play a key role in the
news production process. A number of authors have highlighted
points of convergence between sources and news organizations (for
example, Ericson et al. 1989, Gans 1980, Peters 1995, Schudson 1996).
In addition to journalists becoming socialized into the culture of the
source organization, three other major forms of convergence are of
interest (see Ericson et al. 1989).

First, journalists frequently rely upon sources to function as "reporters" in assembling together "raw" news material. Second, there is
often a high degree of overlap between the elites who control the
media and the elites who preside over government bureaucracies,
though empirical evidence of direct links is often difficult to acquire.
Finally, on occasions, overt convergence is evident when sources gain
additional employment in news organizations through writing regular columns or feature articles.

A seminal study by Hall et al. (1978) *Policing the crisis* argues that
powerful "accredited" sources, such as government departments or
the courts, enjoy privileged access to the media. They command
greater access to the media by virtue of their claims to expert knowledge, their powerful position in society, or their representative status.

Thus Hall et al. (1978: 58) suggest that powerful sources become over-accessed by the media and, as a result, they become "primary definers" of key issues:

> . . . media statements are, wherever possible, grounded in "objective" and "authoritative" statements from "accredited" sources. This means constantly turning to accredited social representatives of major social institutions – MPs for political topics, employers and trade union leaders for industrial matters and so on . . . Ironically, the very rules which aim to preserve the impartiality of the media and which grew out of the desires for greater professional neutrality, also serve powerfully to orientate the media in the "definitions of social reality" that their "accredited sources" – the institutional spokesmen – provide.

However, by concentrating upon primary definition in the media, the structuralist model overlooks the processes of negotiation and conflict prior to the definitions appearing in the media. As Schlesinger (1990: 68) suggests:

> The model given by Hall et al. is one in which primary definitions are conceived of as commanding the field and as producing a dominant ideological effect. While this offers a coherent critique of various forms of pluralism, an uncritical adherence to this model involves paying a price. For this structuralist approach is profoundly incurious about the processes whereby sources engage in ideological conflict *prior to or contemporaneous with the appearance of definitions in the media*. It therefore rules out asking questions about how contestation over definitions takes place *within* institutions and organizations reported by the media as well as the concrete strategies pursued as they contend for space. [original emphasis]

In interviews environment correspondents typically claim they are as sceptical of government sources as of any other news source, and are critical of their competence in managing the news (Cracknell 1993). For example, a former environment correspondent for the British national daily newspaper, the *Independent*, claimed: " A lot of the time government is not sitting on information because news is bad. They often sit on news that does them favours. They are just bad communicators"(Warren 1995: 57). According to media practitioners, objective reporting is encouraged through giving airtime or column inches to major news sources who can put things in their own words, rather than relying upon journalists' speculation or subjective personal opinion. However, news sources have vested interests in the issues they are promoting and can exert differing levers of power on the media and the wider policy-making machinery. As Lichtenberg (1996) observes, journalists have to make important choices about whether a statement is controversial enough to warrant balancing it with an opposing view. In part, this becomes a judgement about the credibility of a source. The less credible the source, the more likely it is to be balanced with an alternative viewpoint. Also, what is viewed as controversial changes over time, as does the credibility of particular sources. For example, a correspondent for ITN claimed that his view of environmental pressure groups had become "increasingly tainted", explaining:

> Partly because they've become more shrill and more extreme as the mainstream political parties have stolen their political agendas . . . and I think that means people who are editing programmes are more suspicious of them and less trusting. And also they have become a business. (Interview, 19 February 1993)

Most journalists claim that their role is simply to relay information leaving the audience to make up its own mind (Gans 1980). However, in practice if x is simply balanced against y, and the journalist offers no interpretative commentary, the audience are left bewildered not knowing who to believe.

Ericson et al. (1989) suggest that in recent years there has been some recognition of the problems resulting from presenting news in this formulaic way. Although news is still predominantly grounded in official interpretive frames, some journalists have done away with presenting news with an air of objectivity. In some cases, they note increased emphasis on giving voice to the views of the "people" in addition to official perspectives. As Ericson et al. point out, this can be seen in part as a response to charges of bias resulting from the standard framing of reports around two opposing sources.

Secrecy and information management

Many commentators observe a tendency among Western governments to make increasing use of public relations techniques and information

69

management in an attempt to control public opinion (Nohrstedt 1993). Often, for example, there are long delays in the production of information for public scrutiny. Also, intensive information campaigns are mounted. Gandy (1982) draws attention to the inequalities in source access to the media through his concept of "information subsidies". This is defined as: "an attempt to produce influence over the actions of others by controlling their access to and use of information relevant to those actions." (ibid.: 61). Gandy's argument is that government sources, who seek to control the content and availability of information that affects their interests, tend to be routinely relied upon by the news media. These sources have the economic base necessary to package news in such a way that it can be used by journalists with ease. For example, creating spectacular pseudo events is costly and time-consuming. Also, the more a given source is used by the news media the more it develops its status as a credible news source.

In Britain, for example, the Department of the Environment manages the news to a considerable extent. A former environment correspondent for the *Times* claimed:

> . . . the press office at the Department of the Environment is specifically targeting me and my colleagues all the time and trying to get us to report the news in the way they want it reported, and so are ministers, all the time. (Interview, 22 February 1991)

A well-known tactic used by government is to time the release of unfavourable news to come out on public holidays, or on Fridays. However, when I interviewed a press officer at the Department of the Environment about the extent to which news is managed in this way, the charge was denied. He maintained that:

> . . . there always used to be this long running joke that, you know, you release bad news at kind of three o'clock on a Friday afternoon . . . just before a parliamentary recess so it goes unnoticed. But I think the journalists are far too sharp. You couldn't get away with that and we really can't just, you know, slow things up and try and cover things over . . . I mean I just don't think we could, you know, I think it's absolutely impossible to time it like that, you know, to actually know there's going to be events around . . . other big news stories. I mean who can predict the news? (Interview, 28 May 1991)

70

Another way in which sources manipulate the agenda is through "off-the-record" briefings. Press officers at the Department of the Environment spend a considerable amount of time providing such briefings for journalists. Also, they advise and brief ministers about their media appearances and negotiate terms.

Government agencies may not always be very successful in managing the news but this should not imply that they do not deliberately attempt to suppress negative news, or dampen its effect. Nohrstedt (1993) suggests that the communication crisis in Sweden following the Chernobyl disaster was caused by the authorities producing changing accounts of levels of radiation and making a number of mistaken predictions. Clearly the Chernobyl disaster and, more recently, the Brent Spar affair have prompted increased recognition of the importance of coordinated corporate strategy and image.

Summary

In this chapter I have considered some of the major ways in which news is socially constructed. The charge that the news media are biased is frequently made by politicians from all sides of the political spectrum. Reporters tend to adopt a liberal-pluralist conception of the news media and the concept of "objectivity" is enshrined in their professional codes. It is often used as a means of legitimating their role and underpins their claims to independence from the state.

The question of the extent to which objectivity is possible, or even desired, is a central debate within the sociology of journalism. This draws upon a wider philosophical debate in the social sciences about the nature of "truth" and the existence of an external "reality". The degree to which individuals believe objectivity is achievable reflects their underlying assumptions about the nature of knowledge. Idealists reject the notion that objectivity is attainable, while realists claim there is an external reality "out there" that the sociologist can seek to uncover. Environmental "facts" are often very complex and contested by a range of different claimsmakers. Although I suggested all "facts" have evaluative dimensions, I argued that extreme versions of idealism are inadequate for they lead us to conclude that it is impossible to arrive at an understanding of external reality.

Many of the difficulties in the bias/objectivity debate stem from the confused, and often ambiguous use, of key concepts such as "objectivity", "impartiality" and "neutrality". Often these terms are used interchangeably as though they mean the same thing. Objectivity should not be confused with total accuracy or with complete value-freedom. An objective account of reality may not necessarily be neutral as it may come down on the side of one particular set of interests. Impartiality implies that competing interests are represented in an adequate and just way. I would contend that it is more useful to view objectivity in terms of a continuum rather than the absolute standards of "true" and "false".

This is not, however, to deny that news is socially and culturally constructed. In some senses I think the news media always offer us a biased view of "reality". The picture they present us with is inevitably selective through the application of news values, and the various organizational and occupational constraints that govern the news-making process. The news media are complexly differentiated according to news formats, style, genre, news values and external constraints. Issues of objectivity, impartiality and neutrality impact differently upon different media.

Media practitioners have their own values and personal commitments which, to a degree, inevitably impact upon their coverage of environment and risk. Conscious and unconscious value positions influence the kind of judgements that are made concerning the credibility of news sources. For example, official news sources, such as government officials, are more likely to be viewed as "objective" than are pressure groups. Moreover, these official sources tend to gain advantaged access to the news media on a routine basis as "primary definers" because of their claims to expert knowledge, representative status and their powerful social position. Such news sources engage in various information-management techniques in an attempt to control public opinion.

However, in my view the structuralist model of source–media relations is too mediacentric. In other words, it tends to result in an exaggerated focus upon the media in relative isolation from broader structures of power that incorporate pressure politics. While this approach usefully draws our attention to the agenda-building power of official "accredited" sources, it overlooks the processes of contestation and negotiation that take place before, or at the same time as, primary definitions appear in the media. Moreover this approach tends to neglect a consideration of factors governing the relative success or failure of non-official sources, such as environmental pressure groups, in making social problem claims. At the same time we should avoid a perspective that is too heavily "source-centred". Also, there are limitations with the pluralist position adopted by, for example, Gans (1980). This approach views society in terms of range of competing groups and interests, with no one interest gaining dominance on a consistent basis. In the next chapter I examine the rise of environmentalism and offer a critical assessment of the contemporary environmental lobby.

Suggested further reading

H. J. Gans, *Deciding what's news* (London: Constable, 1980) is still one of the most readable studies of general news-making processes from a US perspective. For a good introduction to the bias and objectivity debate see M. Harrison, *Television news: whose bias?* (Hermitage: Policy Journals, 1985). Also, J. Curran & M. Gurevitch (eds), *Mass media and society* (London: Edward Arnold, 1996, 2nd edition) contains a number of thought-provoking essays on news production and objectivity (particularly chs 7 & 11).

A detailed discussion of the relationship between news sources and the news media can be found in R. V. Ericson, P. M. Baranek & J. B. Chan's excellent study of crime reporting entitled *Negotiating control* (Milton Keynes: Open University Press, 1989). Finally, C. LaMay & E. Dennis (eds), *Media and the environment* (Washington DC: Island Press, 1991) considers key issues concerning news production processes from the media practitioners' perspective.

Chapter 3

The environmental lobby

In the second half of 1988 it had become increasingly clear that the environment, as a separate issue, had developed a political importance all of its own. . . . It was an accumulative, growing movement which suddenly burst forth. . . . Anything that Mrs Thatcher touched was news anyway, from a newsman's point of view, so if Mrs Thatcher touched the environment it was news. But I don't think one should make the mistake of thinking it was only the Thatcher connection that gave it news . . . It's a massive world-wide movement really, a massive and unstoppable upsurge of feeling about a particular issue. (Interview, former environment correspondent for the *Times*, 22 February 1991)

Introduction

Since the late 1980s large environmental non-governmental organizations (NGOs) have become increasingly prominent in the field of international environmental politics. A sense of global crisis has led to the emergence of new sources of conflict and the "environment" has become a major battleground on which all sorts of resistive struggles are played out. Over recent decades there has been growing awareness of the scale of transnational environmental problems and their relationship with our globalized economy. The gap between the wealthy industrialized nations of the North and the impoverished South continues to widen, and social class remains an important source of conflict within late modernity. However, contemporary forms of collective action represent more than simply reactions to traditional divisive forces. In my view environmentalism has to be understood within the context of global capitalism, new systems of mass communication and the rise of consumer culture. These wide-ranging changes suggest that traditional theories of the position of ideology in social change, class conflict and value change need to be re-examined. Such approaches have variously suggested that social movements can be explained away according to class-based theories, to wider shifts in societal values, or to psychological tensions. Indeed, over recent decades there has been a growing recognition of the sheer complexity of contemporary social movements and the inadequacy of traditional mono-causal explanations. Environmentalism provides an excellent example which we can use to work through some of the key problems with earlier approaches.

In the UK and USA the environmental lobby evolved from a relatively small number of wildlife protection and nature preservation groups (see Pepper 1984). These early organizations were essentially concerned with domestic issues. However, by the 1960s many environmental organizations had broadened their focus to include a wider set of issues. Environmental threats such as global warming, far from being a new discovery, have a long history in scientific circles. However, it was in the late 1960s and early 1970s that environmentalism first took off in Britain with the publication of the *Limits to growth report* (Meadows et al. 1972), then *Blueprint for survival* (The *Ecologist* 1972), and in the USA with *Small is beautiful* (Schumacher 1974). After the most recent peak of environmental concern during the late 1980s and early 1990s, initial enthusiasm has waned.

However, by the early 1990s the environmental lobby consisted of an array of campaigning organizations employing a diverse range of strategies and tactics to achieve their aims. Many of these organizations had forged alliances across the globe and, with mass public support, wielded considerable potential bargaining power over particular issues. By the mid 1990s many such groups had become increasingly significant players in the policy-making arena. In part this reflects the growing institutionalization of environmental demands and international governmental pressure. Also, large environmental NGOs have become increasingly adept in their media management techniques. In particular, the use of accredited scientific "experts" problematizes reporting conventions based upon dichotomizing lay versus expert knowledge.

I want to begin this chapter by briefly discussing some of the difficulties involved in defining "social movements". Following this, I want to trace the early organization and tactics of the environmental lobby through to the more contemporary strands of green politics. In particular I will concentrate upon the post-war period, placing the discussion within the context of the new social movements of the 1980s and the revolution in global systems of communi cations. Finally, I want to conclude by taking a critical look at evidence for the rise in environmentalism and major explanatory frameworks.

Defining social movements

So far in this book I have focused upon environmental pressure groups, but what is a social movement? Social movements represent a broad mobilization of interests around a particular goal. Social movements are organized, collective forms of action. Unlike political parties, social movements operate outside of mainstream political institutions. However, they may permeate the corridors of power through a variety of channels including lobby group activity. What differentiates a social movement from a pressure group is the negotiation of universal moral principles (Eder 1993).

New social movements (or NSMs) are often contrasted with "old" social movements in typologies of political organization. The environmental movement is often taken as an archetypal new social movement (see, for example, Eyerman & Jamison 1991). Other NSMs include the women's movement, the civil rights movement, and the peace movement. NSMs have generally been founded since the 1960s and the 1970s and may be differentiated from "old" movements in four basic ways: position in the socio-political structure, goals and ideology, organizational framework and political strategy (see Table 3.1)

Thus new social movements may be characterized by less rigid organizational structures, grassroots activism outside of established political institutions, and the pursuit of wider cultural and lifestyle changes. Contemporary environmentalism is characterized by holistic approaches with an emphasis upon political ecology. A diverse range of environmental groups (including proliferating grassroots

Table 3.1 New and old social movements.

	Old social movements	New social movements
Location	Polity	Civil society
Ideology and aims	Political integration	Autonomy civil society
	Economic rights	New values/lifestyles
Organization of movement	Formal and hierarchical	Informal network and grassroots
Medium of change	Participation in political institutions	Direct action and cultural politics

Source: Martell 1994: 112.

groups) mobilize action at several different levels including local, national, state and international. As environmentalism has become institutionalized, mainstream organizations have tended to develop stronger links with statutory authorities. In contrast, the broad consciousness-raising movements of the 1980s have emphasized the role of the individual and expressivism (cf. Szerszynski 1996, Berking 1996). This stress on the politics of lifestyle represents a movement away from identity centred on state, and is perhaps epitomized by New Age Travellers with their romantic views of the countryside and emphasis upon spirituality.

The environmental movement clearly possesses some of the attributes of both "old" and "new" social movements. It embraces traditional conservation organizations who favour a top-down approach, and radical grassroots networks with a bottom-up approach and the absence of a fixed fee paying membership. Thus within a social movement there may be a variety of social movement organizations (or SMOs) who favour different political strategies that may reflect a degree of tension and conflict.

There are certain difficulties, then, with placing the environmental movement within a new/old typology. As Martell (1994) points out, NSMs cannot necessarily be seen as exclusively contained within civil society. While NSMs may seek autonomy from the state, they are frequently concerned with political reform and influencing the legislative system. Slotting the environmental movement into one or other of these categories fails to account for the complexity and multiplicity of meanings contained within contemporary collective action.

Two competing traditions

Broadly speaking there are two overarching traditions in the study of social movements. The European tradition focuses upon collective action and identity; in particular the capacity of social movements to bring about full-scale transformation of society, for example, Touraine (1978) and Habermas (1976). This approach suggests that social movements are produced by structural contradictions within the social system; the emergence of new forms of collective action reflects institutional change in post-industrial capitalism. Essentially, social movements are seen as arising in response to crises in the socio-economic or political realm. According to this view the role of the researcher should involve active participation in bringing about major social change.

In contrast to the structural approach, the US tradition takes a more disinterested approach and defines social movements in terms of organizational factors. Unlike the former model, it concentrates upon the question of how, not why, social movements evolve and are sustained. For example, the resource mobilization approach stresses the importance of material and symbolic resources (including time, finance, political skills, education and so on), rational action to achieve clearly defined goals, and the position of the individual within the organization (see McCarthy & Zald 1982).

The rise of the green movement in Western Europe and the USA

Post-war consensus politics

The anti-war and civil rights movements of the early 1960s reflected a profound dissatisfaction with the established political structures and the two-party system. At the same time, increasing scientific evidence about the deterioration of the environment became available. Of particular note was Rachel Carson's *Silent spring* (1962) which described the harmful side effects of pesticides and which had considerable political impact. While the environmental movement had strong links with the anti-war movement, it had little in common with the civil rights movement – some activists accused it of an inbuilt middle-class, white, bias. But the climate of awareness generated by the civil rights

Figure 3.1 Cartoon from *New Statesman and Society*, 23 June 1989, pp. 10–11. Reproduced with kind permission from Andrzej Krauze.

movement opened up the channels of political protest, and provided a model of effective peaceful campaigning. The protests against the Vietnam War in the USA, coupled with the rise of the Campaign for Nuclear Disarmament (CND) in Britain, mobilized considerable numbers of disaffected students (see McCormick 1989). Support was mainly drawn from young, middle-class, well-educated people. For many the environment, like the Vietnam War and racial inequality, was seen as reflecting an unhealthy, unjust and uncomfortably materialistic society.

These social movements occurred at a time when the conduct of politics was in transition, and when the electronic media were replacing the print media as the main source of information in society (see Eyerman & Jamison 1991). The very foundations of the old order were being shaken. During the late 1950s Britain and the USA were coming towards the end of a period of sustained economic growth. The consensus and unbridled affluence of the 1950s was beginning to be challenged. With the expansion of higher education and the growth in leisure time, many young people were starting to develop a more critical attitude towards Western society. Moreover, the seeds of this transformation were sown during the 1950s; a time when people in such countries were said to have never had it so good. By the 1960s people's expectations about the quality of life had been considerably raised and many were mobilized to take part in mass demonstrations.

Many of those who had previously been involved in the peace and civil rights and women's movements brought resources, skills and experience to the movement. The period from roughly 1975 to 1980 has been labelled the "social movement" phase in the rise of environmentalism, since it was marked by the increasing politicization of the environmental lobby (cf. Jamison 1996). Conflicts in Western Europe and the USA (mass demonstrations and strikes) in the late 1960s led to renewed sociological attention towards social movements. At the same time, the era of the mass media, youth culture and conspicuous consumption had arrived. The scale of the success of the early civil rights and anti-war movements gave rise to a new set of demands from a number of citizen groups that were formed in the 1970s. These groups mobilized around a number of issues including: environmental and consumer affairs; racial equality; abortion; women's rights; and poverty. The rise of these new groups corresponded with a decline in voters' attachments to the main political parties. The emergence of new campaigning organizations in the USA, as well as in Britain, reflected a growing alienation from the established parties.

By the 1970s the environment had, to a large extent, become institutionalized. It was not until this period, for example, that the UK general election manifestos of the major political parties directly referred to "environmental" policy (Robinson 1992). Administrative provisions began to become consolidated under single agencies, such as the UK Department of the Environment (DoE) which was founded in 1970. These developments reflected an increased awareness that the environment was interlinked with other policy areas. Also, this period marked a growth in commissions and committees charged with deliberating on environmental problems. While in 1970 only 15 countries had established environmental management institutions, by 1980 this figure had increased to 115 (Robinson 1992). There is a marked tendency for groups to become more conservative once they have become established; institutionalization tends to be accompanied by greater bureaucracy, which may dampen more radical strategies for change.

So far I have suggested that the rise of modern environmentalism was in many ways related to post war social and political developments. However, it was not until television became widely available that it was to gain a new symbolic force.

Visual politics and the mass media

Social movements during the early nineteenth century produced most of their own publicity, since they did not enjoy the benefit of the modern mass media. In the USA the suffragettes, the campaign for the abolition of slavery, and early evangelical associations published their own newsletters and tracts, since newspapers tended to be narrowly focused upon political propaganda and business news. In Britain, too, the established newspapers gave little coverage to such movements, but the underground radical press actively campaigned for working-class rights (see Hollis 1974). Curran & Seaton (1991: 20) observe:

> Movements ranging from early trade unions to political organizations, like the National Union of the Working Classes and the Chartist Movement, partly depended for their success on the publicity they obtained from the radical press.

However, with the rise of mass-circulated newspapers in the late nineteenth century the communication strategies of protest organizations were transformed. Increasingly campaigning organizations could not afford to ignore the growing permeation of the mass media in almost every aspect of social life. Clearly by the 1950s it was insufficient for them to rely upon their own publications; they had to take steps to publicize themselves through the mainstream media and take their message to a wider audience.

It was here that the electronic media provided a major breakthrough in their ability to capture large audiences and to cover "live" events. By the late 1950s televisions were widespread in Britain and the USA, and commercial broadcasting was attracting large audiences. Until this time political broadcasting was at its infancy, but the era of televised political debate was beginning to dawn. The televising of the first Campaign for Nuclear Disarmament (CND) march at Aldermaston, UK, in 1958 is often seen as heralding in the new age of "visual politics" (see Seymour-Ure 1991). CND organized the march from Aldermaston to Trafalgar Square in a way that was likely to generate maximum publicity. As Seymour-Ure (1991: 169) observes,

> Until the decline of CND it remained a superb instrument of pressure group publicity – visually varied; sustained over several days in a dead news period (a bank holiday weekend); embracing both ordinary people and several kinds of social and political elite; combining the predictable and the unexpected and culminating in spectacle and oratory in the greatest public space of the capital.

In the USA the civil rights movement was television's first major recurring news story. The symbolic power of mass demonstration captured the visual requirements of television news (see Kielbowicz & Scherer 1986). Communication between individual supporters, the general public and the leadership of such organizations was increasingly relayed through the mass media. Thus, Eyerman & Jamison (1991: 40) note: "Contemporary social movements very early on develop media-conscious strategies and even organizational roles for handling problems of communication". Also, Todd Gitlin's (1980) study of the student movement in the USA reinforces the way in which the mass media can influence movement tactics. As Hershey (1993: 145) observes,

> In addition to radio and newspapers, television was becoming a more important source of information about candidates and issues, and after the mid-1960s, direct mail provided still more cues. The mass media were coming to rival the parties as intermediaries between government and citizens – and access to the media did not depend on party loyalty. Parties became less important to voters, cognitively and emotionally, than they had been in the 1950s.

By the 1970s, then, there was a growing recognition among large campaigning environmental organizations, such as Friends of the Earth and Greenpeace, of the need to develop proactive approaches to the media. Direct-mail techniques had also become a popular means of mobilizing environmental support (Mitchell et al. 1992, Hershey 1993, Shaiko 1993). Such organizations began to widen the focus from traditional issues of wildlife and conservation to broader questions challenging our assumptions about nature and society.

A number of international events gradually fostered a new understanding of the global environment. In particular, the 1972 United Nations Conference on the Human Environment in Stockholm represented a landmark in international environmental policy. The conference established the United Nations Environment Programme (UNEP) and went a long way towards conferring political legitimacy upon the environmental movement. Throughout the 1970s a whole series of intergovernmental conferences on issues such as world population, water and food, continued to push environmental issues to the forefront. However, environmentalism was still largely seen as a fringe concern and few environmental NGOs were truly transnational in focus.

The transformation of the environmental lobby

By the late 1980s the environmental lobby consisted of an array of campaigning organizations employing a diverse range of strategies to achieve their aims. The Brundtland report on environment and development entitled *Our common future* (Brundtland 1987) addressed global issues that went well beyond local interests. By the early 1990s many large environmental organizations in the South had forged alliances across the globe and, with mass public support, wielded considerable bargaining power over particular issues (see Ekins 1992). Many view the rise of the ecology movement as part of a broad shift in society towards "postmodernity". Postmodernism rejects grand "metanarratives", or totalizing views of the world, and emphasizes the increasingly fragmented stream of images in contemporary culture and art (see Ch. 7). Globalization and the rise of new media technologies has meant a growing emphasis upon global marketing reach, and the production and consumption of what Sklair (1994) terms "cultural-ideological" goods. The fact that many mainstream environmental organizations had become significant players in the policy-making process partly reflected the growing institutionalization of environmental demands (Eder 1996).

Transnational NGOs such as the World Wide Fund for Nature (WWF) and Greenpeace International had become increasingly incorporated into the policy-making process, partly as a result of their sophisticated public relations techniques. As Jamison (1996: 226) observes:

Large environmental NGOs, as expert consultants, publicists and problem formulators, and knowledge producers are directly involved in the initiation and the implementation of major programmes of scientific research and technological development, often funded by development assistance agencies and/or multinational development banks. . . . The NGOs have developed highly effective media strategies, which have helped to give their activities and their definitions of the problems a broad public visibility which less professional organizations have difficulty achieving.

These environmental pressure groups have become increasingly attuned to the news values of large media organizations (cf. Anderson 1991, 1993a, 1993b). Greenpeace, perhaps more than any other environmental pressure group, has recognized the role the global media

84

can play in exerting pressure on the global market. Today, Greenpeace has approximately 30 offices worldwide; the largest are located in the UK, Netherlands, Germany and the USA. Greenpeace Communications, a division of Greenpeace International based in Amsterdam, has a full in-house film, video and photographic capability incorporating a small television studio, three editing suites, a digital sound studio and a commercial film and television archive. These facilities also include compressed digital satellite encoders and decoders and three-dimensional computer graphics. The Greenpeace press desk operates on a 24-hour basis to accommodate the deadlines of media organizations around the world. Also, the pressure group employs a range of experienced staff with professional video and photographic skills who work on the video news releases (VNRs) that became so controversial during the Brent Spar affair. Such organizations have increasingly modelled themselves on transnational corporations (cf. Sklair 1994, 1995).

At the same time that these movements were emerging in the 1980s a revolution in global media technologies was shrinking time and space. Television became more affordable for many people in less developed countries and new technological advances made possible the staging of world media "events" such as the "Live Aid" rock concert broadcast across the globe in July 1985 (Spybey 1996). The same movements that have in many respects been critical of technological "advances" have begun to explore ways of exploiting these channels of influence. At present little is known about grass-roots campaigners' use of new media technologies such as cam-corders, mobile telephones and the internet. Although these collectivities of indi-viduals have far fewer resources than powerful transnational environmental organizations, they too are tapping into these communicative technologies through, for example, sending video footage to news desks. The UK organization, Small World, provides assistance to activists in using camcorders to record events and distributes its own videos teaching groups campaigning techniques. Of course, campaigning groups have often developed their own channels of communication, anticipating a hostile response from the mainstream media (cf. Olien et al. 1989). Grassroots activists tend to lack the credibility and institutional backing of larger more established organizations who deal with the media on a routine basis.

Party politics

A series of disasters during the late 1970s and the 1980s, including Chernobyl, Bhopal and Three Mile Island, together with the growing popularization of scientific evidence regarding global environmental change, served to highlight the transnational scale of environmental issues. During the 1980s the greens became a much stronger force within European politics. However, the extent to which they gained parliamentary representation considerably varied between countries depending upon their political structures. For example, in Germany and the Netherlands environmental issues are more tied into traditional political structures than in Britain or Belgium (Lowe & Flynn 1989, Nas & Dekker 1995).

The success of the environmental movement is, to a large extent, related to party political gains. In 1983 the Green Party won representation to the national Bundestag in West Germany with 27 seats. By the late 1980s the greens had won significant parliamentary representation in Sweden, West Germany, Belgium, Italy, Switzerland and Austria. In June 1989 the UK Green Party polled 14.5 per cent of the vote in the elections to the European Parliament and boasted a membership of almost 20,000. However, in the same year there were no greens in the UK parliament, reflecting the fact that small parties do not do well in a two-party, first-past-the-post system. In the UK, as in the USA, the political structure tends to encourage pressure groups since minority political parties are discriminated against by the electoral system. By contrast, West Germany's political system provided greater opportunity for greens to challenge existing parties (Spretnak & Capra 1986).

Of all the green parties probably the most well known is the West German "Die Grunen". Under the West German system parties only needed to pass a threshold of 5 per cent of the vote to gain representation and financial aid from the state. Though Die Grunen enjoyed considerable popularity during the 1980s, in 1990 they failed to achieve the 5 per cent threshold for representation in the Bundestag, catching only 3.9 per cent of the vote. Internal conflicts between radicals and pragmatics divided the party. After months of bitter wrangling the pragmatics won and called for their policies to be closer to those of the Social Democratic Party (SDP). By the early 1990s the political force of Die Grunen was severely weakened and their identity less sharply defined.

While much of the activity surrounding green awareness has occurred in the wealthy Northern hemisphere (especially in Europe), green politics has become more established in the South. For example, signs of green politics are evident in Mongolia, India, Brazil and Mexico. Also, environmental NGOs have become a major feature of the political landscape in many less developed countries (LDCs). Friends of the Earth International, for example, has member groups in Argentina, Brazil and Pakistan (Yearley 1991). In India some broad alliances have been established that have overridden traditional caste/tribal divisions – for example, the Jhardhandi and Narmada valley movements (see Sachs 1993). However, there is little evidence of a movement towards solidarity since many people in LDCs are highly critical of what they see as attempts by the North to solve its own problems at their expense (Yearley 1994).

A new politics?

The contemporary environmental movement is characterized by enormous diversity. Environmental NGOs employ a multitude of different goals and strategies. Some organizations have a strong international focus, while others operate on a local level. Some organizations focus upon a single issue, while others are more broad-based and campaign on a diverse range of fields (Gottlieb 1991). As I suggested earlier, the environmental movement embraces elements of old-style and new-style politics. Environmental protest has become increasingly centred around localized, grassroots groups as particular facets of environmentalism have become institutionalized. Unlike many previous movements they have attracted a heterogeneous support base that crosses over traditional political allegiances.

The much looser networks of the 1980s, which co-exist alongside the more formally organized movements of the 1970s, can be distinguished from them in a number of important respects (cf. Hegedus 1990). Unlike organizations such as Greenpeace and Friends of the Earth, these grassroots movements do not have a fixed fee-paying membership. Distinct leaders are absent; they come and go. There is no hierarchical structure as with the more formal organizations of the 1970s. These networks defy simplistic analysis for they encompass a varied mixture of individuals united only at times seemingly by a deeply held political cynicism and a rejection of consumerism. There is also a sense in which they represent a longing for the past.

Hegedus (1990) argues that one of the central difficulties is that the NSMs of the 1980s cannot be adequately analyzed using the conceptual tools of the 1970s. Although they undoubtedly share some similarities they exhibit important differences. In contrast to many movements in the 1970s, the networks of the 1980s were not based around "new" issues nor were they to be found in "cultural" fields, they tended to emphasize individual subjectivity and expressivism rather than collective responsibility, and they engaged in actions that went well beyond the boundaries of the nation-state. A further problem is that many researchers tend to view NSMs as a phenomenon of Western societies and ignore the developing world. While Hegedus is right to make these distinctions in my view she is over-optimistic in concluding that such "movements" contain within them an emancipatory potential that will result in new forms of solidarity across the globe.

In the USA mainstream lobby groups such as the Sierra Club, the National Wildlife Federation and the Wilderness Society have dominated the environmental scene in recent years. Typically, these lobby groups have a professional staff, a top-down organizational structure, and a credible image (Boggs 1993). However, because the US political system tends to circumvent debate on environmental matters, grass-roots action is popular. Increasingly since the 1960s social movement protest has tended to be localized and diffuse such that it is difficult to define strategies, ideologies and organization. Boggs argues that local action tends to be ideologically unfocused and follows no clear strategy – instead it tends to value spontaneity and identity. As Boggs (1993: 107) observes:

> . . . localism remains very much alive in the United States and elsewhere – simply *because* the public sphere is so closed. The argument for sustainable development *must* take place outside the realm of normal politics. The party system, with abundant help from the mass media, manipulates consciousness and the rules of the game sufficiently to keep genuine conflict out of public discourse, so that politics regularly degenerates into a spectacle dominated by superficial images and symbols. In this milieu a strictly electoral or institutionally based strategy cannot go very far, hence the allure of a purely local approach which allows for more clarity of discourse and action. [original emphasis]

Organizations such as the Sea Shepherd Conservation Society and Earth First! represent the radical wing of the environment movement and favour direct action over lobbying. These groups are almost always splinters of mainstream organizations where a major struggle over policy and strategy has occurred. Earth First! was established in 1980 and attempts to prevent the exploitation of natural resources directly by "monkey-wrenching" tactics. These include sabotaging logging equipment or activists chaining themselves to trees and bull-dozers (see Dobson 1995, Killingsworth & Palmer 1992).

Greenpeace is undoubtedly one of the most well-known environmental organizations across the globe to employ non-violent direct action. Today, it is a large wealthy organization still very much associated with spectacular media images (see Shaiko 1993). In its early days the organization was probably best known for its campaigning against whaling and French nuclear testing. One of the most spectacular images was provided in 1985 when the French sank the Greenpeace vessel *Rainbow Warrior* in New Zealand's Auckland harbour. The vessel had been about to head a flotilla of boats in protest against French nuclear tests at Moruroa when the two bombs hit it. Greenpeace photographer, Fernando Pereira, was killed as he attempted to retrieve his photographic equipment from the water. Compensation, which was later acquired from the French government, was used to fund a replacement vessel and to launch a special fund for photographic work in memory of Pereira (Edwards 1988). After this incident the organization doubled its membership in just 18 months (Porritt & Winner 1988). Despite the climb-down over Brent Spar, Greenpeace has become a highly successful issue-entrepreneur and has managed to win a great deal of public support.

As with the USA, the environmental movement in the UK is very diverse, ranging from single-issue groups to those with a much broader agenda. Although most objectives are complementary there is considerable variation in strategy and methods. One of the best overviews of the environmental lobby is provided by John McCormick in his *British politics and the environment*. McCormick traces the British environmental lobby from its roots in nineteenth century wildlife and nature preservation groups through to the new style campaigning organizations of the 1970s such as Friends of the Earth and Greenpeace. Early organizations include the Royal Society for the Prevention of Cruelty to Animals (RSPCA), the League Against Cruel Sports (LACS) and the Commons, Open Spaces and Footpaths

Figure 3.2 Photograph from *New Statesman and Society*, 29 July 1988, p. 16.

Preservation Society. In contrast to earlier organizations, the new groups of the 1970s generally adopted more radical campaigning with a proactive approach towards the news media (Greenberg 1985). This new style gradually spread to some of the older organizations who became more actively involved in high profile campaigning. Finally, there are a small number of radical groups who eschew a credible public image such as the Hunt Saboteurs Association, and the militant, loosely structured, Animal Liberation Front (ALF) (see Thomas 1983). More recently, a number of grassroots groups such as Reclaim the Streets have participated in anti-roads protests.

Evidence for the rise of a broad-based environmental movement

One way of assessing levels of support for environmental issues is to look at opinion poll data. A variety of public opinion surveys indicate an underlying concern for environmental issues particularly among Western European and North American citizens (see for example Anthony 1982, Jones & Dunlap 1992, Keeter 1984, Kessel 1985, Worcester 1994). Evidence from the USA suggests that environmental concern rose significantly between the mid 1960s and the early 1970s when it began to level off – picking up again during the 1980s (Anthony 1982). Opinion surveys in West Germany and Britain suggest that interest in the environment generally increased during the 1980s (see Hansen 1990a). In Britain environmental concern appears to have peaked during the summer of 1989 when a record number of people (35 per cent) stated that the environment was among the most important issues facing the country. By the autumn of 1990 only 9 per cent of people responded in this way as law and order, health care and unemployment took precedence. This figure fell even lower by May 1994 when only 4 per cent stated that environmental issues were among the most important problems (Worcester 1994).

Public interest in the environment tends to fluctuate according to social and economic circumstances. The most recent peak in Britain occurred towards the end of a period of sustained economic growth. Economic recession has undoubtedly played some part in dampening levels of concern. However, according to MORI, working-class people in Britain are slightly more likely to state that "we should protect the environment, regardless of economic circumstances" than middle-class people. Also, those over the age of 55 are more likely to be classified as "deep greens" than those aged between 18 and 34. But how accurate are the findings of opinion surveys? Do they provide a reliable indicator of environmentalism?

It is important at the outset to distinguish between trends in opinions on environmental issues and trends in behaviour, including green activism. What people say does not always correspond with what they do. Indeed, opinions on environmental matters are not always very reliable indicators of the strength of people's feeling (Heberlein 1981, Keeter 1984). Also the conclusions drawn are likely to be affected by how the "environment" is conceptualized since it includes a diverse range of issues from nature conservation, to wildlife protection, to poverty and development (see Funkhouser 1973). In some cases, public opinion surveys may prompt individuals to declare an interest in issues which ordinarily they may not have had brought to their attention.

Recent public opinion surveys carried out in over 20 different countries have incorporated measures designed to map trends in green activism through identifying "green consumers" and "green activists" (Worcester 1994). British surveys, between 1988 and 1994, indicate a substantial increase in the proportion of people who say they have engaged in various environmental activities including buying green products, watching environmental television programmes and walking in the countryside/along the coast. According to this typology "green activists" are most likely to be middle-aged, but almost as likely to be working-class as they are middle-class, and male as they are female. According to these findings, "green consumers" tend to be middle-class, female and below the age of 45.

The 1992 Eurobarometer survey on "Europeans and the environment" suggests that the majority of Europeans (69 per cent) think that "economic development must be ensured but the environment protected at the same time" (Worcester 1994: 38). The survey found considerable international variations in the types of environmental actions people claimed to have engaged in. Table 3.2 reveals some interesting differences between countries, reflecting social and cultural factors.

However, in my view these findings need to be treated with caution. While they provide a useful guide to environmental attitudes and behaviour they only reveal what people "say" they do. Also, an individual only needs to have bought several green products on one occasion to be classified as a green consumer. To some extent the rise in the proportion of "green consumers" reflects the increasing availability of environmentally friendly products. Public attitudes do not exist within a social and political vacuum. Neither can we assume that they are always rational, or that they are necessarily reliable indicators of environmental activism. Fluctuations in concern for environmental issues are likely to, in some measure, reflect the following sorts of factors:

• competing issues on public, media and political agendas.
• economic conditions.
• high profile publicity of mediagenic environmental issues.

Another way of measuring the strength of support for environmental issues is to look at trends in the membership of environmental organizations. In 1995 Britain's Royal Society for the Protection of Birds (RSPB) boasted a membership of 890,000; more than all the political parties put together, And according to *Social trends*, between 1981 and 1992 Greenpeace membership in Britain grew fourteen-fold (*Social trends* 1994). In early 1990 it was estimated that approximately 8 per cent of the population in Britain belonged to one or more environmental group. More recently, pressure groups such as Friends of the Earth have experienced a fall in financial contributions (Rudig 1995). The cross-over in support for various causes has, however, clearly enabled wider political movements to emerge concerned with

Table 3.2 Actions taken to protect the environment (%).

	Bel.	Den.	France	Ger.	Greece	Ire.	Italy	Lux.	Neth.	Port.	Spain	UK	EC 12
A	85	86	90	88	90	85	89	84	79	88	86	88	88
B	62	77	87	74	55	55	54	55	65	58	54	73	65
C	58	71	58	87	12	33	55	75	82	34	31	54	60
D	50	53	54	67	58	38	57	55	47	71	70	46	58
E	49	43	65	54	78	40	59	53	39	69	67	52	58
F	41	54	45	54	28	42	43	66	52	25	30	57	46
G	35	36	41	50	42	22	39	41	43	43	34	38	41
H	15	18	7	46	11	10	5	27	22	6	5	17	19
I	32	13	32	26	25	8	30	27	13	32	15	11	23
J	11	7	8	16	8	11	10	21	5	6	5	9	10
K	12	5	13	12	10	6	10	18	4	7	7	5	9
L	15	23	5	13	12	15	7	37	22	5	4	14	10
M	10	16	5	7	2	5	6	18	20	2	4	8	7
Index	37	39	39	46	33	28	36	44	38	34	32	36	38

Source: Eurobarometer: Europeans and the environment. Cited in Worcester 1994: 40.

A Avoid dropping papers or other waste on the ground
B Save energy, for example by using less hot water, by closing doors and windows to save heat
C Sort out certain types of household waste (glass, paper, motor oil, batteries) for recycling
D Save tap water
E Not make too much noise
F Buy an environmentally friendly product even if it is more expensive
G Use less polluting means of transport (walking, bicycle, public transport) than your car, whenever possible
H Have your car fitted with equipment to limit the pollution such as, for example, a catalytic converter
I Go on a type of holiday that is less harmful to the environment
J Take part in a local environmental initiative, for example, cleaning a beach or park
K Demonstrate against a project that could harm the environment
L Financially support an association for the protection of the environment
M Be a member of an association for the protection of the environment

transforming social attitudes and institutions. According to Inglehart (1990), environmental awareness, expressed through organized pressure, has occurred in almost every developed nation in the globe.

However, I think membership figures supplied by environmental organizations also need to be treated with caution. Such figures tend to be politically sensitive and environmental organizations may be reluctant to release anything but general trend statistics. Sometimes membership figures lump supporters together with fee-paying members making it very difficult to arrive at an accurate estimate of official membership levels. Also, these figures do not tell us anything about the strength of support for grassroots networks that, by their very nature, do not have an official membership (Lowe & Rudig 1986). Participation in environmental politics is likely to be strongly influenced by cultural factors revolving around issues of "identity" (Giddens 1990, 1991, Johnston & Klandermans 1995). Indeed, Ulrich Beck (1992: 198–9; original emphasis) maintains:

These different partial arenas of cultural and social sub-politics – media publicity, judiciary, privacy, citizens' initiative groups and the new social movements – add up to *forms of a new culture*, some extra-institutional, some institutionally protected.

For Anthony Giddens this newly emerging culture is expressed in the realm of "life-politics" – particularly the politicization of gender divisions. Both writers identify a new radical departure towards "reflexive modernization", although they interpret this in rather different ways. Essentially, they are suggesting that the old order is being shaken up by social institutions beginning to take a more critical, self-confrontational engagement with the downside of industrial society. Thus this new form of individualization is not confined to the private realm of the individual or the family; it is increasingly forcing itself into the public sphere and bypassing formal political arenas.

Despite the difficulties with opinion poll data and membership statistics, there is a general consensus that "environmentalism", at least in the West, has moved from being a fringe concern to forming the basis of a major political ideology (see Dobson 1995, Eder 1996). But how adequate are major explanations of the rise of the environmental movement? Here I will restrict my discussion to four major explanatory frameworks: the changing class structure, shifts in value systems, the role of claimsmakers and the objective nature of environmental conditions. I will focus the bulk of my attention on the role of claimsmakers since it is the media which I am primarily concerned with in this context.

Explanations for the rise of environmentalism

The changing class structure

Environmentalism has opened up new cleavages within advanced industrial society. Some theorists argue that environmentalism reflects changes in the class structure, or consciousness of class. One theory, for example, is that far fewer people are voting along traditional class-based lines. Instead they are more likely to develop political allegiances towards movements that express universal values (Heath et al. 1985). Another approach views the growth of the middle classes in Western Europe and the USA as a key factor in spawning the growth of the environmental movement during the 1970s and 1980s. For example, some evidence suggests that environmentalism tends to be most actively supported by the professional middle classes, particularly those in white-collar, public-sector employment (Cotgrove & Duff 1980, Van Liere & Dunlap 1980). Typically, these individuals have the educational background and leisure/lifestyle orientations that make them more attuned to environmentalism. Berger (1987) cites the emergence of a new "knowledge class" (incorporating intellectuals, public-sector employees and those who work in counselling or education) who reject central capitalist values and whose work is marginal to material production. These individuals, it is argued, favour extending the welfare state and maintaining an environment where educational qualifications are valued in order to protect their position.

While there is some empirical evidence to support both of these theories, I think they must be accompanied by a number of qualifications (see Martell 1994). In particular, the middle classes are fractured by various divisions. Clearly, as we have seen, those most likely to support environmentalism tend to work in the public as opposed to the private sector. Also, there are important differences between those members of the middle classes who support traditional conservationist organizations and those who support radical groups who engage in direct action. Furthermore, in my view these explanations fail to account fully for the new consciousness-raising "movements" of the 1980s that straddle conventional class distinctions. So while social class positioning undoubtedly plays a part in collective action, it would be rather simplistic to suggest that a deterministic relationship exists. Additionally, we need to look at the role of values, identity and knowledge in understanding the growth of environmentalism.

Shifts in value systems

Another influential approach is to view the rise of environmentalism as part of a large-scale transformation of value systems in advanced industrial society. Thus postmaterialists argue that such societies are becoming more "inner directed"; once basic material needs have been met individuals become more altruistic and concerned with quality of life issues. Ronald Inglehart, for example, views the development of new social movements as part of a wider cultural shift in the values and ideologies of Western publics (cf. Inglehart 1977, 1990). He claims that one can identify a gradual transition from "materialist" to "post-materialist" values, evident when one compares the value matrix of the young compared with older generations. He sees this trend as reflecting the expansion of education, a rise in living standards, the growth of the middle classes and the blurring of traditional political divisions. In *Culture shift in advanced industrial society* Inglehart examines data from his longitudinal cross-national survey of public opinion and ideologies. He argues that these data support the theory that young people in Western society are becoming more concerned with quality of life issues, less materialistic and more concerned with self-development. In short, Inglehart suggests that there has been a gradual transition from "materialist" to "postmaterialist" values. The rise of "postmaterialist" values is linked with the trend towards increased economic and political stability in post-war advanced industrial societies. Thus Inglehart (1990: 11) claims,

Advanced industrial societies are undergoing a gradual shift from emphasis on economic and physical security above all, towards greater emphasis on belonging, self-expression and the quality of life. This shift can be traced to the unprecedented levels of economic and physical security that have generally prevailed in these countries since World War II, and to the emergence of the welfare state. Whereas previous generations

96

were relatively willing to make trade offs that sacrificed individual autonomy for the sake of economic and physical security, the publics of advanced industrial society are increasingly likely to take this kind of security for granted – and to accord a high priority to self-expression both in their work and in political life.

The rise of new social movements is explained in terms of the gradual influence of postmaterialist values. According to Inglehart postmaterialists are more likely to be concerned about the state of the environment than their predecessors, and campaigners are more likely to favour an informal, less hierarchical organizational structure. While acknowledging that protest groups reflect the existence of objective problems, Inglehart argues that they also mirror changes in social attitudes, training and skills:

> The rise of the ecology movement, for example, is not simply due to the fact that the environment is in worse condition than it used to be; it is not even clear that it is. Partly, this development has taken place because the public has become more sensitive to the quality of the environment than it was a generation ago. (Inglehart 1990: 372–3)

While this postmaterialist model partially accounts for the rise of environmentalism in Britain and the USA, it is limited in several respects. A first difficulty is that the period of sustained economic growth, on which Inglehart bases his theory, has been replaced by recession, mass unemployment and increased economic insecurity. Recent protests have centred around unemployment and the poll tax, as well as road-building and animal welfare.

A second problem is that the postmaterialism thesis fails to take account of the possibility that the public are responding to "new threats" or the deterioration of existing environmental conditions. The apparent concern with "higher order" needs may simply reflect growing public anxiety about environmental risks that are perceived to have the potential to affect individuals in a direct way (Offe 1987).

One of the key difficulties with theories that try and connect postmaterialism with environmentalism is the problem of circularity. Did postmaterialism create the conditions for the environmental revolution, or did the changes in attitudes towards the environment facilitate postmaterialism? To view the development purely in terms of a shift in public attitudes disassociates it from the real physical world in which environmental problems exist. As Lowe & Rudig (1986: 517–18) argue, in an important review of the literature:

One of our main reservations is that this effectively divorces environmental concern from ecological problems. The environment is seen as just one among many 'post-materialist' issues which suddenly emerged to prominence, unrelated to any change in the environment, through a shift in values among people who had nothing else to worry about.

Third, Inglehart's evidence suggests that the postmaterialism model applies particularly weakly to the British case as economic growth has been slower than that experienced by many other Western European countries.

A further problem is that the theory does not account for the heaviest strains placed upon the political system. The most threatening acts of protest tend to come from underprivileged or marginalized groups within society, rather than the affluent and well educated (Moran 1989). In particular, violent protest that occurs among the urban poor in developing countries is often linked to battles for local empowerment (Boggs, 1993).

Finally, even if we accept the evidence that a growth in postmaterialist values has in fact occurred, it could be that new social movements have promoted postmaterialist values rather than postmaterialism forming the basis for the emergence of contemporary forms of collective action (cf. Martell 1994). Fundamentally, I think the model tends to underplay the role of education, the media and environmental politics. As we shall see, these provide an important basis for understanding contemporary political activity. Any account of shifts in value systems directs attention towards institutions that play a central part in manufacturing values, knowledge and identities. Recent theories have attempted to analyze the complex linkages between structure, meaning and action. As Eder (1993: 8) observes:

... the level of culture plays a decisive role in bridging the micro and macro levels of analysis. A promising way to conceptualize this intermediate level of "culture" is in terms of communication and discourse processes.

In some important respects developments in the study of social

98

movements have tended to be relatively isolated from developments in the sociology of the media. In both these fields there has been a growing recognition over recent years that we need to pay greater attention to the production of "non-expert" sources of knowledge. A number of social movement analysts, for example, have argued that knowledge produced by environmental organizations has rarely been subjected to detailed analysis as it is regarded as "non-expert" (for example, Jamison 1996, Wynne 1996). Also, as we saw in Chapter 2, recently mass communications researchers have highlighted the media–centric focus characteristic of much of the sociology of journalism, and the failure to analyze source–media relations from the perspectives of sources themselves (for example, Anderson 1993b, Cracknell 1993, Schlesinger 1990). As Schlesinger (1990: 71) argues:

> Built into the sociology of journalism (even where its assumptions are broadly Marxist) is the potential for opening up a distinctive problematic: that of the social organization of non-official sources and the ways in which they achieve (or fail to achieve) their impact.

Indeed, there are clearly dangers involved in focusing too heavily upon the media to assess the effectiveness of pressure groups, and ignoring the wider policy-making arena (cf. Cracknell 1993). In my opinion one key advantage of what Martell (1994) loosely labels "action" approaches is to situate the rise of the environmental movement in terms of the broader processes of political communication incorporating education, media and the activities of news sources such as politicians, scientists or environmental pressure groups.

The role of claimsmakers

From an action-based perspective the rise of the environmental movement cannot simply be explained by external structural forces. In contrast to structuralist and socio-cultural frameworks, this type of approach places greater emphasis upon individual agency and the construction of meaning. Frequently public concern about the environment is triggered by the actions of environmental pressure groups, responses to events such as environmental disasters and resulting media publicity. Action theories are concerned with issue entrepreneurs who make social problems claims about the environment. In

Britain during the 1970s and 1980s it was primarily environmental NGOs who gathered together much of the evidence about key environmental issues later acknowledged by governments and official scientific institutions (Grove-White 1993).

Studies of the environmental lobby have tended to adopt two major approaches: an internal approach (for example, Wilson 1984), and an external approach (for example, Dawkins 1987). The internal approach is concerned with the inner structure and workings of environmental groups. Studies that fall into this category discuss factors such as the internal decision-making structure of pressure groups, the amount of resources held, public relations activities, the degree of conflict or cooperation between related interest groups and between environmental groups and government.

In contrast to this, the external approach, typically adopted by political scientists, analyzes social movements in the policy-making process carried out at the level of local and national government. This often involves an analysis of the factors that lead some pressure groups to influence politicians, and the governmental structures that facilitate or prevent this. Although these are the two main perspectives that have been taken there is a degree of overlap. Some combine both approaches in their analysis of the environmental movement (for example, Lowe & Goyder 1983).

One of the most comprehensive studies of environmental pressure groups and the media was conducted by Lowe & Goyder in the late 1970s. The authors surveyed 77 national voluntary groups involved with the environment, between 1979 and 1980 (see Lowe & Goyder 1983). Senior representatives of these groups were interviewed about a number of issues, including access to the media; membership; internal democracy; staff; relationships with government departments; and cooperation between different environmental organizations.

The relationship between culture and social movements has increasingly become the focus of recent studies in the US constructionist tradition (for example, Gamson 1992, Gamson & Modigliani 1989, Gamson & Wolfsfeld 1993, Johnston & Klandermans 1995, Kielbowicz & Scherer 1986, Wolfsfeld 1984). This type of approach suggests we need to deconstruct collective meanings through discourse or frame analysis (see Eder 1993: 9). Constructionist theorists view media arenas as prime sites where symbolic contest is played out. Claimsmakers use different discourses of legitimacy based upon, for example, scientific or moral appeals. Several theorists have noted how competition is played out between social actors over "symbolic packages" that are framed around particular overarching themes (see, for example, Gamson & Modigliani 1989, Eder 1996). In relation specifically to environmentalism, Klaus Eder's work provides a useful starting point for thinking about the ways in which environmental ideologies are packaged. Eder (1996) distinguishes between three major "packages" concerning the environment: conservationism, political ecology and deep ecology. For Eder, environmentalism is more than simply an interpretive package; it has become what he calls a new "masterframe" in public discourse. Of the three packages identified, Eder suggests that political ecology has achieved the highest profile because it enables environmental issues to become part of mainstream political discourse. Environmentalism is fast losing its identity as a counter-discourse and becoming a political ideology. We might also identify particular "packages" concerning animal welfare that still remain in the realm of counter-discourse

The analysis of media–movement relations forms an important part of action theory. For example, Gamson & Wolfsfeld (1993) examine power transactions between media and social movements. They argue that this relationship tends to be based upon unequal power relations since movements are more dependent on media than vice versa. Also, they convincingly argue that movements frequently have different cultures that conflict with mainstream political culture and with media cultures. They conclude that the media play a key role in mediating symbolic contests, but their relationship with social movements is characterized by a "fundamental ambivalence":

> Movement activists tend to view mainstream media not as autonomous and neutral actors but as agents and handmaidens of dominant groups whom they are challenging. The media carry the cultural codes being challenged, maintaining and reproducing them. In this sense, they are a target as much as a medium of communication. But they are also the latter and, in this sense, one tries to speak through the media rather than to them. (Gamson & Wolfsfeld 1993: 119)

However, in my view such models of media–movement interactions do not apply very well to looser grassroots networks. It is questionable whether grassroots networks are always more dependent upon the media than the media are on them. Although in cases where mainstream media seek to cover their views or activities they may well have less power, since they are unlikely to have pre-identified spokespersons for the "movement". In some cases campaigners are actively hostile to the mainstream media and rely heavily upon their own underground channels of communication. Indeed, there are often serious rifts within a movement over the extent to which individuals favour working within or outside of formal structures of power. Ultimately, of course, campaigners cannot ignore the mainstream media if they are to succeed in broadening their support-base. Yet one cannot simply judge the success of a movement through the amount of media coverage it enjoys (cf. Cracknell 1993). In particular, behind-the-scenes lobbying (extensively practised by groups such as Friends of the Earth) can be extremely effective if the support of influential contacts is gained. On occasions prominent political figures become "information conduits", significantly increasing the chances of ideologies gaining wide circulation in the news media.

Resource-mobilization and organizational-based theories are also weak when it comes to analyzing grassroots networks (for example, McCarthy & Zald 1982). These approaches stress the importance of material and symbolic resources, rational action to reach clearly defined goals, and the position of the individual within the organization. They tend to reduce behaviour to cost–benefit analysis and fail to explain how collective identity is produced and sustained. Essentially these approaches are grounded upon the more formal social movement organizations of the 1970s and shed little light on NSMs.

A further example of an action perspective can be found in Eyerman & Jamison's (1991) approach to the study of social movements, based on a study of Denmark, Sweden and the Netherlands. They argue that social movements are not merely shaped by external structures and political contexts, but are continually recreated by the actions of movement members. Eyerman & Jamison develop the notion of "cognitive praxis", by which they mean the intellectual knowledge and consciousness that form the basis of individual and collective action. They argue that social movements developed in Denmark and the Netherlands when environmentalists combined three forms of knowledge – organizational (with the goal of bringing about new open forms of democracy), cosmological (building a philosophy of social ecology) and technological (furthering knowledge about the technological aspects of environmental issues and proposing alternative technologies). In Sweden these forms of knowledge were incorporated within the mainstream political framework (see also Jamison et al. 1990).

However, I think Eyerman & Jamison tend to overemphasize the role of cognitive praxis and underestimate the extent to which a multidimensional framework is needed. Environmentalism, I would argue, has also become more widespread due to the popularization of scientific evidence about global environmental change.

Objective evidence concerning environmental conditions

Many of the explanatory frameworks that have been developed have emphasized external structural factors to the point where objective environmental conditions are glossed over (for example, Yearley 1991). However, Martell (1994) in my view correctly argues that, in addition to the sorts of factors I outlined above, the rise of environmentalism reflects objective environmental conditions. According to this view the most recent outpouring of environmental concern in Western Europe and the USA coincides with increasing popularized scientific evidence about ozone depletion and global warming. I concur with Martell that "social problems" cannot be totally divorced from real-world indicators. One of the problems with extreme versions of social constructionism is that they ignore the role objective factors play. Although our views are inevitably shaped by cultural, social and political judgements, we cannot totally abandon the notion of objectivity. From a critical realist perspective I would argue that although we can identify a number of social causes that go some way towards explaining the rise of environmentalism, it would be mistaken to ignore the real independent properties of nature.

A multidimensional approach

In my review of explanations for the rise of environmentalism I have suggested we need to consider a range of factors. Fundamentally I have argued that we cannot treat the environmental "movement" as one "actor"; for it incorporates a range of organizations and loose networks with quite differing strategies and goals. Universal theories of collective action offer only a limited framework. There are a great variety of environmental protest groups within and between countries with their own peculiar political structures and party systems. Also, the relationship between attitudes to the environment and environmental behaviour, and individual and collective action, is complex. As Nas & Dekker (1995: 18) argue, "instead of treating present models of collective action as competing explanations, different models may be correct for separate segments of the population".

We might best think of the environmental movement as a social movement industry with a fluid competitive dynamics. Theories of risk society and postmaterialism assume that culture is given and tend to ignore the issue of agency. Eder (1993: 10) proposes a "funnel" model:

> Going from action to structure through texture is a "funnel" model of explanation. We start with the collective action events, relate them to symbolically defined action spaces (that are produced and reproduced by collective action events) and then ask what is the connection between symbolically defined action spaces and class differences.

Constructionist studies have usefully directed attention to the ways in which environmental discourses are symbolically packaged in the media. However, extreme versions of social constructionism and relativism ignore objective "real-world" factors. I have argued that it is necessary to pay detailed attention to the ways in which environmentalism is shaped by social action, but at the same time to acknowledge the role of external natural forces.

Summary

In the introduction to this book I argued that the cultural sphere has tended to be neglected within the sociology of risk and the environment until relatively recently. Moreover, developments within the study of social movements have tended to be isolated from developments in the sociology of the media. Recently, however, there has been a growing recognition that we need to pay attention to "non-expert" sources of knowledge as well as "expert" official discourse. Content analyses of environmental reporting and interviews with media practitioners provide an indication of patterns of source access. However, there is also a need to complement these media–centric approaches through analyzing source–media relations from the perspectives of sources themselves through interviews and/or observation. Here, though, I suggest we need to distinguish between formal structured environmental organizations and looser grassroots networks. Clearly it would be mistaken to treat the environmental movement as "one" social actor.

The conceptual frameworks of the 1970s have failed to account adequately for the rise of NSMs. In my view a multidimensional framework is necessary to account for the rise of environmentalism. Extreme relativist or social constructionist positions are problematic since they ignore the role of objective environmental factors. Grassroots consciousness-raising environmental "movements" are likely to continue to grow over the next few years. Although there is a potential for convergence of interests, my assessment of the current situation indicates that they do not form the basis for a new global solidarity.

Suggested further reading

Two of the best overviews of environmentalism from a sociological perspective are L. Martell, *Ecology and society* (Cambridge: Polity Press, 1994) and S. Yearley, *The green case: a sociology of environmental issues, arguments and politics* (London: HarperCollins, 1991). Useful historical accounts of the rise of environmentalism from a human geography perspective are provided by J. McCormick, *The global environmental movement* (Chichester: John Wiley, 1995, 2nd edition) and D. Lowenthal, "Awareness of human impacts: changing attitudes and emphases", in *The earth as transformed by human action*, B. L. Turner (ed.), 121–35 (New York: Cambridge University Press, 1990).

A useful collection of essays on social movements from a cultural perspective is H. Johnston & B. Klandermans' *Social movements and culture* (London: UCL Press, 1995). Finally, M. Redclift & T. Benton (eds), *Social theory and the global environment* (London: Routledge, 1994), and S. Lash, B. Szerszynski, B. Wynne (eds), *Risk, environment and modernity* (London: Sage, 1996), explore more wide-ranging issues concerning the relationship between social theory and ecology.

Chapter 4

News and the social
construction of the environment

... the sorts of stories that I spent much time or attention on are
the ones which I think are going to be picked up by a bulletin or
programme or producer or editor. So there is an awful lot of
what I would consider environmental stories that I don't bother
with. Not because I don't think they're interesting but because I
don't think they are going to get anywhere ... Fashions come
and go. I mean some years ago I used to think mad cows were a
dead cert every time they came up. They are not now. (Interview, BBC environment correspondent, 5 February 1993)

Introduction

In the first two chapters I highlighted ways in which the news media
are embedded within political structures. Moreover, I suggested that
news is a product of a complex array of social, organizational and cultural processes. The news media present us with particular versions of
reality which are necessarily selective. However I have argued that
the concept of objectivity should not be totally abandoned, as it is
often possible to substantiate that a given account of reality is more
"objective" than another on the basis of the available evidence. Also,
when considering the representation of environmental issues I think
we must avoid glossing over the real independent properties of
nature. It is for these reasons, then, that I believe extreme versions of
social constructionism are unsatisfactory.

The aim of this chapter is to consider in more depth how risk and the environment are represented in the news media, particularly in relation to the sorts of issues that have previously been raised. How do journalists and broadcasters decide which stories are most newsworthy? Is there an underlying consensus about what makes the headlines? And how is the role of the expert framed?

Risk and the environment as a social construct

As we saw in Chapter 2, the news media present us with particular versions of "reality". In some senses, then, the media offer us social constructions of the world around us. Our thinking about the "environment" and "risk" is also to some degree influenced by cultural, economic and socio-political factors. Studies of risk perception suggest that attitudes to the "environment" do not exist within a vacuum (Sjoberg 1987, Slovic et al. 1976, Wilkins & Patterson 1991). Inevitably, we are selective in the sorts of issues that dominate our attention in any given culture or historical period.

In the first part of this chapter I want to consider some of the reasons why certain issues come to be defined as social problems in the public sphere, while others attract little or no attention. Indeed, research suggests that the degree to which social issues command attention cannot necessarily be equated with their importance or the seriousness of the risks they pose (Hansen 1990a). As I noted in Chapter 1, researchers such as Anthony Downs have suggested that social problems typically pass through a series of identifiable stages. These natural history models are at best rather crude (Hilgartner & Bosk 1988). Early sociological study of social problems suggested that the emergence of social problems coincided with periods of major tension in societal values. However, these studies were unable to explain why it was that such tension generated particular sorts of responses at particular points in time.

Culture and risk

More recently, a number of anthropological studies (for example, Douglas 1975, 1985, 1992, Douglas & Wildavsky 1982, Thompson & Wildavsky 1982, Wynne 1982b) have focused upon the question of how particular social problems come to be defined as risks. Pollution beliefs, it has been argued, function to maintain social boundaries and to protect vested interests. A study by Douglas & Wildavsky (1982) suggests that our selection of risks is influenced by social values and the way in which different cultures operate. In essence, they argue that competing public perceptions of risk are all equally biased because they reflect different cultural meaning systems. Pollution beliefs, they argue, often serve to maintain the stability of society. For example, the nomadic Hima people will not let women near the cattle because they hold the belief that women will contaminate the cattle and cause them to die. This belief frees women from working in the productive sphere, so that they can devote their attention to making themselves beautiful. This is important since the Hima men make their wives sexually available to other herdsmen in order to encourage them to share their herds with each other, for there is great pressure on the Hima men to bargain and ensure that they have enough friends around them to work together, rather than establishing rival herds. Thus, Douglas & Wildavsky argue that these beliefs function to control women's sexuality so that men can make their agreements in the productive sphere. But the Hima people also believe that the human population needs to be kept down so that there is enough of their staple food, derived from cattle products, to feed everyone. The number of separate households with child-bearing women is reduced through the practice of old men having sexual access to their sons' wives, rather than taking a second wife. Their beliefs, then, function to control reproductive behaviour but also reflect actual physical dangers:

> Their theories of danger, so curious to us, have the usual triple compulsion: first, they keep apart social categories which they want to keep apart; second, they refer to real dangers, for cows do die and get lost and their milk does dry up; third, there is the metaphorical message that always reminds the men and the women that human reproduction must be kept down. (Douglas & Wildavsky 1982: 42–3)

Douglas & Wildavsky maintain that a similar process is at work in modern industrialized society. Indeed, they view the rise of environmentalism in terms of the social control of information and political value-systems. Douglas & Wildavsky claim that traditional American values are being eroded and that concern about environmental issues is being used as a surrogate for a wider attack on these beliefs: ". . . the critics of our society are using nature in the old primitive way: impurities in the physical world or chemical carcinogens in the body are directly traced to immoral forms of economic and political power" (1982: 47). A similar approach is taken by Rothman & Lichter (1987), who claim increased concern over nuclear energy is being used partly as a surrogate for wider ideological criticisms of US institutions.

One of the main problems with this type of approach is that although theorists provide plenty of examples to demonstrate the selective nature of pollution beliefs in less developed countries, rarely do they offer specific instances relating to the modern, industrialized world. Indeed they tend to take it for granted that these findings are applicable to modern industrial society, even though it is more complex and differentiated. Also, it fails to explain why it appears that environmentalism is being used as a surrogate attack on established beliefs. They portray environmentalism as essentially irrational and tend to deny the objective existence of environmental problems.

As we saw in Chapter 3, extreme versions of social constructionism suffer from a number of difficulties. We cannot ignore or totally explain away the "objective" existence of environmental problems (Martell 1994). Though the sheer complexity of many environmental issues makes absolute certainty difficult to achieve, extreme relativism is clearly unsatisfactory. Risk perception is influenced by a multitude of different factors (sociological, psychological, cultural, political, economic) but may also reflect the existence of "objective" problems.

Nature promotion

Although concerns about environmental issues may have objective roots, they are shaped both by the promotional activities of issue sponsors, and through culture representations (including advertising, photography and art). Alex Wilson, in his seminal book entitled *The culture of nature*, explores some of the ways in which "nature" is culturally constructed in modern society. He argues that nature cannot be separated from culture since it is mediated through major social institutions (such as the education system or the tourist industry) and the culture industry (including advertising, photography and art). Wilson's work is important in suggesting that issues resonate differently in particular countries, and at particular points in time, depending upon broader cultural and economic factors. Since the Second

World War, Wilson claims, one can identify a number of significant changes in the ways in which we perceive nature.

First, there has been a great expansion in nature tourism with emphasis upon the mass production of sightseeing experiences such as safari parks or Disney World (see Urry 1995).

Second, since the 1970s, at least in some Western countries such as the USA and the UK, increased stress has been placed upon environmental education and promotion (aided by the activities of various environmental organizations).

Finally, alongside this, there has been a growing recognition of the need to "manage" public opinion concerning the environment. Since the mid 1980s significant energies have been channelled into the substantial risk-management industry and corporate green advertising. Wilson (1992: 86) concludes:

> Alongside the environment of the biosphere, though, there is now also an environment of promotion and advertising and speech about nature – its management, its protection, its fragility, its sacredness, its marketability. It is an environment that encompasses the print and electronic media and suffuses the language of both corporations and social movements. It is also an environment in which we must intervene.

The nuclear power industry provides an example *par excellence* of the growing emphasis upon advocacy within the commercial sector. Various information crises have forced particular sections of industry to take a more proactive approach to marketing and communications. This is reflected in what Donn Tilson (1993) labels "eco-nuclear publicity" accompanying the emergence of visitors' centres designed to promote the green credentials of the nuclear industry. The green consumer has clearly exerted considerable influence upon industry, even if the process has been gradual. For example, in 1995 if it had not been for the number of Germans boycotting Shell petrol stations the company may not have made its dramatic U-turn on plans to sink the Brent Spar oil rig in the Atlantic.

The German boycott of Shell garages is said to have cost Shell Germany approximately 30 per cent of its usual revenue. As mentioned in the introduction to this book, Greenpeace protests against the intended sinking of the Brent Spar oil platform at sea sparked off a major controversy. Video news releases of two Greenpeace vessels sprayed with high pressure water cannons, together with protesters occupying the platform, made dramatic television news footage. At the start of the campaign 20 journalists were invited to board a Greenpeace vessel. The pressure group ensured that the media were kept directly informed through sending live satellite pictures to news desks. Shell's dramatic turnaround attracted considerable attention from the news media.

In Britain the story was a front page lead in all of the national mid-market and broadsheet newspapers on 21 June. The *Daily Mail*'s front page headline was "Shell U-turn sinks Major", while the *Times* chose to lead with the headline: "Shell abandons sinking Brent Spar" (followed by the sub-heading: "Ministers furious over capitulation to Greens").

The Dutch newspaper, *de Volkskrant*, reported:

With Germany as a benchmark, Dutch public opinion has risen against Shell . . . Shell has tried to mount an information campaign to explain its decision, raising the fear that Shell is missing the point. The conflict is based upon an ethical point of view: the sea is not a dumping ground.

Similarly, the German *Der Standard* stated:

In environmentally aware countries every child knows that you should not throw rubbish in the sea. While the British have made a rational economic exercise out of the whole thing, for us the Brent Spar affair is a question of good behaviour.

As mentioned in the Introduction, Shell's announcement was followed a few months later by an admission from Greenpeace that their calculation of the amount of oil on the platform had been inaccurate. While Greenpeace estimated that the amount of hydrocarbons was in the region of 5,000 tonnes, an independent investigation by the Norwegian certification company, DNV (Det Norske Veritas), revealed there were only around 75–100 tonnes of oil on board. Shell's original estimate of around 50 tonnes of oil thus proved to be considerably closer to the final figure. Greenpeace wrote to Shell apologizing for the error. Lord Melchett, Director of Greenpeace UK was reported to have stated:

The activists were working in atrocious conditions. They tried to sample three pipes. Two were blocked and the third wasn't in the pipes. They thought their device was in the tank. Now we realise it was probably in a pipe leading to the tanks rather than the tank itself . . . . It was only a few days before the campaign ended that this analysis became available. Our argument was always that Shell was wrong in principle to seek to dump the installation at sea. (*Guardian*, 6 September 1995: 2)

Following Greenpeace's admission some journalists claimed that the news media had been too ready to accept video news releases supplied by the pressure group, and had failed to report the affair "objectively". This opened up a period of intense scepticism within the news media, prompting Greenpeace to increasingly rely on their own Web site on the Internet as a key vehicle to get their message across (see Pearce 1996). Clearly, different criteria were being used to inform judgements about the relative costs and benefits of deep-sea disposal. I think Shell failed to take account of the strength of public feeling (especially in Germany) against the deep-sea disposal option. Although we must treat public opinion survey material with caution, a 1994 MORI survey in 21 countries found that 16 per cent of respondents claimed they would "boycott a product or country targeted by Greenpeace" (Worcester 1994). Socio-cultural processes clearly impact upon how societies select and deal with risk. As we shall see in the next section, research suggests that lay perceptions of risk tend to incorporate judgements about the relative trustworthiness of institutions. A MORI survey in August 1995 suggested that a relatively small number of British people claimed to have a "great deal" or a "fair" amount of trust in scientists working for industry (48 per cent) or government (38 per cent). By contrast, 82 per cent of the sample claimed to trust scientists working for environmental groups.

Furthermore, Shell's bureaucratic culture meant public relations activity tended to be slow and largely reactive. The company's approach displayed little willingness to engage in wide consultation. Key documentation, for example, was regarded as confidential and dialogue with external stakeholders was limited.

A Business and the Environment survey, conducted by MORI a month after the Brent Spar U-turn, produced some interesting findings. When asked "Who won the argument, Shell and the government, or the environmental pressure group Greenpeace?", 63 per cent of the British public sampled stated "Greenpeace". Moreover, when questioned "Do you think Shell should or should not have sunk the Brent Spar oil platform in the Atlantic?", only 17 per cent replied "yes", while 71 per cent answered "no" (Worcester 1994).

Shortly after the Brent Spar climbdown, there was a further international outburst from consumers at the news that France had decided to resume nuclear testing in the South Pacific. This news led to a convergence of anti-nuclear campaigners joining the Campaign for Nuclear Disarmament (CND) to protest against the plans, and to a call for a boycott of French goods. President Chirac's decision also attracted widespread criticism from world leaders. Greenpeace launched its largest campaign yet against the nuclear tests, costing millions of pounds. However, it was not long before the group's vessel, the MV Greenpeace, their helicopter and various inflatables, were seized at Muroroa by French commandos when protestors entered a 12-mile exclusion zone. Here again, the claims-making activities of Greenpeace played a major role in alerting the public to what was going on.

So far in this book I have discussed some of the reasons why certain issues come to be seen as social problems at particular points in time. To conclude briefly, issues or events come to be perceived as social problems partly through the activities of various issue-entrepreneurs (discussed in Ch. 1) including industry, pressure groups and government representatives. As we saw in Chapter 3, the rise of environmentalism can be seen as the outcome of a complex combination of various factors including perceived levels of public opinion, political expediency, media publicity and the qualities of the issue itself in terms of the degree to which it "fits" established news values. However, I have concluded that objective conditions also have some bearing upon the rise of environmentalism as a social issue.

Media framing of risk and the environment

Before we turn to focus upon key approaches towards understanding story selection, I want to consider briefly the major characteristics of media discourse on risk and the environment. How do the news media construct these issues? Which types of environmental issues feature prominently on media agendas? And how adequate is the content of information provided about risk?

I shall concentrate upon environmental risk since media reporting is often risk-led, based on anxieties concerning threats to health posed by major incidents, accidents or disasters. However, it is useful to make a distinction between these types of events, which draw attention to themselves, and more "routine" environmental issues that only become publicly visible through claims-making activity (Hansen 1991).

The category "environment" often overlaps with or incorporates the category "risk", which is often dealt with as a subcategory of "science" reporting (Dunwoody & Peters 1992). Risk to health covers a very wide spectrum of areas represented in the mass media including environmental issues and controversial technologies. The environment, like other substantive areas of media reporting, is largely mediated through the "expert" as the voice of authority. This may have the effect of discouraging critical thinking and marginalizing lay views (see Ch. 6). Risk and threat feature prominently in media constructions of the environment. In recent years a major controversy has developed over the disjuncture between "expert" and "lay discourse".

According to Susan Cutter (1993), the debate over expert versus lay views of environmental risk reflects important social shifts over the last 30 or so years. In particular, Cutter singles out the following factors: rising affluence in advanced industrial society, resulting in a growth in concern over quality-of-life issues; increasing mistrust of institutions with responsibility for "managing" environmental risk; the institutionalization of scientific conflict through traditional policy-making channels; and the increasing use of technology at home, in work and at leisure. As Cutter suggests, the institutionalization of divisions in scientific opinion has had one of the most significant impacts. Conflicts of opinion have become more difficult to keep within the scientific community, and media publicity provides further fuel for declining public confidence in the "expert".

At the same time, risk "experts" are often critical of mass media, arguing that risks tend to be distorted and the media are too reliant upon pseudo-experts (Dunwoody & Peters 1992). Media practitioners have been criticized for treating issues in an emotive way (through exploiting the human interest angle), giving some stories undue prominence (for example, an escape of toxic gas that impacts upon a relatively small number of people presented as a lead news item), or the inappropriate use of misleading images (such as presenting images of a nuclear explosion while reporting on an accident at a nuclear power station) (ibid., Salome et al. 1990).

115

A number of researchers have attempted to compare "objective" data on environmental risks with news media representations. A content analysis of US network television evening news, conducted by Greenberg and colleagues, found that coverage of risk issues was strongly influenced by traditional news values (Greenberg et al. 1989a). The study suggests that television news tends to focus upon particular types of risks, especially those that are connected with unexpected, dramatic disasters such as large chemical spillages. Yet, as Greenberg et al. observe, the number of deaths resulting from these sorts of disasters are often far fewer than deaths from asbestos or smoking, which receive less prominence. Indeed, television news coverage of environmental risks tends to be *event-* rather than *issue-led*. Also, in a large-scale study of 15 media outlets (including television, newspapers and magazines), Singer & Endreny (1987) found that the news media tended to highlight relatively rare hazards such as toxic shock syndrome, and generally provided inadequate information about risks.

Many public officials and scientists accused the media of exaggeration, distortion and bias in the reporting of the Chernobyl accident. Dunwoody & Peters (1992) cite the example of a senior German official, attached to the government information office, who claimed German media reporting had impaired the authority of science since it was inaccurate, oversimplified and gave "pseudo" experts equal treatment to the Government Radiation Protection Commission.

A large number of studies have been conducted worldwide into risk communication following Three Mile Island and the Chernobyl disaster (see Gale 1987, Rubin 1987, Wilkins & Patterson 1987). However, the findings of this research are inconclusive. A number of studies suggest that the media generally fail to supply people with enough risk information. For example, a study by Friedman et al. (1987a) analyzed coverage in five newspapers and three main television networks in the USA over the two week period following the Chernobyl accident. They concluded that television and newspapers did not provide enough space, or explanation, to the effects of radiation upon health and the environment. It appeared that the nuclear industry had succeeded in effectively managing information as most statements tended to reassure the reader or viewer. Although Friedman et al.'s study is relatively sophisticated in treating the mass media as complexly differentiated, more could have been made of the control of information by government and the nuclear industry, and the problems that the media experience in obtaining accurate information. Also, they did not attempt to differentiate between the various groups that the audience or readership is composed of, and they failed to explore how their perceptions of risk may vary and identify factors that may account for this.

A study conducted by Sandman et al. (1987), focusing upon environmental risk in the US press, came to similar conclusions. They found that very few of the articles that included a discussion of environmental risk addressed the amount of danger they posed. Wilkins & Patterson's (1987) study of US television news coverage of the Chernobyl disaster reinforces this finding. Wilkins & Patterson analyzed the coverage of three television newscasts for one month after the Chernobyl accident. They argue that the news media perform inadequately in covering risk situations because they are presented as novelties, issues are often placed outside their wider context, and crucial comparative figures tend to be omitted. Not surprisingly, television was found to be more event-centred than newspapers and was heavily reliant upon visual imagery. For Wilkins & Patterson (1987: 87): "Perhaps the most fundamental problem in the way the mass media report risk is the necessary reliance upon images to convey a story."

A longitudinal content analysis study of German media coverage of the Chernobyl disaster by Merten et al. (1990) found the distribution of alarming and reassuring statements was about equal (see Dunwoody & Peters 1992). However, a review of Swedish research on Chernobyl coverage suggests there was a much larger proportion of worrying compared with comforting statements in the Swedish media (Nohrstedt 1991). As Allan (1955b) observes, we can identify a number of ideological struggles in nuclear discourse which play upon powerful metaphors and euphemisms.

Explanations of story selection

News values

As we saw in Chapter 2, far from news representing a random response to issues and events, it is highly structured by routine organizational practices. Journalists typically operate with a set of unquestioned news values that frame their activity. Although media practitioners work within various guidelines, many values remain implicit. In judging the newsworthiness of particular stories the reporter makes various assumptions about the audience, editorial identity and conventional story telling mechanisms. These values operate at several different levels within the news production process. Bell (1991) divides them into three main categories, though clearly there is some overlap: (1) values in news actors and events; (2) values in the news process; and (3) values in the news text.

An influential news values scheme, developed by Galtung & Ruge (1965), is based upon an analysis of the presentation of three crises in the Scandinavian press. Galtung & Ruge identified eight key factors that shape the news:

1. Frequency – this refers to the extent to which an item fits the news production cycles of a media organization. Generally, the news media tend to rely upon items that fit into a 24-hour cycle. So unless a gradually developing environmental problem is perceived to have come to a climax, it will often tend to be neglected in favour of the more immediate story. However, as I suggested in Chapter 2, there are important differences between and within the news media.

2. Amplitude or size – the degree of amplification (or issue threshold) that an event has to reach before being viewed as newsworthy. For example, this might include the number of people who have to be killed by a natural disaster, or the sheer scale of an oil spillage, before it is deemed sufficiently newsworthy to be prominently reported.

3. Ambiguity – the less ambiguous an event the more it is likely to be covered. Thus issues that can be presented as relatively clear-cut tend to be more newsworthy. An increased recognition of the complexity of environmental issues may have contributed to decreased levels of reporting evident in many Western countries during the early 1990s (Anderson & Gaber 1993).

4. Meaningfulness – this refers to an item's relevance in terms of cultural proximity and its relation to everyday life. Thus there is a tendency for the news media to concentrate upon "closer to home" items with which we have a degree of familiarity, or upon events in far-away places that are perceived to possess a high degree of relevance.

5. Consonance – the more an issue is compatible with preconceived ideas about a nation or social group, from which the individuals

are drawn, the greater its chance of being represented in the news media as a sort of self-fulfilling prophecy. For example, journalists tend to have particular preconceptions about environmental issues, or about demonstrations, and these types of stories tend to be based upon a familiar script (Bell 1991).

6. Unexpectedness – at the same time, the more rare or sudden the event, the more likely it is to gain novelty value and grab headline attention. News quickly becomes stale and the unexpected and recent is valued. For example, repeated stories about climate change are likely to be valued less than a controversial challenge to expected predictions.

7. Continuity – if an issue or event has already commanded media attention there is a greater likelihood that it will continue to be viewed as newsworthy, even if its scale is diminished. Also, as I shall discuss later on, there is a high degree of media interdependence in selecting and structuring news.

8. Composition – news is produced in such a way as to cover a spread of different sorts of items, while maintaining some common links. Therefore, whether or not a particular news story is selected is to some extent dependent upon the distribution and character of competing items.

According to Galtung & Ruge, none of these factors is significantly shaped by cultural variations; that is not, of course, to say that there are not some variations. For example, we may find the same sorts of general parameters shaping the construction of news in North America as in the UK or Australia. However, we may also distinguish particular facets of the news production process that are very much bound by culture. Galtung & Ruge highlight four cultural factors that play a key role in shaping the news, at least in Western society. Thus an item that includes any of the following has enhanced chances of being reported:

- *Elite nations* – this refers to the dominant position enjoyed by elite nations, such as the USA, in news reporting.
- *Elite persons* – similarly elite persons (for example, representatives of the state or the monarchy) tend to occupy a central place in news media discourse.
- *Personification* – this refers to the tendency to concentrate upon the role of social actors in events, whom people can identify with, rather than structural forces. Human interest stories centring around people form the staple diet of many newspapers. This news value cuts across many of the factors already discussed.

119

- *Negativity* – this refers to the frequent emphasis upon bad news in the news media. Thus a large amount of space is devoted to crime, law and justice (Ericson et al. 1991, Schlesinger & Tumber 1994). In a study of environmental reporting in the Canadian press, Einsiedel & Coughlan (1993) found a strong emphasis upon negativity.

According to Galtung & Ruge these values are cumulative, so that the more factors satisfied by a story, the more it is likely to be viewed as newsworthy. If a particular value is not satisfied this may be compensated for by scoring very highly on another.

Although Galtung & Ruge's analysis is clearly of considerable value it is based upon foreign crisis coverage, which is dominated by news agency output, and concentrates upon criteria specific to the press (Negrine 1989). Later studies suggest that a number of other factors may be significant including: timeliness (Tuchman 1978, Schlesinger 1987); physical proximity; factual risk; and the pressures to use directly attributable statements from authoritative sources that can be verified (Bell 1991, Tuchman 1978).

In a study of television news, Bell (1991) identifies four additional values that are associated with the news process:

- co-option – this refers to a long-running major story, such as the greenhouse effect, which generates coverage for all kinds of marginally relevant stories that are hung on this peg (see Schoenfeld et al. 1979).
- competition – this includes competition between news media for exclusives, and competition between stories.
- predictability – although unexpected events often have a very high news value, prescheduled events can be skilfully planned to fit around news media deadlines.
- prefabrication – the availability of ready-to-use text that can be quickly transformed into a story.

To summarize briefly, I have suggested that a number of news values operate at different levels within the news production process. Some news stories have a much greater likelihood of being covered than others because they accord with organizational norms, pressures and routines and/or they possess particular conventional features. As we shall see later on, some news values are more specific to particular mediums. Also, important differences exist between news criteria employed by local and national media.

So far we have considered some of the major production constraints that influence news-making generally. There are, however, a number of factors that exert a particular influence upon the way *environmental* issues are framed. Here I want to focus upon three important aspects of environmental news items.

Characteristics of environmental news items

In my view three factors intrinsic to many environmental issues influence their chances of becoming news stories. First, much environmental coverage is event-centred. Several researchers have found the news media to be preoccupied with dramatic events such as oil spills and, to a lesser extent, pseudo events such as publicity stunts (for example, Anderson 1991, Molotch & Lester 1974, Rubin & Sachs 1973, Sachsman 1976, Shanahan 1993, Wilkins & Patterson 1987). In part this reflects pressures of time within the news organization. As Dunwoody & Griffin (1993) argue, this orientation towards "events" tends to allow news sources greater control in the framing of stories, and exempts journalists from considering wider issues. Moreover, this may encourage members of the audience to blame individuals or individual companies rather than to consider wider structural explanations (Hannigan 1995).

Second, environmental coverage tends to be characterized by a strong visual component. However, differences exist between and within media. For example, research suggests that television news makes greater use of such criteria than do the press (cf. Wilkins & Patterson 1987). Of course, other areas of news reporting revolve around events and visualization, but to a lesser degree. Perhaps not unsurprisingly Galtung & Ruge do not place much importance upon visual criteria since their study was based upon an analysis of the press. However, visual considerations are extremely important for television. Perhaps one of the greatest differences between press and television coverage of environmental issues concerns the relative weight attached to the visual quality of news stories. Since television is a visual medium the availability and quality of pictures is of much greater importance. This can be a particular problem when searching for new angles on environmental issues. For example, a former environment correspondent for BBC News claimed:

> ... we're about pictures ... we're about words as well but words are captions to pictures, essentially. .... Above all environment

stories really need good pictures . . . global warming is very difficult because you can't actually see global warming. You can see
car exhausts and you can see smoking factory chimneys and you
can hear people talking about it. But when you've done that
you've more or less done the kind of story that I've done 20 times
this year because the ingredients are almost always the same . . .
unless you're making a documentary with clever graphics then
it's hard to ring the changes. (Interview, 24 November 1990)

Also, a former environment correspondent for ITN concurred that
the newsworthiness of pictures can be a particularly important factor
in television news story selection. He contrasted stories concerning
updates about global warming with pitched battles in Britain over the
M3 extension at Twyford Down, Hampshire:

Pictorially it's a tricky one to show global warming because
obviously they're showing something of the future. You cannot
show what it is now apart from a few graphics. Once you've
done those fancy graphics and a few bits of East Anglia battered
by rising sea levels there's a sort of limit before you've sort of
really got to use the same pictures again, but different script, different words . . . Twyford Down is fine . . . and particularly when
it became an EC battle. (Interview, 19 February 1993).

Environmental items in current affairs radio programmes tend to
revolve even more around political controversy. An environment
correspondent for BBC Radio suggested:

On programmes like *Today* and *The World this Weekend* it's not
enough to try to sell a story which is about a pressure group saying a vital piece of a habitat is being destroyed. It stands a much
better chance if Clinton says . . . and the Environment Commis-
sioner for the EC disagrees. That's a story . . . If you can start a
story by saying a major row has erupted between the United
States and Europe over global emissions of carbon dioxide then
you've got a story. (Interview, 5 February 1993)

Clearly certain environmental issues receive more television news
coverage than others because of their visual qualities. For example,
the 1988 seal virus attracted a great deal of television coverage

because seals are so visually appealing (see Ch. 5). In contrast, some of the issues surrounding nature conservation have received less coverage, partly because they are difficult to explain in visual terms. For instance, in a study of television news reporting of environmental affairs, Hansen (1990b) found that only 6.5 per cent of environmental coverage on the BBC 9 O'Clock News was about conservation and public access to nature. A science editor at ITN claimed:

> If you're doing habitat it's hard because habitat doesn't move. And also because habitat is difficult to film to give the idea of the complexity of the ecosystem that is really what you're talking about. I mean you're not saying this is a pretty conservable landscape, therefore we should conserve it. You're trying to say this has got a rich complexity of animal communities. All you can show is close-ups of two or three. (Interview, 17 January 1990)

Third, news production tends to be closely tied into a 24-hour daily cycle while environmental issues tend to involve lengthy processes. Television news broadcasts are based around particularly tight daily schedules and time acts as a major constraint (Schlesinger 1987). News bulletins tend to be very short, and summarizing material succinctly without distortion can present a huge problem. The average news item about environmental issues on television news bulletins is only about 110 seconds long, although national news bulletins vary in length (Hansen 1990b). Documentary filmmakers have much more time and space to produce in-depth, analytical news programmes but the audience tends to be much more specialist.

Many environmental problems do not naturally fit this cycle since they involve slow, drawn-out processes. However, Hansen (1991) argues that this does not pose so much of a problem as it did in the early days, since climate-change issues, involving projections into the future, have gained prominent coverage in the news media. Possibly, the immediacy of the threat was brought home to people during the 1988 drought in the USA, which some took as a sign that predicted climate-change was already occurring. Also, as I argued in Chapter 1, news media agendas are often closely linked to political agendas.

Socio-economic and cultural factors

In addition to the qualities of the issues themselves, broader socio-economic and cultural factors influence the selection of environmental news. A variety of studies indicate that important environmental issues have failed to appear on news media agendas at all (cf. Schoenfeld 1979, Hansen 1990b). For example, Hansen (1990b) made a comparative content analysis of environmental coverage by two major television news programmes, Britain's 9 O'Clock News and Denmark's TV Avisen. Hansen found that the degree of relative attention that the two networks devoted to particular environmental issues strongly reflected economic and industrial factors. For instance, he found that environmental coverage on TV Avisen focused largely upon sea pollution, since Denmark's economy is highly dependent upon the fishing industry. In contrast, this issue was given hardly any coverage by the BBC 9 O'Clock News, a fact explained by the relatively minor role that fishing plays in Britain's economy. Also, while the 9 O'Clock News concentrated primarily upon nuclear energy issues, not surprisingly, TV Avisen gave relatively little space to this topic since there is no nuclear industry in Denmark.

Environmental reporting, like other areas of news coverage, is also strongly influenced by cultural values. In an excellent study of the reporting of law-and-order news, Ericson et al. argue that media practitioners, sources and audiences work with what they label "cultural templates", by which they mean frames or models of how they see society as functioning. These frames are guided by widely held cultural "givens". Thus Ericson et al. (1991: 356) claim:

> In choosing among possible stories, journalists, sources and consumers reveal the cultural templates of their understanding. Cultural templates are neither uniform nor fixed. There is no such thing as a conduit in organizational communications. When knowledge moves, it is always through a process of constructive interpretation. Visions of what ought to be, frame stories of what is, and these stories in turn communicate to others what ought to be.

Ericson et al. go on to state that, although these cultural frameworks shift, they are not completely fluid or relative, since they are constrained in important ways by the market and format considerations.

In other words, economic and technological factors combine with cultural criteria in shaping ideological meanings and messages.

A number of studies have suggested that certain environmental issues receive greater media attention because they resonate with wider cultural values and fears of the unknown (Hansen 1991, Burgess 1990a, Corner et al. 1990, Gamson & Modigliani 1989, MacGill 1987). The majority of these studies focus upon nuclear energy and the way perceptions of risks connect with a variety of ready-made discourses, containing powerful symbolic metaphors. Rather than assuming that media coverage has a direct influence upon public attitudes, these studies suggest that discourses about nuclear energy interact in a complex way. For example Gamson & Modigliani (1989: 2) argue:

> Each system interacts with the other: media discourse is part of the process by which individuals construct meaning, and public opinion is part of the process by which journalists and other cultural entrepreneurs develop and crystallize meaning in public discourse.

These culture-based approaches go some way towards explaining the different styles of discourse concerning the nuclear disasters at Three Mile Island and Chernobyl. For example, one of the major ideological frameworks in which the Chernobyl disaster was situated was the myth of the superiority of American over Russian technology (cf. Patterson 1989). Also, a recent study by Corner et al. (1990) included a detailed textual analysis of three documentaries that discussed nuclear energy issues. Corner and colleagues suggest that the symbolic content of texts should not be overlooked. For example, one of the techniques used in the last episode of a BBC documentary, *Taming the dragon*, which was broadcast in 1987, was to intercut interview sequences with the chairman of the then Central Electricity Generating Board, with strong visual images. Lord Marshall suggested in one of the interview sequences that the problem of nuclear radiation should be viewed in terms of the much greater quantities of radiation that occur naturally in the environment. He implied that radiation is a natural phenomenon, created by God, thus it does not constitute a great danger. This comment is intercut with a shot of a lake covered in mist, a device used by the narrator to reframe Lord Marshall's comments, and to introduce the issue of radioactive effluent from nuclear power stations. The narrator comments: "If there's radioactivity in

125

this garden, there's a great deal more of it in this lake. And it's not God but the CEGB that put it there" (Corner et al. 1990: 14).

Dominant cultural "givens" in environmental reporting include traditional assumptions about the march of progress through scientific and technological revolution, and beliefs about human domination over nature (Hansen 1991). Furthermore, much coverage of the developing world presents it as suffering from a series of catastrophes divorced from social and historical contexts bound up with the "development" of the West (ibid.).

Environmental reporting, like law-and-order news, contains an underlying moral structure. As we have seen, sometimes the category "environment" directly overlaps with the category "law and order" when the focus of the media is turned to violent confrontation (see Ch. 2). In other contexts, "environment", "risk" or "nature" may be categorized in seemingly more neutral ways. According to Ericson et al. (1991), representing news involves visualizing, symbolizing and authorizing claims. One of the major ways in which moral social reality is constructed in the news media is through the use of symbols and metaphors. Particular issues that command attention tend to be mediagenic and can be easily situated within an established institutional framework. Often they possess a particular symbolic resonance, like the Brent Spar campaign or protests against nuclear power.

As I argued in Chapter 1, environmental pressure groups such as Greenpeace have become highly attuned to these sorts of news judgements. Chris Rose, a former director of Media Natura, suggested:

What Greenpeace are very good at is that they've invented, if you like, a sort of morality play. . . . You've got to have the pictures, it doesn't matter what they're talking about, you've got to have the pictures. So that takes Greenpeace straight out of the editorial system of gatekeepers . . . and it puts them in the same sort of news as natural disasters and the royal family/entertainment news . . . if you can't deal with it in those terms, and their formula, they can't really campaign on it, which is one reason they've stuck with boats on the high seas and are therefore not affected by things like trespass law. Issues are simplified, they're global problem issues and they're David and Goliath, a sort of pantomime I suppose. (Interview, 24 January 1990)

Confrontational stories of "goodies" versus "baddies" evoke powerful deeply held symbolic frames of reference. Claimsmakers use different discourses of legitimacy based upon, for example, scientific or moral appeals. Gamson & Modigliani (1989) for example, speak of particular issues being organized in interpretive "media packages", around an overarching "frame of reference". They suggest that there are five major mechanisms for framing an issue.

Media packages

1. catchphrases
2. metaphors
3. exemplars (historical examples from which lessons may be drawn)
4. visual images (such as icons)
5. depictions (such as moral appeals)

Framing mechanisms may be analyzed in a number of different ways. One technique is to analyze systematically headlines, keywords or picture captions over a given period of time. For example, in a study of environmental reporting in the Canadian press, Einsiedel & Coughlan (1993) analyzed headlines of environmental items contained in the Canadian Newspaper Index between 1977 and 1990. In addition, they drew upon a content analysis study of environmental reporting in seven Canadian newspapers and examined changing keywords and descriptor phrases that were used to frame the "environment". They found that after the mid 1980s the environment was more likely to be framed in a global context. The terms "earth", "global" and "planet", for example, came to be used much more frequently; the same keywords received very little mention in the newspaper headlines of 1977. Also, they found a proliferation of sub-headings that became associated with the "environment" during the 1980s. These included headings under "eco-tourism", "environmental law", "environmentally friendly products" and "eco-feminism". This is highly significant for it tells us something about the way in which the environment began to be perceived as something that impacted upon a wider range of arenas. Though the analysis of headlines and keywords may run the risk of ignoring the broader context in which stories are packaged, combined with other techniques it offers a valuable tool for identifying overarching discursive frames.

Discourse analysis can also be used to identify popular metaphors. For example, Einsiedel & Coughlan found that metaphors to do with conflict and war, or with business and finance, became dominant frames of reference in the Canadian press during the late 1980s. Environmental activities came to be seen as a battle to save the planet through the use of terms such as "fight", "survival" and "defeat" (see also Segal 1991). They note the growing use of such phrases as "environmental terrorists'" as well as terms like "battles", "survival" and "defeat", which were increasingly applied to activities associated with environmental protection (see Ch. 5).

Also, the classification of social actors in hierarchical terms constitutes a further way in which news acts as a moral discourse. As Ericson et al. (1991: 5) observe: " News is fundamentally a discourse of morality, procedure, and hierarchy, providing symbolic representations of order in these terms." There are some striking similarities in the ways in which the news media and law-enforcement agencies represent issues of law and order. Both tend to be highly oriented towards events, institutional procedures and responsibility. Also they tend to address moral authority through personalizing and individualizing conflict rather than looking at problems associated with social structures (ibid.).

News construction and official sources

As we have seen, media discourse on risk and the environment is to a significant extent a discourse dependent upon the voices of official "experts". Scientists are called upon to provide risk assessments that are largely presented as authoritative. As we saw in Chapter 2, often the news media invite "expert" evidence to be presented from both sides of the argument where issues involve a "for" and "against" dimension. Media practitioners are faced with great problems in interpreting and explaining these competing claims. Relatively few journalists and broadcasters have scientific training. For example, a study by Sandman (1974) found that the majority of environmental reporters in the San Francisco Bay area of the USA did not have any scientific training. Research also suggests that few environment correspondents in the UK have a scientific background (Anderson 1993a). In the USA this low level of scientific training among reporters is accompanied by a high degree of faith in science (Dunwoody & Peters 1992, Sjoberg 1987). Clearly, this may present particular problems for the journalist since there is often a great deal of disagreement among scientists over environmental risk assessments. Given the ever present constraints of time and resources, journalists tend to rely upon a few well-known scientists rather than a vast network of contacts. Some evidence suggests that journalists tend to make more use of source material from "establishment" scientists, attached to official government organizations, rather than "independent" scientists (Dunwoody 1986). Also, they tend to view scientists who have already been used as sources by the media as vested with greater credibility (ibid.). This is likely to be particularly the case for news items in national daily newspapers and television news where journalists are tied to very tight news-processing structures and routines. In contrast, independent documentary makers may often have more scope to challenge received wisdoms and search out alternative views. Occasional features in daily newspapers may also perform this sort of function. As Russell (1986: 89) argues,

> Problems in science coverage often arrive when inexperienced general reporters get a "scoop" on a local science or medical story that they perceive to be of major significance. Because of their lack of background, general assignment reporters are more likely to portray a story as "newer" or "bigger" than it actually is . . . . Nevertheless, many good general assignment reporters are able to tackle tough subjects of any kind and often outdo speciality reporters by asking basic questions that readers want answered.

However, unless the reporter checks the story with a number of scientists, both orthodox and non-conventional, there is the danger that he/she may too readily accept scientific information, particularly when facing particularly tight deadlines. A former environment correspondent for the *Sunday Times* admitted:

> . . . particularly where you're doing things about toxic waste I find it very difficult sometimes because I haven't got a clue what all these chemicals do and what they are and it's easy to be taken in by somebody telling you these chemicals are going to kill somebody. (Interview, 14 February 1989)

In the UK since the most recent surge of media interest has waned, a number of environment correspondents have been replaced by general reporters. This particularly applies to popular and mid-market newspapers and independent television news. A correspondent for BBC news claimed:

When we're spending the amount of money and time on specialist subjects I think in some circles it's supposed that anybody, a general reporter, can do any story . . . if they're an experienced, seasoned journalist then they can be sent out in specialist areas. And to a certain extent that's true because of the limits of time. If we have to get a story in one minute, fifteen seconds (or even twice that length for radio, as is common), there's not a need to flex your specialist muscles . . . So people in senior management have been asking themselves, I think, the question why are we paying if we could use general reporters. Counter to this the specialist does have the contacts and, if he or she is doing the job properly, comes across all the current issues and doesn't have to desperately search for background material, and that is important. (Interview, 5 February 1993)

Perhaps one of the greatest difficulties is that by simplifying complex scientific information one inevitably distorts it. As we saw in Chapter 2, decisions about "factual evidence" inevitably involve evaluative judgements. A former environment correspondent for the *Observer* claimed: "I think the main problem is that you cannot simplify without distorting to some degree, but you have to do it honestly and with the least distortion that you possibly can" (Interview, 17 January 1989).

Environmental stories are often covered by non-specialist reporters (especially in the local press) who may simply regurgitate official press releases. Also, as we saw in Chapter 2, there is the ever-present danger of journalists becoming too sensitized to issues of risk and that all stories are treated in the same manner, despite variations in the level of danger posed.

Journalistic over-reliance upon press releases from official sources is influenced by a number of factors. As Gans (1980) observes, sources tend to take the lead in seeking access to journalists rather than the other way round. The closer the source is to the journalist, in social and often geographical terms, the more likely they are to gain access. Also, the extent to which access is successfully obtained tends to centre around the perceived reliability and trustworthiness of the source. Extremely tight time schedules, coupled with the pressures of professional codes concerning impartiality and objectivity, often lead powerful institutional sources to become over-accessed.

As I suggested in Chapter 2, the news media also enjoy close links with government. A speech made by the former Prime Minister, Margaret Thatcher, to the Royal Society in September 1988, was to make a significant impact upon the media – swaying many newspapers and television stations to appoint specialist environment correspondents for the first time. Writing in the late 1980s, a former environment correspondent for the *Daily Mail* suggested:

> I think the main obvious thing that happened was Thatcher's speech to the Royal Society which suddenly made all politicians think about the environmental implications of what was happening in the areas of their own departmental responsibility . . . . And I think it made newspaper editors think about their coverage of the environment. Very often the Prime Ministerial lead is taken and then followed by newspapers. (Interview, 25 July 1989)

Similarly, a former environment correspondent for the *Daily Express* commented:

> I think it's become high profile for newspapers, if you're talking about newspapers like ours, I think what did push it right up the top of the agenda was initially the speech that the Prime Minister made . . . . And I think it was the acceptance of the fact that the government suddenly realised the environment was a pressing issue that prompted what I might call the pop to the middle of the road media to take it seriously . . . . Being a Tory supporting newspaper we realized the government was now elevating it to a very high priority and therefore that it ought to be reflected in our coverage. (Interview, 31 October 1989)

By the beginning of 1991 many of the environment correspondents appointed by tabloid newspapers during the height of the most recent peak of concern had been moved to other posts and not replaced.

As we saw in Chapter 2, Hall and colleagues in a seminal study, entitled *Policing the crisis*, argued that official sources tend to gain advantaged access to the news media. Research in a number of different countries indicates that official sources, such as government or scientists, are cited by print journalists and broadcasters as primary sources much more often than environmental groups (Gandy 1980, Greenberg et al. 1989a, b, Hansen 1990b, Wang 1989). For example,

Hansen's study of television news coverage of environmental affairs in Denmark and Britain, found that 23 per cent of primary sources were representatives of public authorities, 21 per cent were government representatives, 17 per cent were independent scientists or experts and only 6 per cent were representatives of environmental organizations.

Most studies of source-use have focused upon national media. Relatively few researchers have focused upon the question of how environmental coverage by regional and national media differs. However, US and UK studies on regional media coverage of environmental issues suggest that environmental groups tend to enjoy qualitatively greater access to local media, at least for some issues (for example, Anderson 1993a, Cottle 1993b, Friedman et al. 1987, Molotch & Lester 1975, Sandman et al. 1987, Spears et al. 1987). Scientific and expert opinions are markedly less prominent in regional compared to national environmental reporting. Research also indicates that the local press devote a proportionately greater amount of space to environmental issues than national newspapers (for example Molotch & Lester 1975, Singh et al. 1989).

However, in my view Hall's theory of primary definers suffers from some limitations. First, Hall et al.'s theory is time bound. In the example given by Hall et al. reference is made to the Confederation of British Industry and the Trade Union Congress (TUC) as key "accredited" institutions. While this was clearly applicable in the 1970s, since then the structure of access has changed. In particular, over recent years the TUC has become less of a major institutional voice in the media. Moreover, the theory is unable to account for the shifts in access that environmental pressure groups, such as Friends of the Earth and Greenpeace, have experienced in recent years. As Schlesinger (1990: 67; original emphasis) argues,

> The structuralist model is *atemporal*, for it tacitly assumes the permanent presence of certain forces in the power structure. But when these are displaced by new forces how are we to explain the dynamics behind their emergence? The notion that primary definers are simply "accredited" to their dominant ideological place in virtue of an institutional location is at the root of this unresolved issue.

A second point concerns the failure of Hall et al. to consider instances where the influence of primary definers is not clearly visible, such as "off-the-record" briefings (Schlesinger 1990). For example, as we saw in Chapter 2, it is widely known that senior government officials representing the Department of the Environment frequently use "off-the-record" briefings to manage the news.

Third, the concept of "primary definition" implies that there exists a consensus among official sources; it leaves no room for cases where there is a conflict of interest among institutional representatives (ibid.). Who then is the primary definer? And can there be more than one? I discuss this further in Chapter 5 where I analyze press reporting of the seal plague story.

A fourth problem with Hall et al.'s theory is that it cannot account for inequalities of access among the "accredited" sources themselves (cf. Schlesinger 1990). Clearly, there are times when some actors enjoy much more privileged access than others. During the late 1980s Greenpeace and Friends of the Earth attracted considerable media attention in the UK. Since then they have not generally experienced such ease of access because the environment has been overshadowed by other issues such as the recession.

Fifth, Hall et al. assume that primary definitions always originate from the political system. However, as Schlesinger (1990) points out, there are cases where media act as primary definers through challenging institutional representatives and causing them to respond, or through developing themes that "accredited" sources later adopt (see Ch. 5).

A final problem is that Hall et al. deduce patterns of source access from quantitative content analysis, and assume that one can generalize about source–media interactions across the media. An examination based purely on the content of media coverage paints a rather one-sided picture. This sort of analysis needs to be supplemented by interviews with news sources themselves, as well as with media practitioners. While content analysis is a useful way of measuring the manifest content of texts, it does not reveal latent meanings or the overall context in which they are placed.

The notion that "primary definers" necessarily secure advantaged access to the media, then, is not without its problems. However, as Schlesinger (1990: 77; original emphasis) argues,

> . . . it is necessary that sources be conceived as occupying fields in which *competition for access* to the media takes place, but in which material and symbolic advantages are unequally distrib-

uted. But the most advantaged do not secure a primary definition in virtue of their positions alone. Rather, if they do so, it is
because of successful *strategic action* in an imperfectly competitive field . . . . Thus, while we may certainly accept that the state
dominates institutional news coverage, this does not render
irrelevant questions about differently endowed contending
groups in the building and modification of political agendas.

In the following chapter I will present some of the findings of my
own research that focused upon the relationship between news
sources and the news media.

Summary

In this chapter I have suggested that the news media are highly selective in the representation of risk and the environment. Risks that are
relatively rare and connected with unexpected, dramatic disasters
(such as large chemical spillages) tend to be over-reported. Also the
event-centred nature of environmental reporting tends to divorce
issues from their wider social and political context, and rarely incorporates a consideration of multiple explanations. News is not the
product of a series of random events; it is the outcome of routine
organizational processes and taken-for-granted assumptions. News
values, a kind of sixth sense about what constitutes a "good" news
story, play a central role in the selection of material. Moreover, filter-
ing occurs at each level of the news production process.

News media representations of the environment are shaped by
socio-political and cultural values. Particular social issues that succeed in commanding attention tend to be mediagenic and can be
easily situated within an established institutional framework. Often
they resonate with powerful deeply held cultural beliefs and work at a
symbolic level. Much media reporting of risk and the environment
places symbolic themes in juxtaposition. The image, for example, of
an idyllic, close-knit rural community counterpoised against the
image of isolated individuals existing in a kind of urban chaos.

I have argued that media discourse on risk and the environment is
largely a discourse framed in science. The representation of many
environmental issues involves the voice of science, the "expert", to

interpret complex phenomena. Studies of environmental news coverage in a variety of countries have found that official sources (particularly government departments and scientists) tend to enjoy advantaged access to the media and become "primary definers" of the issue in question. By contrast, environmental pressure groups are much less likely to receive "primary definer" status. However, studies of environmental reporting in local news media paint a rather different picture; they suggest that environmental pressure groups may well experience comparatively greater access at the regional level.

Claimsmakers use different discourses of legitimacy based upon, for example, scientific or moral appeals. Many large environmental groups such as Friends of the Earth or Greenpeace place increasing emphasis upon scientific research. On occasions, claims advanced by environmental pressure groups may be framed with the kind of legitimacy that the media usually reserve for claimsmakers in the science forum or the political forum. In the next chapter I focus on one such case that involved a variety of competing claims advanced by politicians, Dutch scientists and Greenpeace activists.

Suggested further reading

J. Galtung & M. Ruge "Structuring and selecting news", in *The manufacture of news*, S. Cohen & J. Young (eds), 62–72 (London: Constable, 1973) and G. Tuchman, *Making the news: a study in the construction of reality* (New York: Free Press, 1978) still remain classics in the general news-making literature.

Excellent analyses of news media representations of the environment are provided by two linguists, A. Bell, *The language of news media* (Oxford: Blackwell, 1991) and R. Fowler, *Language in the news: discourse and ideology in the press* (London: Routledge, 1991). While Bell's study focuses upon television news, Fowler looks at discourse and ideology in the press. Also A. Hansen (ed.), *The mass media and environmental issues* (Leicester: Leicester University Press, 1993) provides a good overview of recent research on the role of the media and the rise of the environment as a social issue. For a comprehensive account of the social constructionist perspective on media and the environment see chapter 3 in J. A. Hannigan, *Environmental sociology: a social constructionist perspective* (London: Routledge, 1995).

Chapter 5

Contested ground:
news sources and the media

Introduction

In previous chapters I have considered ways in which the news media
and the environment may, in some senses, be considered to be socially
constructed. Also, I have suggested that news sources play a central
role in the news production process. In this chapter I want to focus
more closely upon the relationship between news sources (here I concentrate upon environmental pressure groups) and the news media.
In this discussion, I will draw upon my own research into the national
daily press reporting of an epidemic among North Sea common seals
during the summer of 1988. The outbreak of the disease began off the
coast of Denmark and before long seals were discovered washed
ashore on German, Swedish, Norwegian and British coastlines. The
case study was based upon in-depth, semi-structured interviews with
journalists covering environmental issues in the UK national daily
press and Sunday newspapers; broadcasters covering environmental
affairs; and representatives of environmental pressure groups, related
interest groups, and scientists and industry. In addition, the study
included a textual analysis of the reporting of the seal virus by the
national daily and Sunday press during the month of August 1988.

A convergence of approaches

My research into the press reporting of the seal plague combined a
range of methods. The advantages of combining methods can be considerable since it can allow a particular topic to be approached from

different angles thus enhancing the validity of the overall analysis. The case study was based upon the qualitative analysis of interview material in conjunction with media texts. Content analysis is an established research technique within mass communications research and has traditionally been grounded in quantitative or pseudo-quantitative approaches (Bell 1991). This research technique has been widely used by researchers to study how a range of issues are represented in the news media (for example, Burgess & Gold 1985, Gans 1980, Halloran et al. 1970, Glasgow University Media Group 1976, 1980, 1982, Schlesinger et al. 1991, Tumber 1982). Content analysis uses predetermined categories in order to measure the frequency with which particular characteristics appear in texts, and the amount of space devoted to them. Holsti (1969: 14) provides this definition: "Content analysis is any technique for making inferences by objectively and systematically identifying specified characteristics of messages."

In my case study of the seal virus content analysis provided a useful means of identifying important characteristics of the news coverage. The month of August was selected because a pilot content analysis of the *Daily Mail*'s archives indicated that the majority of the press took up the story during this month. The newspapers analysed were London editions so may not be completely representative of other regional editions. The coding schedule was drawn up which was designed to provide information on: the item length; whereabouts the item was located in the newspaper; the type of item; who was responsible for writing the item; the main stimulus for the item; the major themes explored in the item; whose views were quoted or presented and how they were referred to; the number and length of accompanying photographs or illustrations; the type of illustrative content and the subjects shown. Only items which made specific reference to the seal virus were coded. Finally, the coding schedule was designed to be flexible. For example, up to four main themes could be coded for each item. Also further categories and variables were incorporated as they arose during the study, thus allowing for a degree of reflexivity.

While content analysis has a number of advantages it does suffer from some important drawbacks. This approach assumes that the study of the manifest text is significant; that one can make inferences upon the basis of an analysis of the surface-level content and that the frequency with which particular themes occur is meaningful (Holsti 1969). Content analysis is a valuable way of measuring the amount of attention given to particular themes in media texts. It enables the researcher to identify important characteristics of manifest content. However, it is most useful when combined with qualitative techniques such as discourse analysis, or in-depth interviews (see Lindlof & Meyer 1987). As with all methods, the chosen categories reflect the particular biases and interests of the researcher and there is no neutral way in which they can be classified. As Siedman (cited in Walker 1985: 13) maintains,

> ... few have questioned the inherent subjectivity of quantification which requires "selection" of parameters and baseline data, the interpretation of findings, and selection of facts and evidence. There is much to be gained by destroying the myth of objectivity since subjectivity is always intricately involved – but disallowed.

The content and textual analysis was supplemented with in-depth, semi-structured interviews with reporters, NGO representatives and press officers at the Department of the Environment. Interviews were conducted with scientists and representatives of industry but this was limited due to problems of access and the fact that they tended to be unforthcoming about their media relations. Interviewing the sources and producers of news is an established research technique (see, for example, Ericson et al. 1989, Schlesinger & Tumber 1994). As Newcomb (1991: 101) maintains,

> The primary strength of *interviewing* as a method is its capacity to range over *multiple perspectives* on a given topic. Multiple interviews can be used to increase information and broaden a point of view. All interviews can be used as heuristic devices, as new information leads to new perspectives and questions for later subjects . . . . All these factors lead to what is perhaps the interview technique's greatest strength – the gathering of more comprehensive information than might be possible in participation observation. Because even the most rigid interview schedule can be altered in progress, the researcher is free to follow leads and expand questions [original emphasis].

The case study illustrates how national press coverage can, in particular instances, have a direct effect upon the political agenda. It suggests that there is complex interaction between the scientific agenda, political priorities, media coverage and public attitudes towards environmental issues. Also, it is suggested that the *Daily Mail's* sustained "Save our seals" campaign played a major part in raising environmental issues to the top of the political list of priorities in the UK, as did the activities of representatives of environmental pressure groups. The "Save our seals" campaign mobilized huge public support that alerted Conservative back-benchers to the strength of the *Daily Mail* readers' concern about wider environmental issues.

The background

In April 1988 a large number of common seals around the coast of Denmark were found to be dying from a mystery disease that affected their immune systems. Later, in July and August 1988, the disease was discovered to be affecting great numbers of common seals along the Norfolk coast in Britain. Between April and December 1988 18,000 seals around the coasts of Northern Europe were discovered dead (Hall, Pomeroy, Harwood 1992). The symptoms of the disease varied but included respiratory problems, skin lesions, lethargy and abortion. At first marine biologists thought that the Danish epidemic was caused by pollution because it occurred around the same time as an outbreak of algae blooms in the Baltic. However, once the disease began to spread to Sweden, Norway, the Dutch Waddensea, and to the North coast of the Federal Republic of Germany, virologists maintained that it was probably caused by a viral infection since there was no clear evidence that these waters were polluted. Initially two viruses were identified in the dead seals: herpes virus and picorna virus. By September 1988 the current scientific theory was that it was a form of canine distemper (a disease with similar symptoms that affects dogs). Some scientists also thought that pollution had lowered the seals' immunity to the disease and there were fears that the virus might spread to dolphins and porpoises.

At this time environmental issues, such as the pollution of the North Sea, were growing in political importance across Europe. The environment became one of the key issues in the Swedish and Danish General Elections in September 1988. Indeed, an article in the *Guardian* (20 August 1988: 18) suggested:

140

It is especially difficult for a Swedish Prime Minister with an election just around the corner to dismiss the image, flashed onto TV screens each night as more and more seals, both dead and dying, wash up on the local beaches.

The Dutch and Danish preoccupation with the North Sea is closely tied up with economic and cultural factors. The Dutch and Danes viewed the state of the North Sea as more of a political priority since the fishing industry is vital to their economies (cf. Hansen 1990b). In Britain, this cultural climate did not exist and political attention was largely sparked off through the *Daily Mail*'s campaign.

By October 1988 virologists in Britain had identified a phocine distemper virus (PDV), similar to the canine distemper virus (CDV) that affects dogs, but unique to seals. PDV is a morbillivirus similar to measles in humans. However, the precise cause of the virus, and the role that pollution played, is still far from clear. In the UK various projects were commissioned by the Department of the Environment as part of their programme of research on the North Sea in conjunction with the Natural Environment Research Council's Sea Mammal Unit. Research suggests that there were significant differences in the concentration of organochlorines (such as chlorinated biphenyls) in the blubber of seals found dead in the 1988 epidemic, when compared to seals who were exposed to the virus and survived (Hall, Law et al. 1992). These differences could not be fully explained by either condition-related transformations in blubber thickness or seasonal changes. Despite this the evidence is still inconclusive, partly due to deficiencies of data in the UK, and a number of other factors that could not be ruled out (cf. Thompson & Hall 1993, Hall, Pomeroy, Harwood 1992). For example, a research review published in 1993 concludes:

> ... while organochlorine pollution may have affected seal immune function, there are also likely to be natural variations in transmission rates and susceptibility which may explain this pattern. Further studies of the biological effects of contaminants are clearly required before this question can be answered. (Thompson & Hall 1993: 153)

The agenda-setting role of the popular press

The case study of the seal plague illustrates the way in which the press can, in certain instances, play an important part in moulding the political agenda (Lang & Lang 1981, Solesbury 1976, Downs 1973, Stringer & Richardson 1980, Schoenfeld et al. 1979), although there is no simple correlation between the political agenda and the media agenda. There are complex interactions between the political, public, scientific and media agendas. In what follows the concept "political agenda" is defined as the parliamentary table of priorities, "public agenda" as the degree of concern attached to various social issues by the public, "scientific agenda" as the ranking of the importance of scientific knowledge by scientists and the "media agenda" as the range of topics that the media present us with.

It has been widely acknowledged that the *Daily Mail*'s "Save our seals" campaign, launched in August 1988 and sustained for over a year, alerted members of the public and Conservative politicians to the wider network of issues concerning the quality of the environment as a whole. Indeed, it appears that one of the factors that led the former British Prime Minister, Mrs Thatcher, to make her "green" speech was the *Daily Mail*'s campaign, which brought to her attention the strength of public concern about environmental issues. Richard North, former environment correspondent at the *Independent*, claimed on Radio Four's *Today* programme that it was the *Daily Mail*'s coverage of the *Karin B* affair [the ship carrying a cargo of toxic waste that was refused entrance at Liverpool Port in August 1988] and the seal virus, which forced Mrs Thatcher to take action:

> She would read the same thing millions of times in the *Guardian*, the *Times* and the *Independent* and say these people are whingers. But when the *Daily Mail* takes it up she realizes it must be a genuine popular concern and she is sensible enough a politician to follow their lead. (Quoted in the *Daily Mail*, 29 September 1988)

Indeed, a former environment correspondent for the *Times* argued that:

> The *Daily Mail* was the newspaper that took up this campaign and really put this onto the public agenda and it is down to David English and the *Daily Mail*, it seems to me, as much as

anyone else in the news media, for putting the environment on the agenda with the seals campaign. (Interview, 22 February 1991)

When questioned about this two years later, the correspondent still maintained:

What put it on the agenda without any question in my mind was the *Daily Mail* with the seals campaign. I was on the news desk at the *Times* and I remember when the story first surfaced and it was painted as a not very important story at all. David English, who was editor of the *Mail*, decided one day to do a splash on it. And about three or four days later everybody else followed. And that is undoubtedly one of the turning points . . . and that was a case of the media actually leading the agenda. But on the whole it tends to follow. (Interview, 28 July 1993)

However, we cannot assume that the *Daily Mail* campaign had a direct effect upon readers. Public opinion polls suggest that concern about environmental issues had been gradually rising over a long period of time as the general quality of life improved (Anthony 1982). Indeed, as Lang & Lang (1981) have argued, one weakness of agenda-setting studies has been that they have tended to assume that the public are directly influenced by media agendas (cf. McQuail 1991). Furthermore, such studies have devoted little attention to analyzing the process through which agendas are built and social problems are transformed into political issues:

. . . the agenda-setting hypothesis – the bland and unqualified statement that the mass media set the agenda for political campaigns – attributes to the media at one and the same time too little and too much influence. The whole question of how issues originate is sidestepped, nor is there any recognition of the process through which agendas are built or through which an object that has caught public attention, by being big news, gives rise to a political issue. In other words, while agenda-setting research, like most research, suffers from methodological shortcomings, the more basic problems are conceptual. (Lang & Lang 1981: 448)

In the lead up to the *Daily Mail* campaign environmental issues

143

were gradually becoming more prominent in Europe and there was increasing scientific evidence that global warming was taking place. In both political and scientific terms, then, the environment came to be seen as a legitimate and pressing issue. As early as October 1987 the *Mail on Sunday* carried a feature that used the seals story as a way of focusing attention on environmental issues in general. It claimed: "Pollution is being blamed for an unprecedented number of common seals found dead or dying on the North Norfolk coast." This was followed by a series of "Doomwatch" reports in the *Mail on Sunday* between October 1987 and August 1988. These were accompanied by the logo: "The environment: the newspaper that cares". However, it was not until the summer of 1988 that the seals crisis hit saturation coverage and the *Daily Mail* turned it into a sustained campaign. This prompted other rival popular newspapers such as the *Daily Express* and the *Daily Star* to launch their own campaigns. An environment correspondent for the *Daily Express*, effectively admitted that the newspaper's decision to set up a "Save our Seas" campaign was probably influenced by the activities of the *Daily Mail*: "It's quite possible that we were prompted by the fact that other newspapers were running campaigns on the environment and that we ought to have a campaign too ourselves" (Interview, 31 October 1989).

Also, the success of the *Daily Mail* campaign led many of the broadsheets to focus upon the seals issue. A former environment correspondent for the *Times*, maintained:

Well the key thing is that the *Daily Mail* led the way and dragged everybody along behind them. I mean in the end I can remember there was a certain amount of scoffing in the *Times* when that began but then they suddenly realized that they ought to follow it. (Interview, 22 February 1991)

Indeed, the seals issue received widespread coverage in virtually all of the national daily newspapers (see Table 5.1 and Table 5.2).

The content analysis of national newspaper coverage indicated that the highest number of items (28) in the quality press were carried by the *Guardian*, the daily newspaper traditionally most associated with coverage of the environment, and the *Independent*, well known for its team of science reporters. Both of these newspapers had their own specialist reporters for scientific and environmental affairs. However, the *Daily Mail* carried an impressive 24 items, since it did not have a

Table 5.1   National daily press coverage of the seal virus during August 1988.

Newspaper	Number of items
Guardian	28
Daily Mail	24
Independent	21
Daily Telegraph	15
Times	12
Daily Express	12
Today	12
Daily Mirror	10
Daily Star	8
Financial Times	5
Sun	4

Table 5.2   Average item length (including illustrative material) in standard column centimetres, August 1988.

Newspaper	Column centimetres
Daily Mail	1,822
Independent	1,181
Today	1,118
Guardian	1,033
Daily Mirror	880
Times	849
Daily Express	578
Star	487
Daily Telegraph	473
Financial Times	74
Sun	58

specialist science or environment reporter and it did not have as much space as many of the other newspapers. Indeed, it contained twice as many items as its middle-market rivals and it was the only paper to carry two front page leads. The *Star* carried double the number of items (8) as the *Sun* (4), including one editorial on the seal virus. The *Financial Times*, like the *Sun*, gave the issue little coverage; clearly these newspapers viewed the seal virus as of little interest to readers.

145

A former environment correspondent for the *Financial Times* suggested that:

> ... some of the things that are very important are boring, that's the trouble ... I mean I suppose it's slightly easier for me because to some extent we can be a bit more technical than other papers because of our readership, and a bit more weighty perhaps. It's very difficult, I should imagine, to write for a popular paper. That of course is why papers, pop papers, and people like television, love an issue like the seals. You know, there's pictures, and quite mistaken pictures actually. I mean you've got gooey-eyed little seals, apparently they're quite dangerous. You know, if you get too near to them they're quite likely to take your hand off or something. But people will get dewy-eyed about these issues won't they? (Interview, 24 January 1989)

Indeed, the only daily newspapers to publish readers' letters on the seals issue during August were the *Guardian* and the mid-market press. The *Daily Mail* and the *Guardian* printed five letters each, while both *Today* and the *Daily Express* carried two. Indeed, the reason why the *Daily Mail* decided to campaign on the seals issue was clearly related to its market position and to its identity as a Conservative newspaper. Clearly, it wanted to appeal to its largely Conservative readership who were becoming increasingly concerned about the environment, it aimed to attract new readers, and it wanted to put pressure on the government to take action on environmental issues. Also, the newspaper has a history of featuring animal stories (cf. Nicholson 1987).

Table 5.3 indicates that, of the Sunday newspapers, the *Mail on Sunday* and the *Observer* carried the highest number of stories on the seal virus. During August 1988 there were no items on the seal virus in the *People*, while the *News of the World* and the *Sunday Express* only carried one item each.

Some newspapers, such as the *Mail on Sunday*, unequivocally portrayed the seals story as a "political" issue. In an explicit attempt to force politicians to take action on environmental issues, the *Mail on Sunday* used the seals as a way of launching a general attack on the government's indifference about ecological matters:

The man and the woman on the street know that disaster looms

Table 5.3 National press coverage of the seal virus by the Sunday newspapers, August 1988.

Newspaper	Number of items
Mail on Sunday	8
Observer	6
Sunday Times	3
Sunday Mirror	3
Sunday Telegraph	3
News of the World	1
Sunday Express	1
Sunday People	0

unless something is done to protect their environment. They have the wisdom that governments lack ... But those set in political power over them do not listen. Do they even care? It is true that the Rhine and other of Europe's rivers are filthy with pollution. But the rest of the EEC does not dump untreated sewage into the North Sea. (Editorial, *Mail on Sunday*, 28 August 1988)

The seal virus, then, was used by the popular press as a peg to focus upon environmental issues in the broader sense. The seals story marked an issue-threshold for environmental issues, which were already attracting considerable concern from the public.

The seals story as an issue threshold for environmental awareness

An important question raised by previous agenda-setting studies is how certain issues, which have received some initial media interest, come to attract sustained coverage and political attention (Downs 1973, Solesbury 1976, Lang & Lang 1981). It appears that issues are sustained by factors intrinsic to the nature of the issue, by a certain degree of fortuitousness and by external social and political forces. In the case of the seals story one of the factors that kept it alive was that it satisfied a number of news values. The seal plague marked an issue

147

threshold; from the summer of 1988 onwards environmental problems in general came to be viewed as legitimate concerns.

One reason why the seal plague attracted so much media coverage during August 1988 was that it was during this month that the first affected seals in Britain were discovered to be dying in large numbers along the Norfolk coast; this constituted a key news "event" for the British media. Often it is a specific event that draws attention to general issues concerning the environment (Solesbury 1976). Some journalists felt that the *Daily Mail* was prompted to set up a campaign after the seal virus came to Lord Rothermere's attention through his daughter's concern about environmental issues. Whether this was purely anecdotal or not, the newspaper had already decided to start up a wildlife campaign with a strong human interest component and the seals story provided all of these elements. Chris Rose, director of the UK environmental media charity, Media Natura, observed:

> The *Daily Mail* wanted to do something which combined human interest, like AIDS for example, with animals and they already wanted to do that before they heard about the seals. And the seals thing was brought to their attention via I think it was Lord Rothermere's daughter, a friend of whose is interested in environmental issues, or several of her friends are .... You know, they decided they wanted to do something and the seals thing combined animals, which was their traditional way of covering environmental stories, with disease. You know it was a virus so it was a bit like AIDS ... it meant that you were dealing with the fate of animals at an individual level and people can relate to that, and especially *Daily Mail* readers who are largely women and relatively well off. So it was an ideal story for them. (Interview, 24 January 1990)

As we saw in Chapter 4, the visibility of an environmental "event" is another factor that is likely to propel such issues onto the media agenda (Solesbury 1976, Downs 1973). Indeed, press coverage of the seal virus largely centred on the visual appeal of the animals and news reports or features generally included large close-up photographs of seal pups. Indeed, 35 out of 61 items coded in the sample of national daily newspapers contained close-up pictures of seals. A further 11 items contained pictures of dead seals. Often images speak louder than words; dying seals came to represent pathetic innocence. Bruce

Fogle, a broadcaster and vet, recalled some of the images that were portrayed by the media:

> Pictures of dead and dying seals, seen in newspapers and on television over the last few days, sear themselves into our minds. The image of the seal is that of the ultimate innocent. With their prominent large moist brown eyes they look like characters out of a Walt Disney film rather than the carnivores they really are. ("The cruel sea", *London Evening Standard*, 25 August 1988)

The seals became icons for an environment in crisis. News discourse on the seal plague was striking in the use of war metaphors such as "battle", "fight" and "defence". Also "doom" and "hope" were often presented in juxtaposition. The emphasis was on how people could themselves take action on environmental issues. Indeed, a former reporter for the *Daily Mail's* "Save our seals" campaign maintained that the seal plague enabled the public to visualize and identify emotionally with the effects of environmental pollution. He claimed:

> I believe that the seals disaster had one very, very positive effect which was to shock people into the realization that, you know, man cannot go on polluting the environment without, you know, a very heavy price to pay. And you see the scientists can talk about the damage to the ozone layer and, you know, the dangers of dumping chemicals in the sea until they're blue in the face. But, you know, people aren't touched by that, they can't visualize it . . . . And the reason why the seals did was here are these beautiful creatures that people adore, just very, very touching and human-like in their own way, suddenly die. (Interview, 25 July 1989)

Furthermore, a former environment correspondent for the *Daily Mail*, agreed:

> . . . the story had a lot of ingredients which made it an obvious one to choose as a big campaign issue. Seals have sweet friendly faces and doleful eyes and so their plight was a very emotive one. And the pictures, as far as newspapers are concerned, I always think in terms of pictures, and they made quite a lot of

very good pictures. And it seemed at the time that what was happening to them was something to do with pollution of the seas. Although that's very much in doubt now at the time it seemed that was the most obvious cause. And so if you think there's so many animal lovers and increasingly people were being more interested in the environment then those two factors, combined, probably made it a very good story to campaign on. (Interview, 25 July 1989)

Moreover, a former environment correspondent for the *Daily Express* suggested that visually appealing animals, such as seals or dolphins, are often used by the tabloid press as a peg to introduce less emotive issues:

The dolphin is such a cheerful animal, you know, its great big grin on its face, that people can identify with it and as being sort of man's friend in the ocean . . . it's easier to attract sympathy for the dolphin than it might be for an ugly-looking bottle-nosed whale. But since it is the bottle-nosed that is extinct you actually let people know that by doing a story about dolphins as well! It's how you hook the reader and then get them involved in what the real issue is and that is, you know, if you keep killing the bottle-nosed there won't be one left by the turn of the century. (Interview, 31 October 1989)

A further factor that helped sustain the seals story was that many famous individuals, including several from the entertainment industry, were willing to pledge their support. Since there is such a high degree of competition between stories within papers, this gave the seals issue an added dimension. As Downs (1973: 67; original emphasis) argues:

The requirement that a problem be dramatic and exciting is important to the maintenance of public interest in it because *all news is in reality "consumed" by much of the American public (and by publics everywhere) largely as a form of entertainment*. As such, it competes with other types of entertainment for a share of each person's time. Hence, in the fierce struggle for space in the highly limited universe of television viewing time or news print, each issue must vie not only with other social problems but also with a multitude of nonnews items that are often far more pleasant for the public to contemplate.

A number of popular newspapers used an entertainment approach to attract readers to the seals story. For example, the seals campaigns by the *People* and *Today* were launched by the well known naturalist, David Bellamy. And the *People* offered seal badges, posters and stickers to readers. Perhaps the newspaper that became most strongly associated with this approach was the *Daily Mail*. Indeed, the fact that a reporter for the *Daily Mail*'s "Save our seals" campaign was previously the *Daily Mail*'s show business reporter was clearly evident in the paper's coverage of the seal virus. Over 18 of the seal stories printed by the newspaper between August and December 1988 were principally about the involvement of celebrities with the seals issue. And special T-shirts and sweatshirts were designed to promote the campaign. The *Daily Mail* reporter explained:

> . . . it kind of ranged from actors and actresses, all sorts of show business stars, sports personalities, a very, very wide range, some quite interesting people. You know, we got Micky Rooney and Ann Miller for the sweatshirt, Frank Bruno before his title fight. I mean we got into some bizarre situations of people wearing sweatshirts in unusual places, all of which combined to make a very powerful visual image. In the paper the sweatshirt itself had a picture of a pup's face on the front of it and it was a very, very touching sort of image anyway. (Interview, 25 July 1989)

The approach that was taken by the *Daily Mail* clearly generated a huge number of stories and partly explains how the seals issue was sustained over such a long period. According to a former *Daily Mail* reporter,

> . . . we carried a seal story, I think, certainly every day for three months . . . . I struggle to think of another campaign run in recent times by a newspaper that has given such sustained sort of support in the newspaper. But of course it was relatively easy to do because if there wasn't a news story on, you know, what was happening in various parts of the country, if there weren't features on the people who were treating the seals, if there wasn't

151

front line reports on, you know, going out in boats or land rovers, you know, recovering seals with the rescue workers, then there'd be sweatshirt pictures that could be put in the paper or details of the latest fundraising. (Interview, 25 July 1989)

A further news value satisfied by the seals story was human interest, not just in terms of the personalities involved with the story, but concerning the possible effects upon people. The popular press, in particular, played upon the threat water pollution posed to humans. They suggested that if pollution was killing large numbers of seals (which are at the top of the food chain) then it must be doing some harm to us. And in this way the tabloids found a way of connecting their traditional way of covering environmental issues during the summer break with a story that involved an unknown virus spreading among attractive animals. For example, a full-page editorial in the *Mail on Sunday* claimed:

Be in no doubt the problem of the seals is only a tiny part of a potentially calamitous problem. Three weeks ago this newspaper reported that three young boys in Southend-on-Sea, Essex, had developed a mysterious and debilitating ailment,

HEART-RENDING: But seals are only part of a calamitous threat

Figure 5.1 *Mail on Sunday*, 28 August 1988, p. 8.

causing near paralysis in their legs. The cause? Almost certainly a virus contracted while swimming in sewage-polluted seas near their home. (28 August 1988: 8)

A cartoon in the same edition of the newspaper also concentrated upon the threat to humans. It depicted a man wading in the sea. The caption went: "Now wash your hands".

And four days previously a front page lead in the *Daily Mail* claimed: "This is a man-made tragedy of nature. We have made possible a virus destroying a whole species. It is our duty to find the antidote. And there is almost no time" (24 August 1988: 1).

Also, a *Daily Mirror* editorial on the seals issue and the toxic waste carried by the *Karin B* freighter, warned:

> Seals are only the first victims of complacency, greed, neglect and stupidity. There will be other victims – and they could be on the land. Not content on allowing the North Sea to become a cesspool of filth and deadly chemicals, the Government is aiding and abetting the dumping of dangerous waste for profit. (29 August 1988: 2)

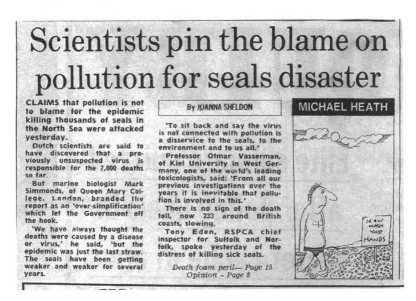

Scientists pin the blame on pollution for seals disaster

CLAIMS that pollution is not to blame for the epidemic killing thousands of seals in the North Sea were attacked yesterday.

Dutch scientists are said to have discovered that a previously unsuspected virus is responsible for the 7,000 deaths so far.

But marine biologist Mark Simmonds, of Queen Mary College, London, branded the report as an 'over-simplification' which let the Government off the hook.

'We have always thought the deaths were caused by a disease or virus,' he said, 'but the epidemic was just the last straw. The seals have been getting weaker and weaker for several years.

By JOANNA SHELDON

'To sit back and say the virus is not connected with pollution is a disservice to the seals, to the environment and to us all.'

Professor Otmar Vasserman, of Kiel University in West Germany, one of the world's leading toxicologists, said: 'From all our previous investigations over the years it is inevitable that pollution is involved in this.'

There is no sign of the death toll, now 233 around British coasts, slowing.

Tony Eden, RSPCA chief inspector for Suffolk and Norfolk, spoke yesterday of the distress of killing sick seals.

Death foam peril— Page 15
Opinion – Page 8

MICHAEL HEATH

Figure 5.2   *Mail on Sunday*, 28 August 1988.

Several popular newspapers even linked the virus to AIDS and some of them quoted the independent scientist, Pat Gowan, who believed that such a connection might exist. The phrases "deadly virus" and "killer plague" commonly featured in tabloid news discourse. The *Daily Star* ran a large feature, entitled "AIDS of the sea", which used two emotive pegs to capture readers' attention; AIDS and pollution (see Figure 5.3).

Three days later, other popular newspapers followed suit. The *News of the World* claimed:

> What baffles scientists the most is why the seals have NO resistance to this virus. Why have their immune systems broken down in the same way that AIDS affects humans? Already there are reports of three young boys being hit by a mysterious paralysis after paddling in the polluted sea at Southend. (28 August 1988: 8)

Similarly, the *Sunday Express* implied that the virus might be linked to AIDS and quoted "independent scientist", Pat Gowan, as stating: "I

Figure 5.3 *Daily Star*, 25 August 1988, p. 73.

believe the virus attacking the seals may well be the AIDS virus which has been put into the North Sea through the human untreated sewage of AIDS victims" (28 August 1988: 5).

The popular press, then, tended to offer the explanation that the virus was linked with pollution even though there was a lot of uncertainty among scientists as to the precise cause of the disease. The tabloid papers did not want to report that a disease was killing common seals but that no one knew what was causing it, as this would not have been so newsworthy. A crucial problem is that newspapers do not like dealing with uncertainties, whereas in the vast majority of cases the causes of environmental problems are contested and some of the solutions are viewed as costing too much. A "Save our seals" reporter of the *Daily Mail* explained:

> . . . you can't write a story saying six seal pups are dying of something and it might be the virus. You make a decision and you say, you know, the virus has returned. And within that story you say tests are still being carried out but the workers at the centre are almost positive that it is the work of the virus. (Interview, 25 July 1989)

Similarly an environment correspondent for the *Daily Express* claimed:

> Nobody quite knew what it was and therefore pollution was, I think, an easy target wasn't it, initially. I mean even some of the scientists themselves in the very early days weren't too sure and said it could well be some chemical pollutant which was doing this. So they weren't terribly sure initially. It wasn't until the laboratories got to work and samples were taken from the seals that they arrived that they were dealing with a distemper that is not that dissimilar to canine distemper. (Interview, 31 October 1989)

Instead of observing that some scientists believed pollution was responsible it was frequently claimed that scientists thought pollution was the cause of the seal deaths. This gave the impression that scientists were in agreement that pollution was involved, although in reality most scientists merely stressed that pollution could not be ruled out at this stage. The *Daily Mail*, in its early coverage, almost overwhelmingly quoted scientists or environmentalists who believed that pollution was responsible. The content analysis indicated that 8 out of the 24 items coded mentioned that pollution may have been a cause of the virus as a major theme. A further four items reported the view that pollution had lowered the seals immunity and only one item mentioned the uncertainty surrounding the cause of the virus as a prominent theme. Moreover, Table 5.4 shows that a total of 19 representatives of environmental or animal welfare organizations were quoted by the *Daily Mail*, while the views of 12 scientists were reported and only 5 government sources and 1 representative of industry were quoted.

Although the *Daily Mail* won the Royal Society for the Prevention of Cruelty to Animals (RSPCA) special media award for its coverage of the seal virus, and raised a tremendous amount of money to fund seal sanctuaries, it has come under attack from some prominent scientists. The *Daily Mail* announced in a front page lead that scientists at the Sea Mammal Research Unit had opted to vaccinate seals against the virus when, in actual fact, they had serious doubts about the viability of this method:

> Today the *Daily Mail* unveils its emergency action programme to save the grey seal population of Britain from the scourge of disease and pollution which could wipe it out . . . . Supplies of vaccine to combat the virus which is destroying adult seals have been ordered from Holland. On the islands, the team will set about protecting the newborn pups from the disease decimating the older generation. (9 September 1988: 1–2)

These assertions angered some scientists and an article in the *New Scientist* criticized the *Daily Mail*'s approach. It stated:

> A national newspaper in Britain is calling for donations from its readers for a fund that would vaccinate wild grey seals against canine distemper virus, which has killed 11,000 common seals in the North Sea since April. But scientists working with the seals say the methods proposed by the Daily Mail to "save our seals" are not practicable and may not even be desirable. ("Folly of a newspaper's plan to save seals", *New Scientist*, 15 September 1988: 29)

Table 5.4   Sources of the *Daily Mail*'s coverage during August 1988.

Source	Number
Government	
Junior minister for the environment	2
Back bench Conservatives	1
Members of the European Parliament	1
Spokesperson for the DoE	1
Total	5
Scientists	
Statement by a foreign scientist	4
Representative of the Sea Mammal Research Unit, Cambridge	3
Scientists in general	5
Total	12
Environmental/animal welfare organizations	
Environmentalists in general	3
Representative of Greenpeace	5
Representative of FoE	1
Representative of the RSPCA	4
Representative of a British seal rescue centre	5
Representative of the Seal Rescue Centre at Pieterburn, Holland	1
Total	19
Other sources	
Representatives of industry	1
Members of the public	4
Environmental Health Officer	1
Celebrities	2
Not clear/cannot code	1
Total	9
Total	45

Indeed, a reporter on the "Save our seals" campaign, admitted that this had been a mistake:

> We ran one story talking about . . . . I mean basically we pinned a lot of hope in there being a vaccine. And I mean scientists and environmentalists were just saying why are they so keen on that because it can't be administered and never could be administered to seals in the wild. But because there were people who thought that possibly it could, you know, it was something that

we did. And in retrospect obviously you wouldn't have done that. (Interview, 25 July 1989)

A former science correspondent for the *Independent* suggested:

For the environmentalists and the popular press this was enough; pollution must have allowed the new epidemic to penetrate and spread. It meshed in with the belief that the millions of tonnes of sewage, industrial waste, fertiliser and pesticide poured into the North Sea had reached a critical level. ("Deadly seal virus returns to the Orkneys", the *Independent*, 29 July 1989: 3)

Indeed David Lavigne, professor of Zoology at the University of Guelph, maintains that there is still no evidence to suggest that the seals immune systems were weakened by such viral infections:

While few seriously considered the involvement of the AIDS virus, the supposition that the seals had depressed immune systems, which left them particularly vulnerable to viral infections, remains. Yet, despite widespread media coverage to the contrary, there is no evidence that immunosuppression predisposed the seals to the plague. (BBC *Wildlife Magazine*, July 1989: 438)

Generally the broadsheet newspapers were more cautious in their coverage of the seal plague. Perhaps this reflected the fact that items on the seal virus in the serious press tended to be written by science correspondents, while stories in the popular press were largely written by various general reporters or features editors. Also, the broadsheets have more scope to discuss weighty scientific issues.

However, many of the broadsheet newspapers suggested that pollution was not responsible for the seal deaths, but this had not been established by scientists any more than had the theory that pollution caused the tragedy. This relates, in part, to inter-paper rivalry but also to the desire to present news in terms of certainties. For example, an article written by the *Daily Telegraph*'s science correspondent was entitled: "Death of seals not caused by pollution". However, an editorial in the *Times* was more wary about making assumptions about the role that pollution played:

Despite confident assertions that pollution is the culprit there is, as yet, no clear evidence of why North Sea seals are dying in such disturbing numbers. There are several contending theories, and none of them can wholly be discounted at this point. (26 August 1988: 13)

The *Independent*'s former environment correspondent took a more sceptical line and criticized the press in general for suggesting that pollution explained the outbreak of the disease:

. . . everybody was rushing round saying the seals are dying, they're clearly being poisoned and that's obviously because the North Sea is getting dirtier. And the problem with that is, yes, the seals were dying but they probably weren't dying of pollution and if they were that would be odd since there's less rather than more pollution in the North Sea. The North Sea is cleaner than it used to be so why are seals suddenly dying? Well you can come up with all sorts of theories about that and people did, as to say well maybe it's an incremental thing and the seals died because they're the straw that broke the camel's back. Actually months later it looks as if pollution wasn't in the frame. It might have been a contributory factor or something like that. So with more coverage you get worse coverage in a way. Now that's partly because there are people running around obeying their editor's commands to come up with environmental stories which isn't at all the business of informing the public about what's going on in the environment. It is the business of discovering sexy issues to put in front of the public even if they have to fib a bit. (Interview, 15 March 1989)

Clearly one of the major reasons why the seals story was sustained by the press was that it fulfilled important news values. The story was triggered by an event, it included a strong visual element that people could identify with, it centred upon human interest and it provided a means by which the popular press could present environmental issues in a lightweight entertainment format.

However, a number of other factors explain how the seal plague came to act as an issue-threshold for environmental issues in general. Had the seal virus not come to light in Britain during the summer break then things might have been quite different. It was fortuitous that the outbreak occurred during the "silly season" when parliament was in recess and there was little political or business news around, for it meant that the seals issue did not have to compete with so many "hard" news items (cf. Lang & Lang 1981: 453). Also, by concentrating upon the pollution angle, the media were able to provide an engaging way of covering the usual summer focus on the state of Britain's beaches.

Once the *Daily Mail* launched its "Save our seals" campaign, and demonstrated the strength of public interest in environmental issues, other newspapers followed. In this sense, the *Daily Mail* can also be seen to have set the agenda for other popular newspapers. As Schoenfeld et al. (1979: 50) have argued,

> Once such a legitimate news category has come into existence, different orders of meaning and association can be made to cluster together, and produce more media space. Hence the discovery of the "environment" as a social problem in 1969–70 had an effect on "news values", perhaps an even greater effect than environmental events would justify at any one time.

However, the seals story did not become an issue-threshold merely through extensive media coverage; the activities of sources were of crucial importance. The seals issue was sustained by the various social actors who were involved because it was, for different reasons, in their interests to do so. As Lavigne maintains,

> I think the reason why TV and the press took up the issues so readily is directly related to the involvement of marine mammals (remember the gray whales in Alaska). This, together with pollution, and the prevailing political environment, made the seal plague a timely story – one which scientists, environmentalists and politicians were happy to keep going for a variety of reasons. (Personal communication, 11 August 1989)

A key weakness of previous agenda-setting studies is that they have tended to pay little attention to the role that sources play in constructing the agenda (Solesbury 1976). The case study of the seal plague indicates that sources play a central role in building media agendas.

The agenda-building role of sources

The process by which the seal virus was transformed from being viewed as a purely scientific issue into being seen as a "political" issue was complex. The activities of sources, be they scientists, environmentalists or politicians, were crucial in this process because it was these sources who first "defined" the nature of the problem, rather than the media, and they continued to influence the subsequent development of the agenda. Moreover, the institutionalization of environmental issues through government departments and non-governmental organizations was important. Since the 1970s environmental groups have become more sophisticated in dealing with the media. Schoenfeld et al. (1979: 51) noted that in the case of America:

Environmental issues gained stable press salience both because the issues had become professionalized – "de-scholared" – and because they had been placed in the care of people who not only "spoke the same language" as reporters and editors but were adept at creating the interpersonal communication that leads to space in the press.

Indeed, the seals story illustrates how the relationship between sources and the media can be of great importance in shaping the political agenda. While the activities of Greenpeace displayed a sophisticated understanding of the workings of the press, the response made by Dutch virologists demonstrated a somewhat undeveloped and suspicious attitude towards the media. One of the major sources that the media used for the seals story was Greenpeace. The environmental organization developed a successful strategy by using the seal deaths to draw attention to their anti-pollution campaign. They mounted an advertising campaign during August 1988 in the national daily press that suggested that pollution was responsible for the plague (see Table 5.5). The Greenpeace advertisement claimed: "The scientists confirm the very strong indications that pollution is contributing to the seals' deaths." (What the advertisement failed to mention was that there was a considerable amount of uncertainty amongst scientists as to what extent pollution was to blame.)

Table 5.5 suggests that the Greenpeace advertising campaign in the tabloids was directed towards the largely Conservative, middle-class,

161

Table 5.5 Greenpeace adverts on the seal virus during August 1988.

Newspaper	Number	Positioning
Guardian	3	Front page
Independent	3	Leader page (2), front page (1)
Times	2	Front page
Today	2	Diary/gossip page
Observer	2	Front page
Daily Telegraph	1	Weekend section
Daily Mail	1	Diary/gossip page
Mail on Sunday	1	Leader page
Sunday Times	1	Front page

female readership of *Today* and the *Daily Mail*. Indeed, Greenpeace's media director, Sue Adams, maintained:

> We advertised knowing we'd get its Tory readers, asking them to ring the DoE to ask what they were doing about it. They were so inundated they couldn't cope and suddenly realized there were a lot of Tory voters out there who really cared about these issues. This forced them to start taking on the green mantle. (Cited by Warren 1995: 61)

Also, it is interesting to note that the advertisements in the mid-market press were all carried on entertainment pages, which reveals something about the way in which these newspapers cover such issues and assumptions about the level of reader interest. Another way that Greenpeace focused attention upon the seals issue was through organizing an international conference held at the Greenpeace scientific unit at Queen Mary College, University of London. And during September 1988 independent scientists, attached to the environmental pressure group, carried out their own research into the links between pollution and the seal deaths. The results of their research, which indicated that there were high concentrations of mercury in the livers of seals in the Wash and the Irish Sea, were promptly sent to the press and received wide coverage. Two years on, Greenpeace still maintained that pollution was a factor, although they to some extent modified their position:

> The factors involved in any epidemic are complex. The potential involvement of pollution in this recent European seal "die-off"

still requires consideration. The continuous movement of persistent chemicals into the marine environment has been seen for some time by some authorities as a potential cause for the eventual extinction of marine mammals. If we add to this possibility an increase in epidemics associated with increased ambient temperatures then the future of whales, dolphins and seals looks far from assured. (Letter by Mark Simmonds, Greenpeace research associate, published in BBC *Wildlife Magazine*, October 1990: 709)

While Greenpeace mounted a proactive campaign to attract media attention, Dutch scientists at the Dutch National Institute for Public Health and Environmental Protection, who doubted that pollution was a central factor, largely shunned the media. When the seal virus was first discovered Dutch scientists began a lengthy research programme to investigate possible explanations. In the UK, research was carried out by the Sea Mammal Research Unit at Cambridge University. Particularly during the early stages of investigation Dutch virologists generally refused to speculate about possible causes of the disease. However, some scientists such as Professor Vasserman at Kiel University, West Germany, suggested to the media that particular theories could not be ruled out, such as the theory that pollution was a cause of the seal virus. Also some scientists suggested that the virus spread from East Canadian harp seals to common seals. This provided some spurious claims with a degree of legitimacy. As Lavigne claims,

> This suggestion required such a convoluted chain of events that it should never have been taken seriously, but taken seriously it was. Newspapers published maps describing the envisaged route of infection, and scientists lent it credibility by mentioning it in the media as a possibility that could not be ruled out. (BBC *Wildlife Magazine*, July 1989: 438)

Dr Osterhaus and colleagues at the Dutch Institute for Public Health and Environmental Protection told journalists that they would not reveal their findings until they were published in the British science journal, *Nature* (which has a policy of not offering unpublished evidence to the media). Finally, the Dutch government put pressure on the scientists to reveal the basis of their findings a couple of days before they were due to be published. This suspicious attitude towards the media, particularly towards the popular newspapers, meant that Greenpeace was able to act as the principal "gatekeeper" in the early "definition" period. The theory that pollution had caused the seal virus provided the tabloid newspapers with a dramatic story, which fitted in with major news values, and manipulated a growing concern about health related issues among the public. A fundamental conflict arose, then, between the scientists' lengthy research cycle and the media cycle of daily news stories. As Lavigne argues,

> The media and some environmentalists were not interested in theories that might take months or even years to examine; they wanted instant explanations and immediate action. (*BBC Wildlife Magazine*, July 1989: 438)

As scientists became more accustomed to dealing with the media, a *Daily Mail* reporter claimed that they became less suspicious of the tabloid press. Although, more cynically, some scientists may have seen this as a way of getting more money. The fact that the *Daily Mail* donated some of the money it raised towards scientific research on the virus may have made scientists feel under obligation towards the newspaper. For example, £50,000 was donated to the Sea Mammal Research Unit at Cambridge. This obviously raises the question of the ethics of scientists accepting money from a national newspaper (cf. *New Scientist*, 15 September 1988).

Greenpeace defined the seal deaths as a *political* issue and this, together with the resulting media coverage, forced politicians to respond. The Department of the Environment claimed that pollution was not responsible for the seal virus. The Secretary and the Under-Secretary of State for the Environment, Nicholas Ridley and Virginia Bottomley, argued that the plague was caused by a virus that had occurred naturally. A press officer at the Department of the Environment suggested that the reason why government sources were not quoted as many times as environmental organizations was that their response was not as newsworthy. The press officer claimed:

> Well that [pollution] made the headlines . . . you could always find an expert to say that, or someone that could call on an expert, particularly if they happen to be attached to one of the organizations which was putting the pressure on . . . . The environmental pressure groups were giving the headlines which they were looking for . . . what we will say will actually kill their

stories. So they tend, if they know that's going to be the case, not to come to us, or if they do they will ignore what we say. (Interview, 28 May 1991)

Of course, it was in their interests to suggest that Britain should wait until there was firm evidence before introducing costly anti-pollution measures. But the definition of the problem as a political issue ensured that it continued to attract prominent media coverage and political attention. As Lang & Lang (1981: 466; original emphasis) suggest:

The process is a continuous one, involving a number of feed-back loops, most important among which are the way political figures see their own image mirrored in the media, the pooling of information within the press corps, and the various indicators of the public response. We argue that a topic, problem, or key concern to which political leaders are or should be paying attention is not yet an *issue*. Important as the media may be in focusing attention, neither awareness nor perceived importance makes an issue. However, once the above-mentioned links are established, a topic may continue to be an issue even if other topics receive greater emphasis from the media.

Indeed, as Solesbury (1976: 383) acknowledges, it is only when a number of conditions have been satisfied that government reacts to an issue:

Issues finally evoke responses from governments when they have become powerful enough to capture public resources, when they become the subject of political debate, when they come to dominate the media, when organizations grow around them conducting campaigns both for and against responses and when they begin to be used to gain influence and money.

The role of sources as "gatekeepers", then, is fundamental to the agenda-building process. NGOs do not generally attract widespread media attention unless their demands are viewed as legitimate by government. However, in the case of the seals issue, Greenpeace managed to secure considerable media interest. This seems, in part, to reflect the fact that other prominent sources, such as government and scientists linked to government bodies, failed to act quickly enough in order to "define" the problem.

Summary

The case study has suggested, then, that the popular press, on some occasions, plays an important role in setting the political agenda. Indeed, in my view the role of the media as definers in the agenda-setting process has been overlooked by Hall et al. (1978). Sometimes the media take up themes that are later adopted by key institutional sources, such as the government. However, if one analyzes the process through which agendas are constructed then it becomes clear that sources play a crucial role in defining problems that are later taken up by the media. Also, sources play a major role in sustaining issues once they are taken up by the media. Therefore, the relationship between the public agenda, the media agenda and the political table of priorities is complex. As Schlesinger (1990: 67; original emphasis) argues,

> ... the model of reproduction of Hall et al. deals with the question of the media's relative autonomy from the political system in a purely *uni-directional* way. The movement of definitions is *uniformly* from power centre to media. Within this conceptual logic, there is no space to account for occasions on which the media may take the initiative in the definitional process by *challenging* the so-called primary definers and forcing them to respond .... At times, too, it is the media which crystallize slogans or themes which are subsequently taken up by the primary definers because it is in their interests to do so.

Hall et al. fail to consider instances where the media influence politicians indirectly through drawing attention to a problem and mobilizing the public to place pressure on the government. In the case of the seals issue, Britain's cultural climate was not favourably disposed towards taking action over North Sea pollution and the *Daily Mail* and the *Mail on Sunday* were largely responsible for provoking an outcry among Conservative voters.

The case study also suggests that the boundaries of definition shift. While a number of studies indicate that government sources tend to be most accessed by the media, in the case of the seals issue, Greenpeace acted as a key "primary definer". Government ministers and scientists linked to government bodies were suspicious of the press and slow to respond. While it was in Greenpeace's interests to act speedily and mobilize public concern about the plight of the seals, it was in the interests of government to stall immediate action and wait for demonstrable evidence to suggest that pollution played a role in the seals' deaths.

When all is said and done, does it matter that there is still no firm evidence to suggest that pollution caused the seal virus? Surely any coverage that heightens people's awareness of environmental issues is desirable? Peter Usher, reporter for the *Daily Mail* "Save our seals" campaign, argued:

> Now it didn't matter that the reason they were dying was a virus and that pollution couldn't be pinned down as the cause of the virus. It didn't matter because it just woke the realization that if you go on dumping chemicals in the seas you'll kill all the creatures in the sea. If you go on dumping chemicals in the land you'll kill all the creatures on the land. It's a very simple kind of realization but I think, I believe, that it was the seals that really drove that point home. (Interview, 25 July 1989)

However, in the long term, I think environmentalists may lose credibility if no proven link between pollution and the virus is found. Also, politicians will argue that this shows there is no urgent need to take action on pollution. And what about the plight of animals that do not evoke such an emotional response? As Dr Sidney Holt, a senior United Nations official involved with the International Whaling Commission and currently scientific advisor to the International Fund for Animal Welfare, maintains,

> Constructive responses to both saving the sea and saving seals may be impeded by precipitate actions. Some environmentalists have opportunistically used the seal deaths to support their anti-pollution campaigns. But if no clear link is demonstrated, politicians will be able to say that the need to deal with pollution is less urgent. That is, of course, untrue because other harm to marine life and to us is undoubted. (Letter published in *Sunday Times*, 4 September 1988)

Similarly, an editorial in the *New Scientist* (1 September 1988: 27) warned:

> Paradoxically those who are rushing to point the finger at chemicals in the current episode just might prolong that flow of effluent. What happens if pollution is found to have no influence on the spread of the disease, and that the seals die irrespective of the amount of PCBs in their bodies? The public may well want pollution reduced, but the lobbyists for the chemicals industry will rush forward to point out that this was yet another false alarm and tell us how expensive it would be to control the release of chemicals.

The problem is that there is a fundamental conflict between the tendency for scientists to qualify everything and the media dependence upon short, sharp events and clear unqualified statements. Scientists tend to have little training in media relations and they are therefore often suspicious of journalists. Scientists need to develop a greater awareness of the workings of the media and similarly journalists need to cultivate a greater understanding of the constraints that influence scientists. Finally, environmentalists should avoid the temptation to manipulate the popular press through offering newsworthy explanations for complex phenomena because, in the long term, this may prove counter-productive.

Suggested further reading

A useful discussion of environmental agenda-setting can be found in W. Solesbury, "The environmental agenda", *Public Administration* **54**, 379–97, 1976. For a discussion of the relationship between scientists and media practitioners see S. Friedman, S. Dunwoody, C. Rogers (eds), *Scientists and journalists: reporting science as news* (New York: Free Press, 1986). The classic work on primary definers is S. Hall, C. Critcher, T. Jefferson, J. Clarke, B. Roberts, *Policing the crisis: mugging, the state, and law and order* (London: Macmillan, 1978). For recent qualifications to this thesis see P. Schlesinger, "Rethinking the sociology of journalism: source strategies and the limits of media centrism" in *Public communication: the new imperatives*, M. Ferguson (ed.), 61–83

(London: Sage, 1990) and A. Hansen (ed.), *The mass media and environmental issues* (Leicester: Leicester University Press, 1993), particularly chs 3, 4 and 6.

Other case studies of the representation of environmental issues in the news media are discussed in R. Fowler, *Language in the news* (London: Routledge, 1991) and J. A. Hannigan, *Environmental sociology* (London: Routledge, 1995).

Chapter 6

Mediating the environment

Introduction

In Chapter 5 we saw how significant numbers of newspaper readers were sufficiently moved by the "Save our seals" campaign to contribute donations. Also, I suggested that there is a fundamental conflict of interests between scientists' tendency to qualify everything and the news media's dependence upon immediate, dramatic events. The environment, like other substantive areas of news reporting, is largely mediated through the voice of the "expert". However, there are various tensions over what is viewed as "expert discourse" and what is perceived as "lay discourse".

So far in this book I have concentrated upon the processes involved in producing and managing the news. The environment as a contested terrain depends upon broader cultural frameworks in society that enable us to make sense of environmental issues. In this chapter I want to address the question of how well the news media inform and educate the public about the environment. As we saw in Chapter 1, the issue of media effects is one of the most heavily researched areas within the mass communications field. Despite decades of research into the impact and influence of the mass media, there remains an underlying lack of consensus about their precise role. Individual audience members have their own meanings and motivations that shape their use of the media, making it difficult to predict how they will respond. Also, as we shall see, audiences relate to particular social issues in different ways depending upon factors such as levels of prior knowledge, social class, gender, ethnicity and age.

Live Aid

As we have seen in previous chapters, many ongoing stories about environment and development fail to attract sustained public and media attention. However, some awareness-raising campaigns have made a major impact, at least if this is measured in terms of the number of people persuaded to donate money. During the mid 1980s a major campaign known as "Live Aid" was launched to draw attention to the plight of human suffering from the Ethiopian famine. Like the "Save our seals" campaign it involved the presence of prominent show business personalities. The campaign was spearheaded by the pop singer Bob Geldof, and culminated in a live rock concert in the USA and the UK in July 1985. This concert was broadcast across the world and in many ways relied upon the power of television to get the message across. Much was made of the sheer technical brilliance that allowed such a "global" event to take place.

The Live Aid campaign clearly moved the audience. Philo & Lamb (1990) note a significant increase in donations to aid charities during the time-span of Live Aid. For example, between May 1984 and April 1995 donations to Oxfam reached £51 million, compared to only £23.9 million the previous year, and £45.2 million the following year. In addition, by late 1986 Band Aid itself had raised $110 million. However, the fact that development charities have to strive continuously to keep famines in the public eye suggests that the effects tend to be relatively short term. There is a perception among some media practitioners that such events do not achieve a great deal in educational terms and the public soon tire of the issues. For example, a correspondent at ITN maintained:

I think there's a general tiredness with that kind of telethon . . . there's actually very little consciousness raising that goes on in that kind of environment. I think it really is just help the starving millions full stop. (Interview, 19 February 1993)

Voluntary-sector campaigners are constantly battling against the tendency for the public to lose interest each time a further appeal is made because they have "already heard it all before". Despite this, many journalists were taken aback at the degree of public response generated. The BBC news reader, Michael Buerk claimed:

Everything about the British and other publics proved to be wrong. I remember talking to NBC, who also ran the piece and had this amazing reaction; they told me: "It"ll only last a week; the American public will soon get bored with that sort of stuff". I almost agreed with them at the time, but they proved to be terribly wrong. (cited by Philo & Lamb 1990: 58)

Live Aid and the "Save our seals" campaign are clearly not typical of the bulk of environmental items that make their way onto news bulletins, or onto the pages of our newspapers. Both involved heart-rendering images of death and destruction, and received sustained high profile treatment by sections of the news media. Also, it seems likely that the entertainment-style approach encouraged members of the audience to develop a closer identification with the issues through the involvement of famous personalities. Finally, both offered concrete ways in which individual members of the audience could make a difference. There remains the problem that many reports on less developed countries fail to examine the causes of poverty and simply present their populations as victims (Philo & Lamb 1990).

As I noted in Chapter 5, during the height of the recent wave of environmental interest, there was a perception among environmental pressure groups that women were particularly concerned about environmental matters. A Senior Information Officer for Friends of the Earth stated:

As soon as green consumerism and aerosols appeared it was very much on the part of the tabloids "this could happen to you", the skin cancers that sort of thing. It's very difficult now, in the light of everything that has happened recently, to actually say what appeals to the press most because we're constantly amazed by the new sort of ways they're finding. But it is very much for the individual how something affects them personally . . . . For women, particularly, it is what will happen to their children if certain environmental problems aren't solved such as pesticides in food, radiation, ozone and the greenhouse effect. There's a tremendous amount of environmental concern among women. (Interview, 17 July 1989)

An information coordinator at Greenpeace concurred:

We have a features writer who works to much longer deadlines and targets specifically women's magazines .... Women seem to be very interested in conservation and environmental issues and women's magazines were crying out for articles and features. We have lots of green pages and things like that. (Interview, 22 January 1991)

The question of the degree to which individuals are influenced by these sorts of campaigns, as well as more routine news coverage, is of crucial importance. Today, the majority of audience research is carried out by the media organizations themselves, or from specialist data agencies providing information on who watches what and for how long. It is based upon a limited number of standard demographic characteristics such as occupation, gender and age (Bell 1991).

Media practitioners' views of the audience

Journalists working in radio or newspapers tend to have a much closer relationship with readers and viewers compared to broadcasters. The letters-to-the-editor page, for example, provides an important forum for the exchange of views. One reason for this may be that the press, especially the broadsheets, tend to receive far more letters about environmental matters than does television. A former BBC environment correspondent maintained:

What they don't get in the same profusion as newspapers get, is letters indicating their audience's deep concerns. I used to edit the letters page on the *Guardian*. I did it for 18 months, and so I saw a lot of letters and even in those long ago days it was getting a lot of letters about environmental concerns and they feed through into the kind of editorial policies the paper decides to adopt . . . so there's a community of interest which develops between the readers and the newspapers which you don't have in news on television, certainly. (Interview, 27 November 1990)

This view is supported by the comments of a former environment correspondent for the *Daily Express*. When questioned at the time of the most recent peak of environmental concern, he claimed:

> What we have noticed is that doing environmental stories in the paper has provoked huge reader response and people are very, very concerned ... the generating or motivating fact now is very much the fact that readers expect to read about the environment ... we did the good and bad beach guide right in front of the school summer holidays this year and that attracted huge reader response ... there's been a huge amount of reader sympathy for the seal and what was happening to it and dolphins too. (Interview, 31 October 1989)

In the case of television, there are relatively few avenues through which members of the audience can make their own voices directly heard on an equal footing with presenters – with the notable exception of audience discussion programmes and video talkback slots (Bell 1991). Though broadcasters maintain a keen awareness of broad trends in public demand, they rarely make use of audience research and tend to view the audience with a certain amount of disregard (McQuail 1969, Gans 1980, Silverstone 1985, Schlesinger 1987, Westergaard 1977). They are generally much more concerned about audience numbers than about their composition. Also, there is a time lag in the availability of audience data; programming adjustments can only be made in the future (Bell 1991).

On the whole this is not perceived as a major problem; rather, notions of professionalism are invoked in order to assert autonomy, and to maintain social distance from consumers. A former environment correspondent at BBC News claimed: "There's a sense in which broadcasters talk to each other, and talk to politicians, and exclude the vast swathe of the population". (Interview, 27 November 1990) Broadcasters have a much keener sensitivity towards the reaction of their peers, and of public figures, than of the average member of the audience. However, this view of the audience is not necessarily shared by individual correspondents working on the ground. For example a correspondent, who has worked as an environmental reporter for both BBC radio and BBC television, claimed:

> My perception of the audience is different from that of senior editorial management. I believe very strongly, in fact I think I know, that there is an unsatisfied appetite for environment

stories. In television they are picture-led stories which tend to be quite strong, vivid . . . I know from my mail and telephone calls that whenever we transmit a story, for instance, about animal welfare there's a great response. And that people when polled don't believe that there's enough on the news about environmental concerns. That's shown up, it seems to me, by the success of programmes like "Newsround" who get an enormous mail-bag from not only young people but from the adults who watch the programme which they do in large numbers. (Interview, 5 February 1993)

He went on to state:

The public are very well-informed, particularly the younger audiences who are often streets ahead of both the politicians and the press in their perception of the damage that's being done to the global environment. Most polls reveal that people know about, and are alarmed by, what we're doing to our planet . . . and that's at odds with what they want in their own lifestyle and their own aspirations. And in that they're no different from anybody else and the politicians who promise to fulfil those aspirations. (Interview, 5 February 1993)

In a climate where environmental issues are low on the political agenda, producers and editors may suffer from "environmental overload" if there is a shortage of new angles. A correspondent for BBC Television News claimed:

It's no longer the major political issue it once was . . . . You got to the stage, I think, where you got environmental fatigue . . . . Even if you got marvellous pictures the emphasis is gone out of it . . . . People say "not again, we've heard this before" . . . . It doesn't mean the story is not as important as ever, but to sustain a news operation you have to have new stories, and campaigns are all very well but they tend to lose their impetus after a while. (Interview, 5 February 1993)

Indeed, a former environment correspondent for BBC News maintained:

What makes me hold off stories is not thinking that the public
may not be interested as thinking that producers and editors
may not be interested. (Interview, 5 February 1993)

To sum up then, media practitioners tend to inhabit a highly insular
culture, are likely to spend little time "off the job", and typically view
the audience with a degree of indifference.

Public opinion and news media representations
of environmental issues

There is a substantial literature on public attitudes to the environment. An underlying assumption of much of the research is that the
media have a powerful influence upon public attitudes to the environment. Frequently researchers make the assumption that it is possible
to demonstrate a direct causal relationship between media coverage
and public opinion. However, there is little conclusive evidence about
the effects of television (or other media) upon public attitudes to particular environmental issues. Some studies suggest that the media
have played an important role in influencing public opinion about
environmental matters (Atwater et al. 1985, Brosius & Kepplinger
1990, Parlour & Schatzow 1978, Salwen 1988). A German study by
Brosius & Kepplinger (1990) found a relatively strong correlation between public and media agendas for energy supply issues. However,
they note that their findings should be treated with caution since
agenda-setting timescales vary depending upon the category of issue.

A more complex approach towards understanding the flow of information between the media and the public can be found in ideology
diffusion models of communication (see for example, Tichenor et al.
1970), However, these theories tend to suffer from the same basic limitations as those described above. Such studies portray the processes of
mass communication as though they operate in a linear rather than an
interactive fashion. In other words, they map the evolution of social
problems in terms of clearly identifiable 'stages'. For example,
Strodthoff et al. (1985) view the diffusion of environmental information as starting with scientific claimsmakers, channelled through special interest magazines, then to magazines with a more general
auidence, through to the broader public. As Hansen notes: "in their

pursuit of linearity [such approaches] gloss over the interactive nature of meaning construction among and between institutions in society" (1991: 447). This tends to ignore the possibility that there may be considerable overlap between stages.

A rather different approach to the question of media flows, the spiral of silence model, focuses on the level of individual meaning construction (see McQuail & Windahl 1993). This theory, with its origins in social psychology, suggests that individual opinions are highly dependent upon what is perceived to be the "majority" view on any given issue. In other words, the model suggests that individuals actively weigh up the general climate of opinion in coming to express their own judgements. Interpersonal networks and the mass media are seen as the key means through which individuals gain clues as to the relative prominence of particular points of view. If an individual's own position does not seem to accord with the dominant view then they are seen as being much less likely to express their opinions than if they are perceived to have wide support. According to this theory, opinion polls as reported in the media may themselves have a significant impact upon people's voting behaviour.

Noelle-Neumann (1974, 1991) is perhaps best known for her work in this area. In order to test this model, Noelle-Neumann conducted a study into public opinion on nuclear energy. She discovered that newspapers gave increasing coverage to nuclear energy issues during the period 1965–85, matched by a relatively stable trend towards less reassuring statements. Noelle-Neumann claims the majority of the public supported nuclear power until the early 1980s, when there were greater numbers of opponents compared to supporters. The study concludes that this provides further evidence to support the theory that when individuals feel their views are isolated by assessing the perceived climate of opinion, they are likely to conceal or change their attitudes.

While such studies are significant, in that they suggest some of the ways in which the media play a part in the decisions individuals make in prioritizing particular issues, they are limited in scope. In my view they tend to gloss over the complexities of the processes by which different social groupings make sense of environmental meanings as presented in the media. Given such difficulties it is not suprising to find that the results of different studies are often contradictory.

Other studies suggest that the media have little direct influence on public attitudes about specific environmental issues (Gunter & Wober

1983, Protess et al. 1987, Wober & Gunter 1985). A US study by Protess et al. (1987) suggests that television documentaries on environmental issues may have a greater impact on policy-makers than on public opinion. The study focused upon a local investigative television series about the disposal of toxic waste at a Chicago university. Protess and colleagues carried out a random telephone survey of members of the public and follow-up interviews. They found that there was a high degree of journalist involvement with the policy-making elite, and after the programme was broadcast, government agencies took action to ensure that toxic waste disposal regulations were monitored at the university.

Most studies have tended to focus upon television news and current affairs in advanced industrial societies. However, a study by Sekar (1981) researched the role of the press in promoting environmental concern in India. He concluded that, for a number of reasons, the Indian press plays only a limited role in creating mass concern about environmental issues. First, a large proportion of people are preoccupied with daily struggles to satisfy basic needs such as food and shelter, thus the Indian public display some indifference to environmental issues. Second, there are high levels of illiteracy in India; only around 10 per cent of the population are literate newspaper readers and the majority lack the benefit of science education. Finally, the quality of environmental reporting in the Indian press is very variable. A content analysis study conducted in 1979–80 revealed that a large number of environmental items were news reports; most stories were reactive, and there was very little evidence of investigative journalism.

A study by Gooch (1996) casts further doubt on traditional agenda-setting studies that imply there is a linear relationship between public attitudes and the relative prominence of themes and issues in the news media. Gooch investigated the relationship between public perception of environmental risks and the reporting of environmental affairs in the Swedish regional press. The study was based upon a content analysis of two Swedish local newspapers between August and October 1992, followed up by a postal attitude survey at the end of the final month. The findings suggest that local newspapers do not have a strong agenda-setting effect on attitudes towards the environment despite the important role of the regional press as a source of information. While water and waste issues were found to receive the greatest prominence in the local newspapers during the sample period, this did not appear to be reflected in the public's assessment of the perceived "seriousness" of a range of environmental problems. The survey indicated that the public appeared to be much more concerned about air quality than either water or waste. While Gooch rejects linear models of media effects, I think these findings need to be treated with a degree of caution given the drawbacks with surveys of this kind. For example, a question which asks the respondent to rank the perceived seriousness of a given number of issues is likely to elicit a very different response compared to a question on how the respondent "feels" about an issue. Though the survey did include one open-ended question, in which respondents were asked to describe what they saw as the most serious local environmental problem, this does not completely address this difficulty. Also, while such surveys clearly provide some indication of public concern about issues, there is a sense in which they divorce opinions from their socially negotiated setting. Indeed Gooch (1996: 124)acknowledges that:

The important role played by friends, neighbours and relatives as sources of information also demonstrates that interpersonal interaction plays a considerable role in the forming of the public's perception of environmental issues.

As I observed earlier, some evidence suggests that the agenda-setting effect may occur in the opposite direction. In other words, the regional press may in some cases be responding to public concern rather than initiating it; if this is the case it would be necessary to measure public attitudes *before* conducting a content analysis of trends in environmental reporting. Another possibility may be that the agenda-setting effect of regional newspapers operates on a shorter timescale, its longer term impact being closely bound up with the extent to which major news sources succeed in sustaining interest over a lengthy period of time. Interestingly, Gooch found that environmental pressure groups gained little access to the local press over the sample period. In contrast, some British and North American studies of environmental reporting in the regional press have found that environmental groups have obtained relatively high levels of access (for example, Anderson 1993a, Molotch & Lester 1975, Spears et al. 1987). It is likely that the degree of access that environmental groups gain to the local press differs depending upon the complex interaction of a number of factors. These include the following: the nature of the issue; its stage of development in the regional press and the wider news media; the extent to which environmental groups are specifically targeting local newspapers; the degree of activity or non-activity of key players (such as government or industry sources) and their relationship with the local press; editorial policy and the relationship between environmental groups and local media; and the degree to which issue "packages" resonate with news values. The news media, then, form part of a complex web of interacting influences which are glossed over in linear models of media effects.

Most early audience research in the North American social-psychological tradition was based upon social survey methods, which offer only a superficial guide to changes in attitude. Such studies tended to include different combinations of social issues, making comparison difficult. Also, timescales varied from a couple of days to a couple of weeks. Finally, they tended to ignore the possibility that, on occasion, the public may influence media agendas (Lowe & Goyder 1983).

More recently, a small number of audience reaction studies have been made in the UK. For instance, a MORI poll of 2,043 adults, carried out for the Nature Conservancy Council, indicated that 73 per cent of those who claimed they were "very interested" in conservation, viewed television as their main source of information about conservation. A great deal fewer claimed their main source of information was from newspapers, magazines or radio (33 per cent, 10 per cent and 6 per cent, respectively). Indeed, some evidence indicates that viewers became more concerned about nature conservation through watching natural history programmes (Burgess 1990a). A BBC audience survey (1987) found that 50 per cent of viewers of conservation programmes stated that as a consequence they were better informed about the issues involved (Sparks 1987).

It is more difficult to ascertain whether audience members actively respond to such programmes through joining conservation organizations. The 1987 BBC audience survey found that 2 per cent of the viewers of wildlife documentaries claimed that, as a result of watching television, they joined a conservation group. But these figures may simply reflect annual membership increases. One must treat such findings with caution. As we saw in Chapter 3, a major limitation of social survey methods is that they offer little in-depth evidence about the effects of media coverage over time. As Burgess (1990b: 9) argues,

Questionnaire surveys seek to establish the extent to which news coverage, for example, has changed peoples' opinions rather than focusing on the ways in which individuals interpret news items. Closed questions and pre-determined attitude scales cannot reveal how different people interact with different media texts, nor can they explain why some information is felt to be significant enough to be retained and incorporated into people's knowledge and understanding while most is simply ignored.

Recall and understanding

Relatively few studies have been conducted into how much people understand from news reporting. The majority of news diffusion studies have focused upon recall (see McQuail & Windahl 1993). Research suggests that on the whole people do not have a very high level of recall; they can only rarely remember more than 30 per cent of the information even when prompted (see Bell 1991, van Dijk 1988). Large-scale studies in the US, Sweden and Austria suggest that people tend to have relatively low levels of general recall from the news media (see Bell 1994). Typically, people are more likely to remember the setting and the persons involved than what was actually said. People tend to have a stronger identification with place than with time; so the place where an environmental incident occurs (for example, Chernobyl) tends to be more memorable than its timing (Bell 1994). The order in which news items are presented in news bulletins can also affect recall. Studies indicate that the first and final items are remembered the best; levels of recall tend to drop for items in between (for example, Gunter 1987). Overall, the last items in a news bulletin are most likely to be recalled by the audience. However, final items often tend to have a strong human interest appeal (often these are "soft" up-beat stories) that could also account for high levels of recall.

Also, recall is significantly influenced by levels of previous knowledge, and to a lesser extent, an individual's demographic characteristics. Yet levels of recall vary for different categories of news stories. As one might expect, dramatic environmental disasters tend to prompt a relatively high level of recall. For example Wilkins (1987) surveyed two groups of people about their memories of the reporting of the Bhopal disaster seven months after the event. The sample was taken from two different communities in the USA; Eugene (which considers itself as an environmentally aware city), and Charleston (the location of the sister Bhopal plant). Perhaps not surprisingly, Wilkins found a substantial number of people vividly remembered the event, especially the reported long-term impacts on health and the environment. However, levels of specific factual recall tended to be relatively low. Just over a third of the sample correctly estimated the number of people who had died as a result of the incident (between 2,000 and 2,500). Yet, only 4.3 per cent were able to estimate accurately the numbers of injured people (between 2,000 and 2,500).

Recall studies are rather limited as they do not necessarily provide any indication of how well people have comprehended important scientific concepts/data. The findings of studies on news comprehension are complex, but broadly suggest that understanding is enhanced by stories that are visually strong, personalized or deal with issues in concrete ways (see McQuail 1992). In an information-saturated world, stories about environmental issues have to stand out from competing news items.

One interesting pilot survey of levels of environmental understanding was conducted by Allan Bell in the late 1980s (Bell 1991). Bell based his survey upon a small sample of 61 New Zealanders, designed to reflect key demographic characteristics of the country as a whole. The interviewees were asked to answer six questions on climate change issues, and each was given a mark out of ten for every correct reply (no marks were deducted for incorrect answers). In addition, Bell conducted a study into the reporting of climate change in the daily press, radio and television. The analysis of news media representations was conducted over a six month period in the late 1980s.

Bell's study suggests that people tend to exaggerate what they remember from the media, especially if it is very dramatic or negative. For example, some respondents significantly exaggerated reported sea-level rises well beyond the estimates of the Royal Society of New Zealand, or those of the Villach conference in 1985 (see Figure 6.1).

Although Bell found a number of instances of inaccurate news reporting, he concluded that: ". . . public exaggeration considerably exceeds anything for which the balance of media reporting can be held directly responsible" (1991: 243). This has important implications; exaggerated estimates could be counter-productive as media practitioners and scientists are likely to be blamed if these scenarios do not occur.

Bell also found that there were significant differences between the content of news reports and public understanding of ozone destruction. Three-quarters of the sample stated that aerosol cans resulted in ozone loss, while only a fifth attributed it to refrigeration, and still

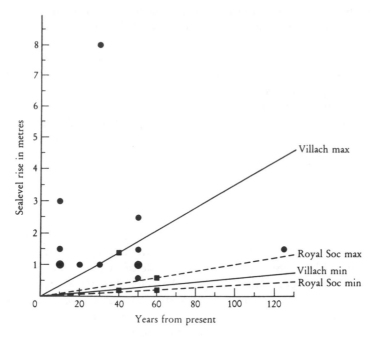

Figure 6.1 Estimates of possible sea-level rises by 14 members of the New Zealand public, plotted against the upper and lower scenarios from the 1985 Villach conference and from the 1988 Royal Society of New Zealand report. *Source:* Bell 1991:244.

fewer to the manufacture of polystyrene. Refrigeration and the manufacture of polystyrene each contribute almost as much to ozone destruction as spray cans. As Figure 6.2 illustrates, fire extinguishers and solvents were not identified as causes by the public at all.

Finally, the public displayed a large amount of confusion between global warming and ozone depletion. Typically people viewed them as indistinct from one another, or they mis-associated causes and effects. These misunderstandings may have serious consequences for preventative behaviour, or for comprehending the real causes of glo-

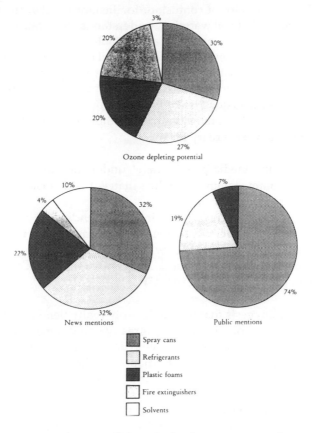

Figure 6.2 Distribution of New Zealand consumption of ozone depleting substances, and distribution of mentions of the substances in news reporting, compared to the public's mentions. *Source*: Bell 1991: 241.

bal warming. I concur with Bell that media exaggeration is not justified. Such exaggeration could easily result in a backlash if predictions are seriously out of line and, in any case, evidence suggests that the public are overemphasizing the scenarios themselves.

Interestingly, Bell (1994) found a significant level of confusion between ozone depletion and the greenhouse effect in news media discourse. Some media practitioners clearly recognize this as an area of potential confusion. For example, an environment correspondent for BBC News maintained:

185

I think you get a lot of confusion, for instance, between the ozone layer and global warming, understandably because it is confusing. But I think there is an appreciable, a sizeable minority of people who know a lot, far more than I do. And we should never underestimate that . . . We should be trying to make sure that what we are saying makes sense to them as well as to the far larger number who don't really know but probably would like to know more and are rather worried without being quite sure why. (Interview, 5 February 1993)

However, some media practitioners' understandings appear to have more in common with the public's than with scientists':

Journalists are laypeople in their understanding of climate change and other scientific matters. They bring to their reporting task lay preconceptions of what is going on. It remains a moot point to what extent journalistic confusion reflects or creates public confusion. (Bell 1994: 47)

Bell's study suggests that the public only really benefit from this type of information provision if they already know something about the issues themselves. Those people who do not have any knowledge of the topics tend to glean little information. In the case of Bell's sample most people knew a little about climate change issues, but on the whole their level of understanding was not high. Bell found evidence of a significant knowledge gap between the higher socio-economic sections of the population and the disadvantaged (Bell 1994). This leads to the conclusion that people only really benefit from media coverage if they already know something of the issue in question. This is also supported by other research focusing upon public awareness about racial issues (van Dijk 1988).

One of the features of the current cycle of environmental concern is a perception that the issues are much more complicated than previously conceived and involve some difficult decisions. As we saw in Chapter 1, Anthony Downs (1972) highlights a stage in public awareness concerning social problems which he labels "realizing the costs of significant progress". According to many of the journalists and broadcasters I interviewed, we are viewed as presently in this part of the cycle. For example, a former BBC News reader claimed:

The deteriorating economic situation has led the audience to believe, and I think the journalists themselves to believe, that a lot of the issues that appeared to be clear-cut in times of prosperity are no longer clear-cut and there are trade-offs between, for example, a protected environment and jobs. (Interview, 29 May 1993)

An environment correspondent at the BBC concurred:

I think perhaps two or three and a half years ago there was something of a feeling that if we all go to the supermarket and buy recycled kitchen towels once a week and eat organic potatoes, then we should be saving the planet. I think now people are realizing it's going to be harder than that. And there are some hard choices involved . . . . There is no environmental free lunch and I think that is coming home to more and more of us now. For every environmental solution there is another problem. (Interview, 5 February 1993)

Moreover, a correspondent at ITN suggested:

Two years ago you could do a story saying "this was the problem". Now people expect you to go a bit further . . . the kind of second stage stories are actually technically and politically quite complicated and are not that easily done on TV. (Interview, 19 February 1993)

So there clearly appears to be a certain amount of consensus, at least among broadcasters covering environmental affairs, that over recent years environmental stories have become much more difficult to "sell" to audiences. This may well have the potential effect of exacerbating many of the problems that inevitably surround levels of recall and understanding.

Risk perception

Several studies suggest that the news media perform an important role in amplifying public perceptions of risk (for example, Sandman et al. 1987). The news media may influence public risk perceptions not just in terms of relaying scientific facts, but in presenting information in ways that encourage the public to imagine scenarios and heighten their memorability through bringing risks closer to home. Studies suggest that lay people make use of factors other than technical information in coming to understandings about risk – for example the unfamiliarity of the risk, its influence on future generations, or potential for catastrophe may all influence judgements (Krimsky & Plough 1988, Krimsky & Golding 1992).

For the German social theorist Ulrich Beck, risk has become a central anchor for conflict in modern industrialized society:

> The social and economic importance of *knowledge* grows similarly, and with it the power over the media to structure knowledge (science and research) and disseminate it (mass media). The risk society is in this sense also the *science, media and information* society. Thus new antagonisms open up between those who *produce* risk definitions and those who *consume* them. (Beck 1992: 46) [original emphasis]

Although Beck is right to observe an increasing consciousness of risk in advanced industrial society, I think he tends to overstate his case. In particular, he describes general processes in Western society as a whole without differentiating between diverging experiences in different countries. Also, he tends to lump the mass media together. A study by Nohrstedt (1991) on the information crisis after Chernobyl, reveals important differences between local and national reporting of the disaster. The Chernobyl disaster was initially widely reported in the national Swedish media but it received more extensive, sustained treatment in local media once the initial panics had begun to subside (see also Spears et al. 1987).

Many studies of risk communication are based upon the underlying assumption that it is possible to judge the quality of reporting through the use of objective measures. In Chapter 2 I argued that we cannot totally dispense with the objectivity ideal. Also, I noted that objectivity is not necessarily the same thing as complete accuracy though the two terms are frequently confused. One measure of media performance is to compare audience assessment of risk with media output. Studies suggest that lay and expert judgements of risky situations tend to be based upon different evaluative schemes. Lay assessments are more likely to take account of factors other than pure statistical measures of risk, including: extent of trust in major social institutions;

degree of uncertainty in risk assessments; potential for large-scale disaster; political controversy and potential wider societal impacts (Dunwoody & Peters 1992). Indeed, according to Durant (1996: 16),

One important reason why professional and lay estimates of risk so often differ is that lay perceptions frequently embody intuitive assessments of the trustworthiness of particular institutions responsible for the safe management of risk. In this sense the concept of risk dissolves the boundaries between science and the wider society; for technical and social judgements are both equally relevant to lay risk assessment.

Studies of risk perception focus upon peoples' attitudes towards specific risks rather than their outlook on environmental issues in general. As we saw in Chapter 4, risk perception varies cross-nationally and is strongly influenced by cultural attitudes and customs. A number of studies suggest that, where some risks are concerned, there are important divergences of perception between policy-makers, scientists and the public (for example, Kempton 1991). In the main, expert perceptions of risk tend to be based upon quantitative measures, whereas lay views are more likely to be influenced by qualitative assessments (Cutter 1993). Also, a variety of opinion surveys suggest that fear and anxiety about the consequences of nuclear fall-out appears to be higher among women (or females feel more comfortable acknowledging this).

However, in my view traditional social-psychological approaches to risk perception suffer from a number of weaknesses. The first major difficulty concerns how risk is defined. On the whole, studies are based upon the assumption that risk is the likelihood of death resulting from particular activities; they do not include any other forms of risk that cause serious, long-term ill-health (ibid.).

A second major limitation concerns the tendency to treat attitudes as though they exist within a vacuum. Although such studies can provide us with a guide to levels of perception they are unable to reveal much about the ways in which meanings are socially and culturally mediated (Douglas & Wildavsky 1982, MacGill 1987).

A third problem is that many of the early samples are unrepresentative consisting of, for example, non-randomly selected college students in Oregon, USA (Cutter 1993). It is questionable as to how far one can generalize beyond these particular groupings, which are skewed by social class, educational background, ethnicity, gender and age.

Fourth, Gamson & Modigliani's (1989) review of survey data on attitudes to nuclear power suggests that there is considerable ambivalence among the public that these studies tend to gloss over.

Texts and readers

New forms of audience and textual analysis are developing which suggest that the audience are not passive but interpret media texts in different ways, depending upon a variety of contextual factors such as class, gender and socialization (Moores 1990). These new approaches are based upon very different assumptions to those underlying traditional effects research. Rather than assuming that the meanings of the text are given, and that audiences passively respond, such studies suggest that there is a complex circuit of communication between readers and texts.

The audience constitutes a central problematic within media and cultural studies. This interest ranges from studies of popular culture and pleasure (for example, Ang 1985, Fiske 1990, Radway 1987); through taking the popular press seriously (for example, Dahlgren & Sparks 1992); to ethnographic reception studies (for example, Morley 1980). There has been a recent shift in cultural geography and cultural studies towards a growing interest in qualitative methods that allow the researcher to focus upon the processes through which audiences actively make sense of media texts (for example, Lindlof & Meyer 1987). Audience ethnography has become increasingly popular since the late 1970s, but is used by different researchers to mean different things (Turner 1992). In its strict sense, an ethnographic study requires the researcher to become involved in a community over a relatively long period of time. According to Burgess & Harrison (1993: 201) an ethnographic study should:

> . . . combine observational and participatory activities with the production of an analysis of oral–visual and written texts, everyday speech and communications to elucidate the bases of local knowledge and experience within a given locality. Further, ethnographic research requires a focus on the practical actions taken by members of the culture over time.

190

Though ethnography is often associated with qualitative methods, ethnographers do employ quantitative techniques, such as statistical sampling methods, as well (Lindlof 1995). Ethnographic studies often involve the use of in-depth or semi-structured interviews, and small-group discussions (for example, Morley 1980, 1986, Silverstone 1985). The main advantage of group interviews is that they are able to explore in detail the social context in which meanings are negotiated in everyday life (Lindlof 1995). In a famous essay entitled "Thick description: towards an interpretive theory of culture", the social anthropologist Clifford Geertz (1973) suggests that a good ethnography is an account that accurately represents social actors' actual meanings, as opposed to potential meanings, at a particular point in time. In the context of studying the media, "thick description" involves in-depth analysis of the ways in which social actors make sense of texts, rather than simply taking them as read.

The differing ways in which an individual may interpret media texts is influenced by what the French social theorist, Bourdieu (1984), refers to as "cultural capital" and "habitus". Cultural capital can be defined as the amount of cultural power possessed by an individual or social group in terms of knowledge, skills and other cultural acquisitions. The *habitus* is a set of "dispositions" that influence individuals to act or react in particular ways. According to Murdock (1989: 93), we may think of the *habitus* as providing "basic conceptual categories and action frames through which individuals think about and respond to the social world". These action frames and ways of thinking are acquired during early socialization and are developed later during education. It is an unconscious process that reflects social conditions. Thus, individuals from a working-class background are likely to acquire dispositions that are significantly different from those from a middle-class background. These inequalities are then, it is claimed, reproduced over time. However, as Murdock (1989) argues, Bourdieu tends to overemphasize the role of social class in stratifying cultural consumption and plays down the influence of gender, ethnicity and age.

Early works on the television audience by David Morley, such as *The "Nationwide" audience* (1980), have come to be regarded as seminal within cultural studies. Morley's early empirical work examined how audiences differentially decode media messages. He concluded that differential readings of a television documentary could not be explained simply in terms of socio-economic factors alone; some

191

individuals within the same broad social-class location responded differently. Though this work suffers from some important limitations, it supports Stuart Hall's contention that members of the audience do not passively decode media texts (see Moores 1990, 1995). More recently, in *Family television* (1986), Morley has turned his focus of attention to the ways in which domestic social processes and relationships inform the viewing context.

Since Morley's influential study, a number of researchers have conducted small-scale studies of audiences in "natural" settings. Silverstone (1994) makes a particularly persuasive case for naturalizing the study of the audience. In particular, he extends the view of the audience as embedded within a number of complex, overlapping, subgroups and subcultures. These structures frame audience experiences in the context of everyday life, and their relationship with macroeconomic and political structures.

For Silverstone, the audience is "passive" and at the same time "active". Or to put it rather differently, the audience is far more heterogeneous than the effects tradition would have us believe. In any case, as Silverstone points out, the notion of an "active" audience is tautological as each member of the audience is, by definition, active in some respects. People often watch television, listen to the radio or read newspapers in a relatively inattentive way while they are engaged in other activities. Yet during this process they may pick up different pieces of information in a casual way. Thus, for Silverstone, "The key issue is not so much whether an audience is active but whether that activity is significant" (1994: 153). I shall return to this issue later in this chapter. But first, I want to discuss the notion that the consumption of media texts forms part of a "circuit of communication".

Circuit of communication

In a seminal piece of work Johnson (1986) maps out the various processes involved in the cultural transformation of meaning through a model of the "circuit of communication"(see Figure 6.3).

Johnson's approach is influenced by the Birmingham University Centre for Contemporary Cultural Studies (CCCS) and extends Stuart Hall's ground-breaking work on the encoding and decoding of meanings in televisual texts. Johnson's diagram represents the production

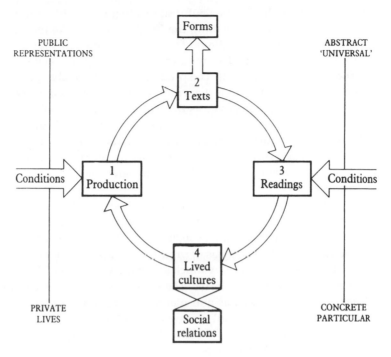

Figure 6.3 Johnson's "Circuit of communication". *Source*: Johnson 1986: 284.

and consumption of cultural objects in terms of a circuit, or an interlocking chain. Each box is used to illustrate a specific stage in the circuit that is dependent upon all the other phases. In short, Johnson argues that transformation of meaning occurs at every moment in the circuit. If we take a television documentary as an example, the first stage refers to the productive processes involved in creating a documentary that are influenced by various internal and external constraints; stage two refers to the documentary itself, which transforms the production processes into a symbolic public representation through images and words; stage three refers to the consumption of the documentary by audiences who bring their different backgrounds and life experiences to it; and finally, stage four involves the integration of these meanings into individuals' private lives. The cycle begins again with people's daily lives providing the raw material for new media products.

If we focus upon the finished cultural product we are blind to the processes that go towards making the finished article. We may, for example, make particular readings of the television documentary that the producer did not intend – I refer to these as "oppositional readings" (Lowe & Morrison 1984). The producer cannot possibly predict all the different interpretations that could be made of the same documentary. Johnson's circuit suggests that cultural and material conditions (what Johnson refers to as "social relations and lived culture") exert a powerful influence upon the ways in which "texts" are read. This includes major social divisions based upon class, gender, ethnicity and age, as well as the power relationship between the "producer" and "reader".

One particular advantage of Johnson's schema is that it directs attention to the complex relationship between structural factors (material conditions) and individual subjectivity (values, beliefs, action). As he points out textual analysis or production-based studies cannot, taken by themselves, tell us very much about the ways in which audiences make sense of cultural forms. The media act as a sort of anchor between local/private arenas and macro structural forces (such as global transnational capitalism) (Burgess et al. 1991).

Stuart Hall (1980) identifies three main political codes that are at work in the interpretation of texts:

1. the dominant code – this is where people accept the "preferred reading" or intended message of the text;
2. the oppositional code – this is where people challenge the "preferred reading";
3. the negotiated code – this is where people recognize the ideological nature of the code but prefer to accept it, letting it go unchallenged.

Figure 6.4 Cartoon on nuclear accidents. *Source*: Larry Wright, *Detroit News*, 8 April 1979 – from Gamson & Modigliani 1989: 28.

To summarize, Hall's basic argument is that individual media texts are open to differential readings; or to put it differently they are "polysemic". It is far too simplistic to suppose that the audience can be viewed as a homogeneous mass who passively accept the dominant ideology. Fiske (1992: 298) observes:

> The television text can only be popular if it is open enough to admit a range of negotiated readings through which various social groups can find meaningful articulations of their own relationships to the dominant ideology. Any television text must, then, be polysemic to a certain extent, for the structured heterogenity of the audience requires a corresponding structured heterogeneity of meanings in the text.

Yet the notion that texts are openly polysemous contains within it a number of difficulties. Media texts are prestructured with an implicit or explicit "preferred meaning", and powerholders in society do their best to ensure that texts are encoded in particular ways. For example, primary definers may frame an environmental story around confrontation and violence, diverting attention away from a consideration of the real issues at stake. Typically, concentration is focused upon the actions of a small minority of extremists, while the arguments of the peaceful majority are ignored. The story thus becomes more about law and order and threats to the dominant culture than about the issues themselves. The fact that particular media forms (such as TV news bulletins) are highly structured, repetitious, and contain "silences" over particular themes, also works towards producing a text that is to some extent closed (Cottle 1993).

Competing discourses about nuclear power

One study that demonstrates how different audiences make sense of media texts in different ways is Corner et al.'s (1990) analysis of the influence of current affairs reporting on nuclear issues.

Corner et al. conducted an in-depth analysis of three very different British documentaries about nuclear energy, taking the framework of David Morley's "Nationwide" audience study as a starting point. The three texts were: a Brass Tacks documentary entitled "Taming the dragon", broadcast by the BBC in 1987; a promotional film produced by the Central Electricity Generating Board called "Energy: the nuclear option", distributed in 1987; and an independent film, "From our own correspondent", produced by Northern Newsreel, and distributed to trade union and Labour Party organizations around the UK. In order to supplement detailed textual analysis of the texts, the authors explored audience responses through 16 discussion groups. The sample represented a broad spectrum of political allegiances and affiliations with community organizations (including workers at a nuclear plant, unemployed people, members of Friends of the Earth, students and a women's group). Each group consisted of five members on average.

In their analysis of viewers' reactions, Corner, Richardson and Fenton identify five major frames that act as interpretative tools:

1. civic frame – main criteria based on balance and fairness.
2. political frame – assessing claims through a political funnel.
3. evidential frame – primary concern with evidence and argument.
4. environmental frame – claims judged according to environmental funnel.
5. personal frame – claims judged against personal experience.

Considerable divergences were found to underlie audience responses. Different groups tended to give higher priority to different explanatory frameworks and were influenced by their own "agendas". For example, the unemployed group displayed a much greater degree of suspicion towards government and state institutions than did members of a broadly middle-class community organization, the Rotary Club. Thus, the unemployed group tended to privilege a "political frame" through a sceptical reading of official perspectives, while the Rotary Club adopted an "evidential frame" through making frequent use of their own professional knowledge to interpret claims.

However, there were some similarities across the different groups. In particular, the civic frame, with its emphasis upon fairness and balance, strongly featured in many responses even where individuals had their own clear allegiances.

Local knowledge

A number of studies of the media representation of social issues suggest that the local community is an important mediating factor in the relationship between audiences and the news media. For example,

Hartmann & Husband's (1974) seminal study into children's knowledge of ethnic minorities concluded:

> . . . the media did not appear to have any direct influence upon attitudes as such. It would appear that the media serve to define for people what the dimensions of situations are. How they feel about the situation, thus defined, would seem to depend on other factors, particularly on where they live. (Ibid.: 111)

An interesting UK study conducted by Burgess & Harrison (1993) traced the development of a debate surrounding a proposal, headed by Music Corporation of America (MCA), to build a theme park in an area of special scientific interest (SSI) in Rainham, Essex (see also Burgess 1992). They combined a comprehensive content analysis of media texts with interviews with media practitioners and news sources, a household survey, and two in-depth focus groups. The focus groups, each composed of ten men and women, met six times during 1991. The first group consisted of "lay" local residents who were largely supportive of the MCA proposal. The second group was also made up of local residents, but they were all fully fledged members of environmental/conservationist organizations.

Burgess & Harrison found that audience members drew strongly upon their own local knowledge to interpret claims. On the whole, members of the "lay" group questioned the claim that the construction of the theme park would lead to species loss. They used their own personal experience/store of knowledge to contest the claims made by conservationists and scientists. Burgess & Harrison were particularly interested to explore local peoples' reactions to a London Weekend Television (LWT) documentary about the Rainham Marshes site. The documentary included library footage of bird species that could be found on the site. However, viewers were given no clues to suggest that this was not actual footage from the marshes; it was cleverly edited to form the background to various interview slots. The lay group gradually recognized what the film-makers had done:

> Vicky: Naw, they weren't there when they filmed 'em. If they were there for a whole week, they wouldn't have seen that many birds. (agreement)

> Tom: It was deception really. Because you're turning round to the public and saying "this is what you're going to lose", you know?

Vicky: Yeah "All these millions of birds. We've only been here a couple of hours and look what we've seen" . . . . But I suppose that's television full stop. You watch it and most of it is a load of rubbish. I mean, you see what they want you to see.

Tom: They can tell you whatever they want.
(Burgess & Harrison 1993: 217)

Burgess & Harrison found that in local culture people tended to view the marshes as a "dump" populated mainly by rats and mice; they did not associate it with "nature". Moreover, the media representations of the marshes reinforced the idea that the conservationists were from outside and did not really know the area. The local newspaper marginalized the conservationists by presenting them as outsiders and cranks. Burgess & Harrison (1993: 218) conclude: "it is practical life lived locally which determines the sense that people make of media texts".

The studies conducted by Corner et al. (1990) and Burgess & Harrison (1993) illustrate how social groups often draw upon their own agendas in making sense of environmental issues. These agendas are influenced by such factors as: political allegiance, employment status, professional competences and group networks, and pre-existing attitudes or cultural dispositions. Also the study by Corner et al. (1990) suggests different interpretive communities vary in how they respond to the *affective* dimension of televisual narratives. For example, while some welcome the use of emotional overtones to encourage viewer involvement, others see this as dangerous and prefer to weigh up a case based on rational argument.

An interesting US study by Gamson (1992) suggests that the sorts of resources which individuals draw upon in making sense of environmental news tend to be issue-specific. Gamson investigated how closely small group discussions among working-class people converged with prominent themes in media discourse. The study focused upon four main issues: the Israeli–Arab conflict, nuclear power, affirmative action and problems in American industry. The study suggests that for some issues people tend to draw heavily upon their own personal experience and associations in the decoding of media texts. Gamson argues that individuals utilize three main strategies to varying degrees depending upon the issue and their dependency upon the media as a source of information:

- personal strategies – draw heavily upon personal experience and tend to be much less likely to be affected by media representations.
- cultural strategies – rely heavily upon media frames for making sense of an issue and attitudes are relatively volatile.
- integrated strategies – influenced by the relative prominence of themes in the media through a process of selective assimilation on the basis of personal experience and appeals to "common sense".

In the case of nuclear power, Gamson found that people tended to adopt cultural strategies.The findings suggest that working-class people tend to draw heavily upon media discourse with regard to this topic and make relatively little reference to their own experience.

A major strength of this research lies in its sensitivity to the structures of meaning and processes of negotiation governing everyday life. However, while such studies provide interesting insights into the ways in which individuals interpret media texts, they do have their limitations. In particular they suffer from three key drawbacks; they are carried out under artificial circumstances, they cannot be replicated under identical conditions, and members of discussion groups may influence each other's reactions. Also if we take the respondents' comments at face value the benefits of this technique are negated (Corner & Richardson 1993).

Environmental education and cultural values

For the final part of this chapter I want to return to a question I raised at the beginning: what stimulates mass public concern over particular environmental issues? And why do we more easily recall, or develop a greater understanding of, some environmental stories rather than others? Both the "Save our seals" campaign and Live Aid were what we might term media "events". The issues became associated with the issue sponsors; in these cases, rock stars and show business personalities. They both had a strong human interest angle and were presented in ways that appealed to popular sentiment.

In my view the degree to which an issue resonates with widely held cultural values helps explain its prominence or lack of prominence in the public sphere. Processes of mass communication contain a strong element of ritual that encourages individuals to draw upon a shared reality in a form of sacred ceremony that affirms collective identity (Carey 1989, Sparks 1995). As we saw in Chapter 4, much of the reporting of risk and the environment in the Western media is framed around beliefs about scientific and technological domination over nature. Some issues connect particularly well with deeply embedded cultural imagery (Hansen 1991, Patterson 1989, Wilkins 1989). For example, the fears associated with all things nuclear, or with food poisoning that are presented in terms of "deep threat". Similarly, news stories featuring wild animals, such as foxes, may invoke commonly held myths about their predatory activities. Finally, many environmental news items resonate with the popular myth that contrasts a bleak urban landscape with an idyllic chocolate-box image of rural bliss. Such imagery plays upon nostalgia for a bygone age where peoples' ways of life are closer to nature. While images must in some senses be familiar, they must also contain an element of distinctiveness, and be dramatized in a symbolic way, if they are to make a major impact (Hannigan 1995).

Also, where television documentaries are concerned, the degree to which individual members of the audience are encouraged to feel they can make a difference is important. A producer of documentaries at the BBC Natural History Unit claimed:

The medium is definitely guilty of encouraging a sort of feeling amongst some people that the only good environment story was a bad environmental story. I think that you've got to offer people some kind of hope especially if you want them to be proactive and involved. . . . So we like to make some effort to say you can do this or there is some light at the end of the tunnel. But I think that feeling of hopelessness is a big problem. . . . I mean our position is we're not campaigners for the environmental movement, we're programme makers and we're journalists and we steer a middle course. (Interview, 23 July 1993)

As I suggested earlier in the chapter, there are significant information gaps between and across cultures. In some less developed countries, such as India, significant numbers of the population are illiterate. Individuals have different cultural repertoires that are available to them in making sense of environmental items. The audience can only be "active" with what they are given. As we have seen, news about risk and the environment is highly managed through direct censorship and the more subtle forms of self-censorship. The degree of prior knowledge and cultural capital that individuals possess is of great importance. Different audiences have varying competences and needs. In my view, there are dangers with taking the notion of the "active" audience too far. As Silverstone (1994) suggests, we must ask, how significant is this activity? Audience engagements with the news media are shaped by various economic, social and political determinants. Environmental stories may be trivialized, if dealt with in the familiar format of "soft" lightweight news, and fail to stimulate critical engagement with the issues. Also, there is a danger that people may become desensitized to environmental issues if they are subjected to overkill. Moreover, periodic media attention to social issues may falsely give the appearance that the issues are being resolved.

Summary

In this chapter I have argued that media practitioners, particularly broadcasters, tend to have a limited knowledge of the audience. Also, traditional attitude theory is inadequate for an understanding of how individuals make sense of risk and interpret media texts. Frequently theorists have attempted to demonstrate linear relationships between public opinion and media coverage of environmental issues, without paying due recognition to the complexity of public attitude formation.

Empirical research within the cultural studies tradition suggests that recall and comprehension of environmental news is significantly affected by levels of prior knowledge. This varies, though, depending upon the category of news story in question. Dramatic, highly visual catastrophic stories tend to prompt relatively high levels of recall but people tend to exaggerate the content of what is remembered. Also, the causes and effects of environmental problems are frequently mis-associated.

I have also suggested that individual responses to representations of the environment in news and current affairs are differentiated according to factors such as social class, gender, ethnicity, age and levels of prior knowledge. People make sense of media texts through drawing upon their own local knowledge, everyday experiences and cultural values. Moreover, people tend to assess actively news media claims through negotiation with others. Where individuals possess little direct experience or knowledge of a given issue or problem there is a greater likelihood that they will be influenced by the media. Also, the more an issue resonates with dominant cultural values that individuals identify with, the more likely it will make a significant impact. However, I have concluded that there are dangers with taking the notion of the "active" audience too far. A number of social, political and economic factors combine to limit the amount of information with which individuals can be "active". Moreover, the tendency to treat environmental items as "soft news" may discourage a critical engagement with the issues. Finally, periodic saturated reporting of environmental stories may result in audience de-sensitization, and foster a belief that the problems are being resolved.

Suggested further reading

J. Lull, *Media, communication, culture* (Cambridge: Polity, 1995), chs 4 and 5, S. Moores, *Interpreting audiences* (London: Sage, 1995) and D. Morley, *Television audiences and cultural studies* (London: Routledge, 1992) provide excellent general reviews of approaches to the audience from a cultural studies perspective. A discussion of the circuit of communication can be found in R. Johnson, "The story so far: and further transformations?", in *Introduction to contemporary cultural studies*, D. Punter (ed.), 277–313 (London: Longman, 1986). And more recently, R. Silverstone, *Television and everyday life* (London: Routledge, 1994) re-evaluates the concept of the "active" viewer.

A. Bell, *The language of news media* (Oxford: Blackwell, 1991) contains a useful discussion of comprehending, forgetting or misconceiving news about environmental issues. J. Corner, K. Richardson, N. Fenton, *Nuclear reactions: form and response in public issue television* (London: Libbey, 1990) explores some of the complexities of programme formats and audience responses.

Conclusion

Over the last decade the issue of the environment has provoked intense public concern and political debate in many Western countries. This book has moved beyond traditional disciplinary boundaries through offering a synthesis of recent debates in cultural theory and media studies with key developments in human geography. I have interweaved those studies that focus on the "environment" with those that seek to address the production, transmission and negotiation of news discourse, and argued that we need to move beyond a narrowly sociological perspective and engage more closely with human geography. My approach is influenced by an interest in culture, space and place, and temporality. I have argued that the media are not monolithic; rather they form a complexly differentiated system governed by particular organizational and societal constraints.

Throughout this book I have suggested that the study of the news media needs to be situated within a complex web of culture, politics and society. Framings of risk and the environment are influenced by social, political and cultural factors, but I have concluded that extreme versions of social constructionism suffer from a number of misconceptions. In Chapter 2 we saw how many critiques of the ideal of objectivity in news reporting are flawed. Although we must scrutinize critically any truth claims in relation to hierarchies of definitional power, this does not make the concept of "objectivity" completely redundant.

This book has considered the production and consumption of environmental meanings in the news media within the context of a social problems perspective. Such an approach, I have suggested, enables us to consider issues in parallel. As we saw in Chapter 1, the environment competes for attention with a range of other issues concerning,

203

for example, deviance, race and gender. Also, different ideologies compete for ascendancy within the broad category of the "environment". Thus I have centred the "environment" as a contested discursive terrain and underscored source–communicator relations.

As we have seen, both Martell (1994) and Benton (1994) claim that many accounts of environmentalism are too strongly social constructionist because they gloss over objective conditions. In response Hannigan (1995) argues that they have misrepresented social constructionism by concentrating upon extreme versions of this approach (for example, Kitsuse & Spector 1981). He claims,

> Unfortunately, these criticisms paint a rather extreme and absolute portrait of the social constructionist perspective. While it is true that some strict constructionists probably go too far in focusing exclusively on the interpretations and practices of participants in social problems construction, contextual constructionists such as Best and Rafter actively encourage the use of empirical data in the evaluation of claims where this is deemed appropriate. (Hannigan 1995: 188)

However, I would go further than this; strict social constructionists undoubtedly go too far in claiming that one cannot empirically verify statements about social problems. All we end up with is a series of contending views that are perceived as equally valid and none of which can be refuted. From this point of view, the assertion in the *Daily Star* that children could catch the AIDS virus from swimming in the sea (discussed in Ch. 5) cannot be refuted. From this perspective, it is as valid as any other claim. Also, the estimated scale of a problem is crucial yet the strict constructionist treats this as unimportant (Goode & Ben-Yehuda 1994). As I argued in Chapter 5, when claims-makers make exaggerated claims about the size and scope of a problem they run the risk of potentially damaging their cause. Consider, for example, the Brent Spar case where Greenpeace was forced to retract an estimate of the amount of oil contained on the platform. How is the researcher to assess the validity of different claims if objective indicators are taken to be unimportant? Although it is acknowledged that there are great problems in assessing evidence about catastrophic threats, such as global warming, and that this makes it much more difficult to judge whether a claim is exaggerated or not, this should not lead us to the conclusion that we cannot form any judgements about objective indicators. In some cases it may not be possible to calculate future threats but in many other instances we are able to form a view about the objective nature of a "problem". From an extreme social constructionist perspective we are unable to conclude whether or not a claim is exaggerated, and the notion of "mass panic" becomes meaningless. On occasions, health stories with an environmental component stimulate mass concern (for example, the recent UK panics over salmonella-in-eggs or BSE, or panics in the USA over Alar in apples). According to Fowler (1991: 148), such hysteria is characterized by highly emotive language: "Hysteria requires an expressive system, a mode of discourse, and, established, exists within that mode of discourse independent of empirical reality".

The strict constructionist approach is littered with contradictions. Why, Goode & Ben-Yehuda ask, do strict constructionists approve of making judgements about social construction claims, but not about their validity?

I accept that social constructionists vary in the degree to which they adopt a relativist position. However, the essential difficulty with social constructionism in general, which Hannigan never really addresses, is it tends to foster an artificial division between the "natural" and the "social". As Benton (1994: 30–31) observes:

> So long as the natural science ("nature")/social science ("society") division of labour *itself* remains unchallenged, it remains possible (and, indeed, comfortable) for social scientists to bracket off "nature" as something the natural scientists deal with while *they* get on with studying the "social" side of things. Subsequently "nature" comes to be understood only by way of its cultural representations in the social movements, environmental organizations, or policy debates which are the primary objects of sociological study. . . . The *interface* between human social practices and their material conditions and consequences is lost to view. [original emphasis]

A second major strand of my argument in this book concerns media, culture and the environmental movement. As I noted in the introduction, "culture" is a very difficult term to define. Culture includes norms, values, ritual, custom and language. Many commentators claim traditional culture has become weakened in modern times. Traditional family and religious ties, for example, are seen as typically exerting less of an influence upon the individual. Giddens and Beck talk about a move to detraditionalization as part of the modernization process. As we saw in Chapter 3, they claim that traditional institutions become increasingly undermined in this phase of modernity. It is not that tradition has altogether disappeared but it has become insecure, leading individuals to look for new ways in which to express their identity. This can be seen, for example, in the New Age movement and radical strands of environmentalism. Also, contemporary debates suggest that political culture is undergoing a profound transformation in many advanced industrial societies. According to Seidman (1994: 235), "Postmodern politics entails a shift away from a class-based, statist politics to a politics centred in diverse movements or groups that are engaged in myriad local, institutional and cultural struggles."

Trust in the "experts" is increasingly questioned as major social institutions undergo rapid change. Over recent decades some significant changes have taken place in cultural attitudes towards gender and racial inequalities, fostered by the women's and civil rights movements. During the 1980s the growth of environmentalism has given rise to a broad critique of modernization. Traditional social movement theory has been unable to explain adequately the growth of the new consciousness-raising networks of the 1980s. As we saw in Chapter 3 these are characterized by the absence of a fixed fee-paying membership, a formal hierarchical structure, or a distinct leadership. Also, in some senses they embrace a longing for the past and elements of old traditions are reasserted (for example, the land rights movement). Environmentalists face two particular dilemmas. One is that they are very much tied to science in terms of their credibility (see Yearley 1992). At the same time, environmentalists are often ambivalent towards scientific knowledge. The other major dilemma concerns their relationship with the news media. In some senses they are bound by their institutional structures, organizational routines and demands for pre-packaged newsworthy material. Yet at the same time they may have misgivings about the ways in which issues are framed.

As I argued in Chapter 3, since the late 1960s the development of mass communications accelerated the circulation of information in the global capitalist system across time and space. A number of commentators claim that contemporary environmental NGOs place increasingly importance upon media images based around the creation of "pseudo events" such as staged campaigns (for example, Milton 1993). Many see this as a feature of "postmodern" society with an increasing emphasis upon the "hyperreal". Undoubtedly, over recent decades many large environmental NGOs have become increasingly sophisticated in their public relations techniques and alliance with science (Anderson 1993a,b). However, as Hannigan (1995) observes, the reliance upon pseudo events is certainly not new. There are examples of pressure groups using these techniques since the early part of the century. And since the late 1960s environmental pressure groups such as Friends of the Earth have engaged in a whole host of actions from abseiling stunts to dressing up as aerosol cans to draw attention to the dangers of CFCs (see Greenberg 1985). Yet the symbolic content of such actions has acquired a new significance. Today's movements have themselves become identified with highly morally charged symbolic messages. As Melucci (1989: 12; original emphasis) maintains,

Contemporary movements operate as signs, in the sense that they translate their actions into symbolic challenges to the dominant codes . . . . In this respect, collective action is a *form* whose models of organization and solidarity deliver a message to the rest of society . . . . Contemporary social movements stimulate radical questions about the ends of personal and social life and, in so doing, they warn of the crucial problems facing complex societies.

One consequence of concentrating upon the symbolic nature of collective action, the formation of collective identities and the development of specialized strategies, is that it leads one to analyze the way in which the media feed into this process. As Hilgartner & Bosk (1988: 74–5) observe:

Specifically, when ecological concepts enter cultural domains, attention should be paid to the conscious manipulation of symbols – the ways in which key operatives select some social problems, formulate them in special ways, and advance them to promote their interests and goals. At the same time, the ecological language calls attention to the resource constraints on operatives as they seek to influence the allocation of collective concern.

207

A political economy perspective primarily focuses upon the resource constraints that govern source–communicator relations. For example, Gandy, (1980, 1982) adopts such an approach in his analysis of the relationship between news sources and the news media. He suggests that non-official and official sources employ distinct strategies towards controlling and manipulating information and signs. Gandy views the relationship between sources and the media as primarily economic; sources exchange information on a cost-cutting basis. Official sources tend to have greater access to the media because they have greater "information subsidies" – it is less costly in terms of time and money for media practitioners to use them on a routine basis. Also, there is an incentive for sources to distance themselves from information by delivering it through scientific channels. This may reduce costs by targeting a government official through the news media.

Although social action cannot simply be reduced to cost–benefit analysis, economic factors clearly play a part in information exchange. As Gandy points out, information subsidies may be direct or indirect. Direct subsidies include placing advertisements in media that policymakers are known to monitor, or personally contacting decision-makers. Indirect subsidies could be off-the-record briefings, or press conferences or news releases where the identity of the source is made known but self-interest is concealed. Gandy (1982: 198) claims that there are two main stages in the provision of information subsidies to media practitioners:

> The use of journalists and media systems involves a two-stage subsidy. The journalist's costs of producing news are reduced through a variety of techniques utilized by sources to manage the information market. The second stage of the subsidy is complete when the target of the subsidy, an actor in the policy process, gains access to the information at a near zero cost, from a credible source, in a convenient accessible form.

One advantage of Gandy's approach is that it recognizes the importance of information strategies. Hall et al.'s (1978) theory of primary definers, discussed in previous chapters, implies that sources do not need strategies since they automatically gain access to the media. One factor that goes some way to explaining the degree to which news sources are successful in their media relations, is the extent to which communicators' and sources' goals become assimilated. Where the goals of media organizations and news sources converge, there is a greater likelihood that sources will succeed in achieving their aims. For example, during the late 1980s in the UK the interests of environmental groups such as Greenpeace converged with some popular newspapers' campaigns. Others have noted the tendency for politicians' and communicators' goals to become assimilated (Gans 1980). As we saw in Chapter 5, with the *Daily Mail*'s "Save our seals" campaign the interests of Greenpeace and a number of backbench Conservative MPs coincided for a short while in the common pursuit of demonstrating the inadequacies of the government's approach to the environment.

However, despite competing against economically powerful official sources, voluntary organizations can sometimes mount successful media campaigns – often through becoming more officially sourced. Once such groups become institutionalized they are more likely to be cited by official sources and brought into the media frame. A carefully targeted strategy aimed at mobilizing an issue to draw attention to wider concerns can be very successful in the realm of symbolic politics, despite relatively small information subsidies.

A related point concerns the importance of a source's internal structure and the degree to which it has developed a clear message, identified a target audience and medium, and prepared the way so that it can have maximum impact (Schlesinger 1990, Wilson 1984). While the effectiveness of a public relations strategy often reflects the size of a group's budget, there is no simple correlation between financial base and successful strategic action. As we saw in Chapter 4, non-official sources may often gain qualitatively greater access to regional news media. However, there are dangers with overemphasizing the role of the media. As I argued in Chapter 3, some grassroots networks eschew the mainstream media and many lobby groups prefer to work behind-the-scenes. Also, there are an array of non-media influences on the policy-making sphere (Cracknell 1993b). Environmental pressure groups are typically involved in targeting a number of different arenas and there is a very real potential for conflict to develop over strategy, and the degree to which resources are ploughed into any given area. The sheer amount of media coverage enjoyed by a pressure group cannot necessarily be taken as an indicator of success. In the long run perhaps the real test is the extent to which it has exerted influence upon the political system and has resulted in real change.

So while the news media play a crucial role in the politics of the environment, I have suggested that they form part of an intricate web of influences. Moreover, there is no linear, clear-cut relationship between public attitudes and media agendas. On occasions, news media may exert a significant influence upon consumer behaviour (as in the case of food scares), but generally evidence suggests that there is often a weak relationship between "attitudes" and behaviour. As I argued in Chapter 6, studies indicate that levels of prior knowledge and direct experience tend significantly to influence audience responses. Also, the extent to which an issue resonates with widely held cultural values helps explain why some issues become more easily defined as "social problems" than others. In order for news sources to obtain their goals a favourable cultural climate must usually exist. News media representations of risk and the environment are often highly symbolic and are grounded upon familiar dualisms. There are many constraints that limit the amount of information the audience can be "active" with. Thus I have concluded that, despite the polysemic nature of media texts, there are problems with taking the notion of the "active" audience too far.

This book has sought to examine the rise of environmentalism over recent decades, and has focused upon the relationship between environmental pressure groups and the news media. I could, of course, have concentrated upon other claims-makers such as politicians or scientists, or analyzed the trajectory of social problem claims-making in other public arenas. However, my concern has been to focus in depth upon what many commentators see as a key site of contestation in a "postmodern" world. Social movements have to some extent shifted their attention from traditional social divisions based upon class, gender or race to the broader realm of cultural politics (Melucci 1989). Moreover, global systems of mass communication have transformed the way in which politics is conducted. The mass media provide a key vehicle for the circulation of meanings and signs to global audiences across time and space (Lash & Urry 1994, Soja 1989).

However, although some very significant changes have occurred, in my view it is difficult to sustain the argument there has been a paradigm shift in the social and cultural spheres. By adopting an historical approach we can see that the emphasis upon symbolic politics is not entirely new. In any given period culture is actively transformed through collective action. Such developments can be viewed as an intensification of characteristics already associated with modernity rather than a new postmodernity (see Lash & Friedman 1992). Interestingly, environmentalists often appear to express hostility towards modernity. As Touraine (1995) observes, they increasingly emphasize the relationship between nature and transformative human action. Those individuals who perceive themselves to be marginalized from mainstream culture often develop their own oppositional beliefs and practices. There is a danger of taking the claims of environmental organizations at face value concerning their unique approach.

In my view the rise of contemporary environmentalism cannot be adequately explained by traditional social movement theory. The consciousness-raising networks of the 1980s stress the role of the individual and expressivism, and their concern with the politics of lifestyle represents a move away from identity centred on the state. Yet the environmental movement possesses some of the characteristics of both "old" and "new" social movements. The cross-over in support for various causes has undoubtedly enabled wider political movements to develop. However, my analysis leads me to conclude that, although there is a potential for convergence of interests, they do not form the basis for a new global solidarity.

This book has raised a number of issues that deserve further investigation. Although studies have undoubtedly shown that the state dominates institutional reportage, it is nevertheless highly relevant to analyze the role of non-official sources in constructing political agendas. Why is it that certain non-official sources enter the institutional arena and others remain on the periphery of debate? What factors explain their success or failure in mounting a public relations campaign? And what role do non-official sources play in the complex negotiation of the political agenda? Answers to these sorts of questions can best be achieved through a combination of textual analysis, observation and interviews with news sources themselves, rather than simply deducing media strategies from a reading of media discourse. This book has suggested that there are important variations between and within the media, thus it is necessary to determine the ways in which news sources (institutional and non-official) target particular media. In order to enable non-official sources to become more heavily accessed we need to have a fuller understanding of these processes. By largely concentrating upon the ways in which the news media make use of sources, the sociology of journalism has ignored a key aspect of the news production process.

211

References

Alderman, G. 1984. *Pressure groups and government in Great Britain*. London: Longman.

Allan, S. 1995a. News, truth and postmodernity: unravelling the will to facticity. In *Theorizing culture: an interdisciplinary critique after postmodernism*, B. Adam & S. Allan (eds), 129–44. London: UCL Press.

Allan, S. 1995b. "No truth, no apocalypse": investigating the language of nuclear war. In *Studies in Communications: the discourse of war and peace*, vol. 5, T. McCormack (ed.), 171–214. Greenwich, Connecticut: JAI Press.

Allen, C. T. & J. D. Weber 1983. How presidential media use affects individuals' beliefs about conservation. *Journalism Quarterly* **60**, 98–104.

Altheide, D. 1985. *Media power*. Beverley Hills: Sage.

Althusser, L. 1965. *For Marx*. London: New Left Books.

Althusser, L. 1971. *Lenin and philosophy and other essays*. London: Verso.

Anderson, A. 1991. Source strategies and the communication of environmental affairs. *Media, Culture and Society* **13**(4), 459–76.

Anderson, A. 1993a. The production of environmental news: a study of source–media relations. PhD thesis, University of Greenwich.

Anderson, A. 1993b. Source–media relations: the production of the environmental agenda. See Hansen (1993), 51–68.

Anderson, A. & I. Gaber 1993. The yellowing of the greens. *British Journalism Review* **4**(2), 49–53.

Ang, I. 1985. *Watching "Dallas": soap opera and the melodramatic imagination*. London: Methuen.

Anthony, R. 1982. Polls, pollution and politics – trends in public opinion on the environment. *Environment* **24**(4), 14–34.

Atwater, T., M. B. Salwen, R. B. Anderson 1985. Media agenda-setting with environmental issues. *Journalism Quarterly* **62**, 393–7.

Beck, U. 1992. *Risk society: towards a new modernity*. London: Sage.

Beck, U. 1995. *Ecological politics in an age of risk*. Cambridge: Polity.

Beck, U., A. Giddens, S. Lash 1994. *Reflexive modernization: politics, tradition and aesthetics in the modern social order*. Cambridge: Polity.

Bell, A. 1991. *The language of news media*. Oxford: Blackwell.

Bell, A. 1994. Climate of opinion: public and media discourse on the global environment. *Discourse and Society* **5** (1), 33–64.

213

Benton, T. 1994. Biology and social theory in the environmental debate. In *Social theory and the global environment*, M. Redclift & T. Benton (eds), 28–50. London: Routledge.

Benton, M. & P. J. Frazier 1976. The agenda-setting function of the mass media at three levels of information holding. *Communication Research* 3, 261–74.

Berger, P. 1987. *The capitalist revolution*. Aldershot: Wildwood House.

Berking, H. 1996. Solitary individualism: the moral impact of cultural modernization in late modernity. In *Risk, environment and modernity: towards a new ecology*, S. Lash, B. Szerszynski, B. Wynne (eds) 189–202. London: Sage.

Berry, J. M. 1993. Citizen groups and the changing nature of interest group politics in America. In *Citizens, protest and democracy*, R. Dalton (ed.). Annals of the American Academy of Political and Social Science 528(July), 30–41.

Best, J. 1989. Afterword: extending the constructionist perspective – a conclusion and an introduction. In *Images of issues: typifying contemporary social problems*, J. Best (ed.), 243–53. New York: Aldine de Gruyter.

Billig, M. 1991. *Ideology and opinions: studies in rhetorical psychology*. London: Sage.

Blaikie, N. 1993. *Approaches to social enquiry*. Cambridge: Polity.

Boggs, C. 1993. The new world order and social movements. *Society and Nature* (5), 91–128.

Bourdieu, P. 1984. *Distinction: a social critique of the judgement of taste*. London: Routledge & Kegan Paul.

Brosius, H. B. & H. M. Kepplinger 1990. The agenda-setting function of television news. *Communication research* 17(2), 183–211.

Brundtland report 1987. *Our common future*. Oxford: Oxford University Press.

Burgess, J. 1985. News from nowhere: the press, the riots and the inner city. In *Geography, the media and popular culture*, J. Burgess & J. Gold (eds), 192–228. London: Croom Helm.

Burgess, J. 1990a. The production and consumption of environmental meanings in the mass media: a research agenda for the 1990s. *Transactions of the Institute of British Geographers* 15, 139–61.

Burgess, J. 1990b. Making sense of environmental issues and landscape representations in the media. *Landscape Research* 15(3), 7–11.

Burgess, J. 1992. The cultural politics of economic development and nature conservation. In *Inventing places: studies in cultural geography*, K. Anderson & F. Gales (eds), 235–51. Melbourne: Longman.

Burgess, J. & J. R. Gold (eds) 1985. *Geography, the media and popular culture*. London: Croom Helm.

Burgess, J. & C. Harrison 1993. The circulation of claims in the cultural politics of environmental change. See Hansen (1993), 198–221.

Burgess, J., C. Harrison, P. Maiteny 1991. Contested meanings: the consumption of news about nature conservation. *Media, Culture and Society* 13(4), 499–519.

Carey, J. W. 1989. *Communication as culture: essays on media and society*. Boston: Unwin-Hyman.

Carson, R. 1962. *Silent spring*. Boston: Houghton Mifflin.

Cloke, P., C. Philo, D. Sadler 1991. *Approaching human geography: an introduction to contemporary theoretical debates*. London: Paul Chapman.

Cohen, S. 1972. *Folk devils and moral panics: the creation of mods and rockers*. London: MacGibbon & Kee.

Colomer, J. M. (ed.) 1996. *Political institutions in Europe*. London: Routledge.

Corner, J. 1986. Codes and cultural analysis. See Collins et al. (1986), 49–62.

Corner, J. & K. Richardson 1993. Environmental communication and the contingency of meaning: a research note. See Hansen (1993), 222–33.

Corner, J., K. Richardson, N. Fenton 1990. *Nuclear reactions: form and response in public issue television*. London: Libbey.

Cotgrove, S. & A. Duff 1980. Environmentalism, middle-class radicalism and politics. *Sociological Review* 28, 333–51.

Cottle, S. 1993a. Sociological perspectives on the news – a critical review. In *New introductory reader in sociology*, M. O'Donnell (ed.), 478–92. Walton-on-Thames: Thomas Nelson.

Cottle, S. 1993b. Mediating the environment: the modalities of TV news. See Hansen (1993), 107–33.

Cracknell, J. 1993. Issue arenas, pressure groups and environmental agendas. See Hansen (1993), 3–21.

Cumberbatch, G. & D. Howitt 1989. *A measure of uncertainty: the effects of the mass media*. London: John Libbey.

Curran, J. & M. Gurevitch (eds) 1996. *Mass media and society*. London: Edward Arnold.

Curran, J., M. Gurevitch, J. Woolacott (eds) 1977. *Mass communication and society*. London: Edward Arnold.

Curran, J., M. Gurevitch, J. Woolacott 1982. The study of the media: theoretical approaches. See Gurevitch et al. (1982), 30–55.

Curran, J. & J. Seaton 1991. *Power without responsibility*. London: Routledge.

Cutter, S. L. 1993. *Living with risk*. London: Edward Arnold.

Dahlgren, P. & C. Sparks (eds) 1992. *Journalism and popular culture*. London: Sage.

Dake, K. 1992. Myths of nature: culture and the social construction of risk. *Journal of Social Issues* 48(4), 21–37.

Davies, M. 1985. *The politics of pressure: the art of lobbying*. London: BBC.

Dawkins, L. A. 1987. The politics of energy conservation and industrial interests in Britain. *Parliamentary Affairs* 40(2), 250–64.

Dickens, P. 1992. *Society and nature: towards a green social theory*. London: Harvester Wheatsheaf.

Dines, G. & J. M. Humez (eds) 1995. *Gender, race and class in media: a text-reader*. London: Sage.

Dobson, A. 1995. *Green political thought*. London: Routledge.

Dominick, J. R. & G. Rauch 1971. The image of women in network TV commercials. *Journal of Broadcasting* 16, 259–65.

Douglas, M. 1975. *Implicit meanings: essays in anthropology*. London: Routledge & Kegan Paul.

Douglas, M. 1985. *Risk acceptability according to the social sciences*. London: Routledge & Kegan Paul.

Douglas, M. 1992. *Risk and blame: essays in cultural theory*. London: Routledge.

Douglas, M. & A. Wildavsky 1982. *Risk and culture: an essay on the selection of technical and environmental dangers*. Berkeley: University of California Press.

Downs, A. 1972. Up and down with ecology – the "issue attention cycle". *Public Interest* **28**, 38–50.

Downs, A. 1973. The political economy of improving our environment. In *Environmental decay: economic causes and remedies*, J. S. Bain (ed.), 59–81. Boston: Little Brown.

Dunwoody, S. 1986. The scientist as source. In *Scientists and journalists: reporting science as news*, S. Friedman, S. Dunwoody, C. Rogers (eds), 3–16. New York: Free Press.

Dunwoody, S. & R. J. Griffin 1993. Journalistic strategies for reporting long-term environmental issues: a case study of three superfund sites. See Hansen (1993), 22–50.

Dunwoody, S. & P. Hans Peters 1992. Mass media coverage of technological and environmental risks: a survey of research in the United States and Germany. *Public Understanding of Science* (1), 199–230.

Durant, J. 1996. Jury out in the cold on science. *Times Higher Education Supplement* **19** (January), 16.

The Ecologist 1972. *Blueprint for survival*. Harmondsworth: Penguin.

Eder, K. 1993. *The new politics of class: social movements and cultural dynamics in advanced societies*. London: Sage.

Eder, K. 1995. Rationality in environmental discourse: a cultural approach. In *Green politics three*, W. Rudig (ed.), 9–37. Edinburgh: Edinburgh University Press.

Eder, K. 1996. The institutionalization of environmentalism: ecological discourse and the second transformation of the public sphere. In *Risk, environment and modernity: towards a new ecology*, S. Lash, B. Szerszynski, B. Wynne (eds), 203–23. London: Sage.

Edwards, R. 1988. Spirit of outrage. *New Statesman & Society*, 29 July, 16–18.

Einsiedel, E. & E. Coughlan 1993. The Canadian press and the environment: reconstructing a social reality. See Hansen (1993), 134–49.

Ekins, P. 1992. *A new world order: grassroots movements for social change*. London: Routledge.

Eldridge, J. 1993. News, truth and power. In *Getting the message: news, truth and power*, J. Eldridge (ed.), 3–33. London: Routledge.

Ericson, R. V., P. M. Baranek, J. B. Chan (eds) 1987. *Visualising deviance: a study of news organization*. Milton Keynes, England: Open University Press.

Ericson, R. V., P. M. Baranek, J. B. Chan (eds) 1989. *Negotiating control: a study of news sources*. Milton Keynes, England: Open University Press.

Ericson, R. V., P. M. Baranek, J. B. Chan (eds) 1991. *Representing order: crime, law and justice and the news media*. Milton Keynes, England: Open University Press.

Eyal, C. H. 1981. The role of newspapers and television in agenda-setting. In *Mass communications review year book*, G. C. Wilhoit & H. de Bock (eds), vol. II, 225–33. London: Sage.

Eyerman, R. & A. Jamison 1991. *Social movements: a cognitive approach*. Cambridge: Polity.

Fejes, F. 1984. Critical mass communications research and media effects: the case of the disappearing audience. *Media, Culture and Society* **6**, 219–32.

Fishman, M. 1980. *Manufacturing the news*. Austin, Texas: University of Texas Press.

Fiske, J. 1990. *Introduction to communication studies*. London: Routledge.

Fiske, J. 1992. British cultural studies and television. In *Channels of discourse, reassembled*, R. C. Allen (ed.), 284–326. London: Routledge.

Fowler, R. 1991. *Language in the news: discourse and ideology in the press*. London: Routledge.

Friedman, S. 1991. Two decades of the environmental beat. In *Media and the environment*, C. LaMay & E. Dennis (eds), 17–28. Washington, DC: Island Press.

Friedman, S. M., S. Dunwoody, C. Rogers (eds) 1986. *Scientists and journalists: reporting science as news*. New York: Free Press.

Friedman, S. M., C. M. Gorney, B. P. Egolf 1987a. Reporting on radiation: a content analysis of Chernobyl coverage. *Journal of Communication* 37, 58–79.

Friedman, S. M., J. Post, M. Vogel, W. F. Evans 1987b. Environmental reporting: the role of local newspapers. *Environment* 29(2), 4–45.

Funkhouser, G. R. 1973. The issues of the sixties: an exploratory study in the dynamics of public opinion. *Public Opinion Quarterly* 37(1), 62–75.

Gale, R. P. 1987. Calculating risk: radiation and Chernobyl. *Journal of Communication* 37, 68–73.

Galtung, J. & M. Ruge 1965. The structure of foreign news. *Journal of Peace Research* 1, 64–90.

Galtung, J. & M. Ruge 1973. Structuring and selecting news. In *The manufacture of news*, S. Cohen & J. Young (eds), 62–72. London: Constable.

Gamson, W. 1988. The 1987 distinguished lecture: a constructionist approach to mass media and public opinion. *Symbolic Interaction* 11(2), 161–74.

Gamson, W. 1990. *The strategy of social protest*. Belmont, Calif.: Wadsworth.

Gamson, W. 1992. *Talking politics*. Cambridge: Cambridge University Press.

Gamson, W. A. & A. Modigliani 1989. Media discourse and public opinion on nuclear power: a constructionist approach. *American Journal of Sociology* 95(1), 1–37.

Gamson, W. & G. Wolfsfeld 1993. Movements and media as interacting systems. In *Citizens, protest and democracy*, R. Dalton (ed.). Annals of the American Academy of Political and Social Science 528(July), 114–25.

Gandy, O. H. 1980. Information in health: subsidized news? *Media, Culture and Society* 2(2), 103–15.

Gandy, O. H. 1982. *Beyond agenda-setting: information subsidies and public policy*. Norwood, NJ: Ablex.

Gans, H. J. 1980. *Deciding what's news: a study of CBS evening news, NBC nightly news, Newsweek and Time*. London: Constable.

Garnham, N. 1986. Contribution to a political economy of mass communications. See Collins et al. (1986), 9–32.

Geertz, C. 1973. *The interpretation of cultures: selected essays*. New York: Basic Books.

Gerbner, G. 1990. Advancing on the path of righteousness, maybe. In *Cultivation analysis: new directions in research*, N. Signorielli & M. Morgan (eds), 249–62. Beverly Hills, Calif.: Sage.

Giddens, A. 1990. *The consequences of modernity*. Cambridge: Polity.

Giddens, A. 1991. *Modernity and self-identity in the late modern age*. Cambridge: Cambridge University Press.

Gitlin, T. 1980. *The whole world is watching: mass media in the making and unmaking of the new left*. Berkeley: University of California Press.

Glasgow University Media Group 1976. *Bad news*. London: Routledge & Kegan Paul.

Glasgow University Media Group 1980. *More bad news*. London: Routledge & Kegan Paul.

Glasgow University Media Group 1982. *Really bad news*. London: Writers and Readers.

Glasser, T. L. 1988. Objectivity precludes responsibility. In *Impact of mass media: current issues*, R. E. Heibert & C. Reuss (eds), 44–51. White Plains, New York: Longman.

Goldenberg, E. N. 1975. *Making the papers: the access of resource-poor groups to the metropolitan press*. London: DC Heath.

Golding, P. & S. Middleton 1982. *Images of welfare: press and public attitudes to poverty*. Oxford: Robertson.

Gooch, G. D. 1996. Environmental concern and the Swedish press: a case study of the effects of newspaper reporting, personal experience and social interaction on the public's perception of environmental risks. *European Journal of Communication* 11(1), 107–27.

Goode, E. & N. Ben-Yehuda 1994. *Moral panics: the social construction of deviance*. Cambridge, Mass.: Blackwell.

Gormley, W. T. 1975. Newspaper agendas and political elites. *Journalism Quarterly* 52, 304–8.

Gottlieb, R. 1991. An odd assortment of allies: American environmentalism in the 1990s. In *Media and the environment*, C. LaMay & E. Dennis (eds), 43–54. Washington: Island Press.

Gray, A. & J. McGuigan 1993. *Studying culture: an introductory reader*. London: Edward Arnold.

Greenberg, D. W. 1985. Staging media events to achieve legitimacy: a case study of Britain's Friends of the Earth. *Political Communication and Persuasion* 2, 347–62.

Greenberg, M. R., D. B. Sachsman, P. M. Sandman, K. L. Salome 1989a. Network evening news coverage of environmental risk. *Risk Analysis* 9(1), 119–26.

Greenberg, M. R, D. B. Sachsman, P. M. Sandman, K. L. Salome 1989b. Risk, drama and geography in the coverage of environmental risk by network TV. *Journalism Quarterly* 66(2), 267–76.

Gregory, D. 1994. *Geographical imaginations*. Oxford: Blackwell.

Gregory, D., R. Martin, G. Smith (eds) 1994. *Human geography: society, space and social science*. London: Macmillan.

Gross, L. 1984. The cultivation of intolerance: television, blacks and gays. In *Cultural indicators: an international symposium*, G. Melischek, K. E. Rosengren, J. Stappers (eds), 345–63. Vienna: Austrian Academy of Sciences.

Grove-White, R. 1993. Environmentalism: a new moral discourse? In *Environmentalism: the view from anthropology*, K. Milton (ed.), 18–30. London: Routledge.

Gunter, B. 1986. *Television and sex-role stereotyping*. London: John Libbey.

Gunter, B. 1987. *Poor reception: misunderstanding and forgetting broadcast news*.

Hillsdale, NJ: Lawrence Erlbaum.

Gunter, B. & M. Wober 1983. Television viewing and perceptions of hazards to life. *Journal of Environmental Psychology* **3**, 325–35.

Gurevitch, M., T. Bennett, J. Curran, J. Woollacott (eds) 1982. *Culture, society and the media*. London: Methuen.

Habermas, J. 1976. *Legitimation crisis*. London: Heinemann.

Hall, A., R. J. Law, D. E. Wells, J. Harwood, H. M. Ross, S. Kennedy, C. R. Allchin, L. A. Campbell, P. P. Pomeroy 1992. Organochlorine levels in common seals (*Phoca vitulina*) which were victims and survivors of the 1988 phocine distemper epizootic. *The Science of the Total Environment* **115**, 145–62.

Hall, A., P. Pomeroy, J. Harwood 1992. The descriptive epizootiology of phocine distemper in the UK during 1988/89. *The Science of the Total Environment* **115**, 31–44.

Hall, J. R. & M. J. Neitz 1993. *Culture: sociological perspectives*. Englewood Cliffs, NJ: Prentice-Hall.

Hall, S. 1977. Culture, the media and the "ideological effect". In *Mass communication and society*, J. Curran, M. Gurevitch, J. Woolacott (eds), 315–48. London: Edward Arnold.

Hall, S. 1980. Encoding/decoding. In *Culture, media, language*, S. Hall, D. Hobson, A. Lowe, P. Willis (eds), 128–38. Centre for Contemporary Cultural Studies, University of Birmingham: Hutchinson.

Hall, S., C. Critcher, T. Jefferson, J. Clarke, B. Roberts 1978. *Policing the crisis: mugging, the state, and law and order*. London: Macmillan.

Halloran, J. D., P. Elliott, G. Murdock 1970. *Demonstration and communication: a case study*. Harmondsworth: Penguin.

Hammersley, M. 1990. *Reading ethnographic research*. Essex: Longman.

Hannigan, J. A. 1995. *Environmental sociology: a social constructionist perspective*. London: Routledge.

Hansen, A. 1990a. Socio-political values underlying media coverage of the environment. *Media Development* **37**, 3–6.

Hansen, A. 1990b. *The news construction of the environment: a comparison of British and Danish television news*. Leicester: Centre for Mass Communications Research, University of Leicester.

Hansen, A. 1991. The media and the social construction of the environment. *Media, Culture and Society* **13**(4), 443–58.

Hansen, A. (ed.) 1993. *The mass media and environmental issues*. Leicester: Leicester University Press.

Harrison, M. 1985. *Television news: whose bias?* Hermitage: Policy Journals.

Hartmann, P. & C. Husband 1974. *Racism and mass media*. London: Davis Poynter.

Harvey, D. 1989. *The condition of postmodernity: an enquiry into the origins of cultural change*. Oxford: Blackwell.

Heath, A., R. Jowell, J. Curtice 1985. *How Britain votes*. London: Pergamon.

Hegedus, Z. 1990. Social movements and social change in self creative society: new civil initiatives in the international arena. In *Globalization, knowledge and society*, M. Albrow & E. King (eds), 263–80. London: Sage.

Herberlein, T. A. 1981. Environmental attitudes. *Zeitschrift fur Unweltpolitik* **4**, 241–70.

Hershey, M. 1993. Citizens' groups and political parties in the United States. In *Citizens, protest and democracy*, R. Dalton (ed.). Annals of the American Academy of Political and Social Science **528** (July), 142–55.

Hilgartner, S. & C. L. Bosk 1988. The rise and fall of social problems: a public arenas model. *American Journal of Sociology* **94**(1), 53–78.

HMSO 1994. *Social trends*. London: HMSO.

Hoggart, R. 1957. *The uses of literacy: aspects of working-class life, with special reference to publications and entertainment*. London: Chatto & Windus.

Hollis, P. (ed.) 1974. *Pressure from without in early Victorian Britain*. London: Edward Arnold.

Holsti, O. R. 1969. *Content analysis for the social sciences and humanities*. Reading, Mass.: Addison-Wesley.

Howitt, D. 1982. *Mass media and social problems*. Oxford: Pergamon.

Inglehart, R. 1977. *The silent revolution: changing values and political styles among Western publics*. Princeton, NJ: Princeton University Press.

Inglehart, R. 1990. *Culture shift in advanced industrial society*. Princeton, NJ: Princeton University Press.

Jamison, A. 1996. The shaping of the global environmental agenda: The role of non-governmental organizations. In *Risk, environment and modernity*, S. Lash, B. Szerszynski, B. Wynne (eds), 224–45. London: Sage.

Jamison, A., R. Eyerman, J. Cramer, J. Lassoe 1990. *The making of the new environmental consciousness: a comparative study of the environmental movements in Sweden, Denmark and the Netherlands*. Edinburgh: Edinburgh University Press.

Johnson, R. 1986. The story so far: and further transformations? In *Introduction to contemporary cultural studies*, D. Punter (ed.), 277–313. London: Longman.

Johnston, H. & B. Klandermans (eds) (1995) *Social movements and culture*. London: UCL Press.

Jones, R. E. & R. E. Dunlap 1992. The social bases of environmental concern: have they changed over time? *Rural Sociology* **57**(1), 28–47.

Katz, E. & P. F. Lazarsfeld 1955. *Personal influence: the part played by people in the flow of mass communication*, Glencoe, Il.: Free Press.

Keeter, S. 1984. Problematic pollution polls: validity in the measurement of public opinion on environmental issues. *Political Methodology* **10**, 267–91.

Kempton, W. 1991. Lay perspectives on global climate change. *Global Environmental Change: Human and Policy Dimensions* **1**, (3), 183–208.

Kessel, H. 1985. Changes in environmental awareness: a comparative study of the FRG, England and the USA. *Land Use Policy* **2**, 103–13.

Kielbowicz, R. B. & C. Scherer 1986. The role of the press in the dynamics of social movements. In *Research in social movements, conflicts and change*, G. Lang & K. Lang (eds), 71–96. Greenwich, Conn.: JAI Press.

Killingsworth, M. J. & J . S. Palmer 1992. *Ecospeak: rhetoric and environmental politics in America*. Carbondale and Edwardsville: Southern Illinois University Press.

Kitsuse, J. I. & M. Spector 1981. The labelling of social problems. In *The study of social problems: five perspectives*, E. Rubington & M. S. Weinberg (eds) 201–8. New York: Oxford University Press.

Krimsky, S. & D. Golding (eds.) 1992. *Social theories of risk*. Westport, Conn.: Praeger.

Krimsky, S. & A. Plough 1988. *Environmental hazards: communicating risk as a social process*. Dover, Mass.: Auburn House.

Kunrether, H. C. & E. V. Ley (eds) 1982. *The risk analysis controversy: an institutional perspective*. Berlin: Springer-Verlag.

Lacey, C. & D. Longman 1993. The press and public access to the environment and development debate. *The Sociological Review* 41(2) 207–43.

LaMay, C. L. 1991. Heat and light: the advocacy–objectivity debate. In *Media and the environment*, C. LaMay & E. Dennis (eds), 103–13. Washington DC: Island Press.

LaMay, C. & E. Dennis (eds) 1991. *Media and the environment*. Washington DC: Island Press.

Lang, G. E. & K. Lang 1981. Watergate: an exploration of the agenda-building process. In *Mass Communication Review Year Book*, G. C. Wilhoit & H. de Bock (eds), vol. II, 447–68. London: Sage.

Lash, S. & J. Friedman (eds) 1992. *Modernity and identity*. Oxford: Blackwell.

Lash, S., B. Szerszynski, B. Wynne (eds) 1996. *Risk, environment and modernity*. London: Sage.

Lash, S. & J. Urry 1994. *Economies of signs and space*. London: Sage.

Lavigne, D. 1989. Dead seals and quick sand. BBC *Wildlife*, July, 438–9.

Lichtenberg, J. 1993. In defense of objectivity. In *Mass media and society*, J. Curran & M. Gurevitch (eds), 216–31. London: Edward Arnold.

Lindlof, T. R. 1995. *Qualitative communication research methods*. London: Sage.

Lindlof, T. R. & T. P Meyer 1987. Mediated communication as ways of seeing, acting and constructing culture: the tools and foundations of qualitative research. In *Natural audiences: qualitative research of media uses and effects*, T. R. Lindlof (ed.), 1–30. Norwood, NJ: Ablex.

Livingstone, S. 1990. *Making sense of television: the psychology of interpretation*. Oxford: Pergamon.

Lowe, P. & A. Flynn 1989. Environmental politics and policy in the 1980s. In *The political geography of contemporary Britain*, J. Mohan (ed.), 255–79. London: Macmillan.

Lowe, P. & J. Goyder 1983. *Environmental groups in politics*. London: Allen & Unwin.

Lowe, P. & D. Morrison 1984. Bad or good news: environmental politics and the mass media. *Sociological Review* 32, 75–90.

Lowe, P. D. & W. Rudig 1986. Review article: political ecology and the social sciences, the state of the art. *British Journal of Political Science* 16, 513 50.

Lowenthal, D. 1990. Awareness of human impacts: changing attitudes and emphases. In *The earth as transformed by human action*, B. L. Turner, W. C. Clark, R. W. Kates, J. F. Richards, J. T. Mathews, W. B. Meyer (eds), 121–35. New York: Cambridge University Press.

Lull, J. 1995. *Media, communication, culture: a global approach*. Cambridge: Polity.

McCarthy, M. 1986. *Campaigning for the poor: CPAG and the politics of welfare*. Kent: Croom Helm.

McCarthy, J. D. & M. N. Zald 1982. Resource mobilization and social movements: a partial theory. *American Journal of Sociology* 1, 212–41.

McClure, R. D. & T. E. Patterson 1976. Setting the political agenda: print versus network news. *Journal of Communication* 26(2), 23–8.

McCombs, M. E. 1977. Newspaper versus television: mass communication effects across time. In *The emergence of American political issues: the agenda-setting function of the press*, D. L. Shaw & M. E. McCombs (eds), 89–105. St Paul, Minn.: West.

McCombs, M. E. & D. L. Shaw 1972. The agenda-setting function of the mass media. *Public Opinion Quarterly* 36, 176–87.

McCormick, J. 1989. *The global environmental movement: reclaiming paradise*. London: Belhaven.

McCormick, J. 1991. *British politics and the environment*. London: Earthscan.

MacGill, S. M. 1987. *The politics of anxiety: Sellafield's cancer-link controversy*. London: Pion.

Macnaghton, P. & J. Urry 1995. Towards a sociology of nature. *Sociology* 29(2), 203–20.

McQuail, D. 1969. Uncertainty about the audience and the organization of mass communications. *The Sociological Review Monograph* 13, 75–84.

McQuail, D. 1991. *Mass communication theory: an introduction*. London: Sage.

McQuail, D. 1992. *Media performance and the public interest*. London: Sage.

McQuail, D. & S. Windahl 1993. *Communications models for the study of mass communications*. Essex: Longman.

Martell, L. 1994. *Ecology and society: an introduction*. Cambridge: Polity.

Maslow, A. H. 1954. *Motivation and personality*. New York: Harper & Row.

Massey, D. 1993. A global sense of place. In *Studying culture: an introductory reader*, A. Gray & J. McGuigan (eds), 232–40. London: Edward Arnold.

Meadows, D. H., D. L. Meadows, R. Randers, W. W. Behrens 1972. *The limits to growth*. New York: New American Library.

Melucci, A. 1989. *Nomads of the present: social movements and individual needs in contemporary society*. London: Century Hutchinson.

Merten, K., H. P. Peters, K. Klosse 1990. Risk information on the Chernobyl disaster in the West German mass media. Paper presented at the XIIth World Congress of Sociology, Madrid, 9–13 July.

Miller, D. 1993. Official sources and "primary definition": the case of Northern Ireland. *Media, Culture and Society* 15, 385–406.

Milton, K. (ed.) 1993. *Environmentalism: the view from anthropology*. London: Routledge.

Mitchell, R. C., A. G. Mertig, R. E. Dunlap 1992. Twenty years of environmental mobilization: trends among national environmental organizations. In *American environmentalism: the US environmental movement, 1970–1990*, R. E. Dunlap & A. G. Mertig (eds), 11–26. Washington, DC: Taylor & Francis.

Molotch, H. & M. Lester 1974. News as purposive behavior: on the strategic use of routine events, accidents and scandals. *American Sociological Review* 39, 101–12.

Molotch, H. & M. Lester 1975. Accidental news: the great oil spill as local occurrence and national event. *American Journal of Sociology* 81, 235–60.

Moores, S. 1990. Texts, readers and contexts of reading: developments in the study of media audiences. *Media, Culture and Society* 12(1), 9–29.

Moores, S. 1995. *Interpreting audiences: the ethnography of media consumption.* London: Sage.

Moran, M. 1989. *Politics and society in Britain: an introduction.* London: Macmillan.

Morgan, M. 1982. Television and adolescents' sex role stereotypes: a longitudinal study. *Journal of Personality and Social Psychology* 43, 947–55.

Morley, D. 1980. *The "Nationwide" audience: structure and decoding.* London: British Film Institute.

Morley, D. 1983. Cultural transformations: the politics of resistance. In *Language, image, media.* H. Davis & P. Walton (eds), 104–17. London: Blackwell.

Morley, D. 1986. *Family television: cultural power and domestic leisure.* London: Comedia.

Morley, D. 1992. *Television, audiences and cultural studies.* London: Routledge.

Mormont, M. & C. Dasnoy 1995. Source strategies and the mediatization of climate change. *Media, Culture and Society* 17(1), 49–64.

Morrison, D. & H. Tumber 1988. *Journalists at war: the dynamics of news reporting during the Falklands Conflict.* London: Sage.

Murdock, G. 1982. Large corporations and control of the communications industries. See Gurevitch et al. (1986), 118–50.

Murdock, G. 1989. Class stratification and cultural consumption: some motifs in the work of Pierre Bourdieu. In *Freedom and constraint: the paradoxes of leisure,* F. Coalter (ed.), 90–101. London: Routledge.

Murdock, G. & P. Golding 1974. For a political economy of mass communications. In *The Socialist Register 1973,* R. Miliband & J. Saville (eds), 205–34. London: Merlin.

Murdock, G. & P. Golding 1977. Capitalism, communication and class relations. In *Mass communication and society,* J. Curran, M. Gurevitch, J. Woolacott (eds), 12–43. London: Edward Arnold.

Nas, M. & P. Dekker 1995. Environmental attitudes and collective action in Europe. Paper presented to the Second European Sociological Conference, Budapest, August.

Negrine, R. 1989. *Politics and the mass media in Britain.* London: Routledge.

Newby, H. 1991 One world, two cultures: sociology and the environment, BSA Bulletin *Network* 50(May), 1–8.

Newcomb, H. 1991. The creation of television drama. In *A handbook of qualitative methodologies for mass communication research,* K. B. Jensen & N. W. Janowski (eds), 93–107. London: Routledge.

Nicholson, M. 1987. *The new environmental age.* Cambridge: Cambridge University Press.

Noelle-Neumann, E. 1974. The spiral of silence: a theory of public opinion. *Journal of Communication* 24, 43–51.

Noelle-Neumann, E. 1991. The theory of public opinion: the concept of the spiral of silence. In *Communication Yearbook 14,* J. Anderson (ed.), 256–87. Newbury Park, Calif.: Sage.

Nohrstedt, S. A. 1991. The information crisis in Sweden after Chernobyl. *Media, Culture and Society* 13 (4), 477–97.

Nohrstedt, S. A. 1993. Communicative action in the risk-society: public relations strategies, the media and nuclear power. See Hansen (1993), 81–104.

Offe, C. 1987. Challenging the boundaries of institutional politics: social movements since the 1960s. In *Changing the boundaries of the political*, C. S. Maier (ed.), 63–105. Cambridge: Cambridge University Press.

Olien, C., P. Tichenor, G. Donohue 1989. Media coverage and social movements. In *Information campaigns: balancing social values and social change*, C. T. Salmon (ed.), 139–63. Newbury Park, Calif.: Sage.

Parlour, J. W. & S. Schatzow 1978. The mass media and public concern for environmental problems in Canada 1960–1972. *International Journal of Environmental Studies* 13, 9–17.

Patterson, P. 1989. Reporting Chernobyl: cutting the government fog to clear the nuclear cloud. In *Bad tidings: communication and catastrophe*, L. M. Walters, L. Wilkins, T. Walters (eds), 131–47. Hillsdale, NJ: Lawrence Erlbaum.

Pearce, F. 1996. Greenpeace mindbombing the media. *Wired* 2(5), 51–88.

Pepper, D. 1984. *The roots of modern environmentalism*. London: Croom Helm.

Peters, Hans Peter 1995. The interaction of journalists and scientific experts: co-operation and conflict between two professional cultures. *Media, Culture and Society* 17(1), 31–48.

Philo, G. 1987. Whose news? *Media, culture and society* 9(4), 397–406.

Philo, G. & R. Lamb 1990. Television and the Ethiopian famine. In *Deception, demonstration and debate: toward a critical environment and development education*, J. Abraham, C. Lacey, R. Williams (eds), 44–61. London: Kogan Page in association with WWF.

Pohoryles, R. 1987. What power the media? The influence of the media in public affairs: an Austrian case study. *Media, Culture and Society* 9, 209–36.

Porritt, J. & D. Winner 1988. *The coming of the greens*. London: Fontana.

Protess, D. L., F . L. Cook, T. R. Curtin, M. T. Gordon, D. R. Leff, M. E. McCombs, P. Miller 1987. The impact of investigative reporting on public opinion and policymaking: targeting toxic waste. *Public Opinion Quarterly* 51, 166–85.

Punter, D. (ed.) 1986. *Introduction to contemporary cultural studies*. Essex: Longman.

Radway, H. 1987. *Reading the romance: women, patriarchy and popular literature*. London: Verso.

Redclift, M. & T. Benton (eds) 1994. *Social theory and the global environment*. London: Routledge.

Rennie-Short, J. 1991. *Imagined country: society, culture and the environment*. London: Routledge.

Robinson, M. 1992. *The greening of British party politics*. Manchester: Manchester University Press.

Rothman, S. & S. R. Lichter 1987. Elite ideology and risk perception in nuclear energy policy. *American Political Science Review* 81, 383–404.

Rubin, D. M. 1987. How the news media reported on Three Mile Island and Chernobyl. *Journal of Communication* 37, 42–57.

Rubin, D. M. & D. P. Sachs 1973. *Mass media and the environment: water resources, land use and atomic energy in California*. New York: Praegar.

Rudig, W. 1995. Editorial. In *Green politics three*, W. Rudig (ed.), 1–8. Edinburgh: Edinburgh University Press.

Russell, C. 1986. The view from the national beat. In *Scientists and journalists: reporting science as news*, S. Friedman, S. Dunwoody, C. Rogers (eds), 61–94. New York: Free Press.

Ryan, C. 1991. *Prime-time activism: media strategies for grassroots organising*. Boston, Mass.: South End Press.

Sachs, W. (ed.) 1993. *Global ecology: a new arena of political conflict*. London: Zed Books.

Sachsman, D. B. 1976. Public relations influence on coverage of environment in the San Francisco area. *Journalism Quarterly* 53, 54–60.

Salome, K. L., M. R. Greenberg, P. M. Sandman, D. B. Sachsman 1990. A question of quality: how journalists and news sources evaluate coverage of environmental risk. *Journal of Communication* 40(4), 117–29.

Salwen, M. B. 1988. Effect of accumulation of coverage on issue salience in agenda-setting. *Journalism Quarterly* 65, 100–6.

Sandman, P. M. 1974. Mass environmental education: can the media do the job? In *Environmental education: strategies towards a more viable future*, J. A. Swan & W. B. Stopp (eds), 207–47. New York: Sage.

Sandman, P. M., D. B. Sachsman, M. R. Greenberg, M. Gochfeld, S. Dunwoody 1987. *Environmental risk and the press: an exploratory assessment*. New Brunswick, NJ: Transaction Books.

Schlesinger, P. 1987. *Putting "reality" together: BBC news*. London: Constable.

Schlesinger, P. 1990. Rethinking the sociology of journalism: source strategies and the limits of media centrism. In *Public communication: the new imperatives*, M. Ferguson (ed.), 61–83. London: Sage.

Schlesinger, P. & H. Tumber 1994. *Reporting crime: the media politics of criminal justice*. Oxford: Clarendon.

Schlesinger, P., H. Tumber, G. Murdock 1991. The media politics of crime and criminal justice. *British Journal of Sociology* 42(3), 397–418.

Schoenfeld, A. C. 1979. The press and NEPA: the case of the missing agenda. *Journalism Quarterly* 56, 577–85.

Schoenfeld, A. C., R. F. Meier, R. J. Griffin 1979. Constructing a social problem: the press and the environment. *Social Problems* 27(1), 38–61.

Schudson, M. 1978. *Discovering the news: a social history of American newspapers*. New York: Basic Books.

Schudson, M. 1996. The sociology of news production revisited. In *Mass media and society*, J. Curran & M. Gurevitch (eds), 141–59. London: Edward Arnold.

Schumacher, E. F. 1974. *Small is beautiful*. London: Abacus.

Segal, J. Z. 1991. The structure of advocacy: a study of environmental rhetoric. *Canadian Journal of Communication* 16, 409–15.

Seidman, S. 1994. Substantive debates: moral order and social crisis – perspectives on modern culture. In *Culture and society: contemporary debates*, J. Alexander & S. Seidman (eds), 217–35. Cambridge: Cambridge University Press.

Sekar, T. 1981. Role of newspapers in creating mass concern with environmental issues in India. *International Journal of Environmental Sciences* 17, 115–20.

Seyd, P. 1976. The CPAG. *Political Quarterly* 47, 189–202.

Seymour-Ure, C. 1974. *The political impact of the mass media*. London: Constable.

Seymour-Ure, C. 1991. *The press and broadcasting since 1945*. London: Basil Blackwell.

Shaiko, R. 1993. Greenpeace USA: something old, new, borrowed. In *Citizens, protest and democracy*, R. Dalton (ed.). Annals of the American Academy of Political and Social Science **528**, 88–100.

Shanahan, J. 1993. Television and the cultivation of environmental concern: 1988–92. See Hansen (1993), 181–221.

Shaw, D. L. & M. E. McCombs (eds) 1977. *The emergence of American political issues: the agenda-setting function of the press*. St Paul: West.

Sigal, L. V. 1973. *Reporters and officials: the organisation and politics of newsmaking*. Lexington, Mass: DC Heath.

Signorielli, N. & M. Morgan (eds) 1990. *Cultivation analysis: new directions in research*. Beverly Hills, Calif.: Sage.

Silverstone, R. 1985. *Framing science: the making of a BBC documentary*. London: British Film Institute.

Silverstone, R. 1994. *Television and everyday life*. London: Routledge.

Simmons, I. G. 1993. *Interpreting nature: cultural constructions of the environment*. London: Routledge.

Singer, E. & P. Endreny 1987. Reporting hazards: their benefits and costs. *Journal of Communication* **37**, 10–16.

Singh, R. P. N., V. K. Dubey, K. N. Pandey 1989. Mass media and environmental issues – a case of India. Paper presented to the Conference of the International Association for Mass Communications Research.

Sjoberg, L. (ed.) 1987. *Risk and society: studies of risk generation and reactions to risk*. London: Allen & Unwin.

Sklair, L. 1994. Global sociology and global environmental change. In *Social theory and the global environment*, M. Redclift & T. Benton (eds), 205–27. London: Routledge.

Sklair, L. 1995. Social movements and global capitalism. *Sociology* **29**(3), 495–512.

Slovic, P., B. Fischoff, S. Lichenstein 1976. Cognitive processes and societal risk taking. In *Cognition and social behaviour*, J. S. Carroll & J. W. Payne (eds), 165–84. Hillsdale, NJ: Lawrence Erlbaum.

Soja, E. 1989. *Postmodern geographies: the reassertion of space in critical social theory*. London: Verso.

Solesbury, W. 1976. The environmental agenda: an illustration of how situations may become political issues or issues may demand responses from government; or how they may not. *Public Administration* **54**, 379–97.

Sopher, K. 1995. *What is nature? Culture, politics and the non-human*. Oxford: Blackwell.

Sparks, J. 1987. Broadcasting and the conservation challenge. *Ecos* **8**(4), 2–6.

Sparks, R. 1995. *Television and the drama of crime: moral tales and the place of crime in public life*. Milton Keynes, England: Open University Press.

Spears, R., J. van Der Plight, R. Eiser 1987. Sources of evaluation of nuclear and renewable energy contained in the local press. *Journal of Environmental Psychology* **7**, 31–43.

Spector, M. & J. I. Kitsuse 1977. *Constructing social problems*. Menlo Park, Calif.: Cummings.

Spretnak, C. & F. Capra 1986. *Green politics: the global promise*. London: Paladin.

Spybey, T. 1996. *Globalization and world society*. Cambridge: Polity.

Steward, F. 1990. Green times. In *New times*. S. Hall & M. Jacques (eds), 67–75. London: Lawrence & Wishart.

Stringer, J. K. & J. J. Richardson 1980. Managing the political agenda: problem definition and policy making in Britain. *Parliamentary Affairs* **33**, 23–39.

Strodhoff, G. G., R. P. Hawkins, A. C. Schoenfeld 1985. Media roles in a social movement: a model of ideology diffusion. *Journal of Communication* **35**(2), 134–53.

Szerszynski, B. 1991. Environmentalism, the mass media and public opinion. Unpublished report, Centre for the Study of Environmental Change, Lancaster University.

Szerszynski, B. 1996. On knowing what to do: environmentalism and the modern problematic. In *Risk, environment and modernity: towards a new ecology*, S. Lash, B. Szerszynski, B. Wynne (eds), 104–38. London: Sage.

Thomas, R. H. 1983. *The politics of hunting*. Aldershot: Gower.

Thompson, P. & A. Hall 1993. Seals and epizootics – what factors might affect the severity of mass mortalities? *Mammal Review* **23**, 149–54.

Thompson, M. & A. Wildavsky 1982. A proposal to create a cultural theory of risk. In *The risk analysis controversy: an institutional perspective*, H. C. Kunrether & E. V. Ley (eds), 145–61. Berlin: Springer-Verlag.

Thornborrow, J. 1994. The woman, the man and the filofax: gender positions in advertising. In *Gendering the reader*, S. Mills (ed.), 128–51. London: Routledge.

Tichenor, P. J., G. A. Donohue, C. N. Olien 1970. Mass media flow and differential growth in knowledge. *Public Opinion Quarterly* **34**, 158–70.

Tilson, D. 1993. The shaping of "eco-nuclear" publicity: the use of visitor centres in public relations. *Media, Culture and Society* **15**, 419–35.

Touraine, A. 1978. *La voix et le regard*. Paris: Editions du Seuill.

Touraine, A. 1995. *Critique of modernity*. Oxford: Blackwell.

Tuchman, G. 1972. Objectivity as strategic ritual: an examination of newsmen's notions of ojectivity. *American Journal of Sociology* **77**, 660–70.

Tuchman, G. 1978. *Making the news: a study in the construction of reality*. New York: Free Press.

Tumber, H. 1982. *Television and the riots*. London: Broadcasting Research Unit.

Tunstall, J. 1971. *Journalists at work*. London: Constable.

Turner, G. 1992. *British cultural studies*. London: Routledge.

Urry, J. 1995. *Consuming places*. London: Routledge.

van Dijk, T. A. 1988. *News analysis: case studies of international and national news in the press*. Hillsdale, NJ: Lawrence Erlbaum.

van Dijk, T. A. 1991. Media contents: the interdisciplinary study of news as discourse. In *A handbook of qualitative methodologies for mass communication research*, K. Jenson & N. Janowski (eds), 108–20. London: Routledge.

Van Liere, K. D. & R. E. Dunlap 1980. The social bases of environmental concern: a review of hypotheses, explanations and empirical evidence. *Public Opinion Quarterly* **44**, 181–98.

Walker, R. (ed.) 1985. *Applied qualitative research*. Aldershot: Gower.

Wang, Z. 1989. The Chinese mass media: environment coverage (a case study). Paper presented to the Conference of the xvith International Association for Mass Communication Research , July.

Warren, S. 1995. *From margin to mainstream: British press coverage of environmental issues*. Sussex: Packard.

Westergaard, J. 1977. Power, class and the media. In *Mass communication and society*, J. Curran, M. Gurevitch, J. Woolacott (eds), 95–115. London: Edward Arnold.

Whiteley, P. & S. Winyard 1987. *Pressure for the poor: the poverty lobby and policy making*. London: Methuen.

Wilkins, L. 1987. *Shared vulnerability*. New York: Greenwood.

Wilkins, L. 1989. Conclusion: accidents will happen. In *Bad tidings: communication and catastrophe*, L. M. Walters, L. Wilkins, T. Walters (eds), 171–7. Hillsdale, NJ: Lawrence Erlbaum.

Wilkins, L. & P. Patterson 1987. Risk analysis and the construction of news. *Journal of Communication* 37, 80–92.

Wilkins, L. & P. Patterson (eds), 1991. *Risky business: communicating issues of science, risk and public policy*. Westport, Conn.: Greenwood Press.

Williams, M. & T. May 1996. *Introduction to the philosophy of social research*. London: UCL Press.

Williams, R. 1974. *Television, technology and cultural form*. London: Fontana.

Wilson, A. 1992. *The culture of nature: North American landscape from Disney to the Exxon Valdez*. Oxford: Blackwell.

Wilson, D. 1984. *Pressure: the a–z of campaigning in Britain*. London: Heinemann.

Wilson, D. & L. Andrews 1993. *Campaigning: the a–z of public advocacy*. London: Hawksmere.

Winch, P. 1990. *The idea of a social science and its relation to philosophy*. London: Routledge.

Wober, M. & B. Gunter 1985. Patterns of television viewing and of perceptions of hazards to life. *Journal of Environmental Psychology* 5, 99–108.

Wolfsfeld, G. 1984. The symbiosis of press and protest: an exchange analysis. *Journalism Quarterly* 61, 550–56.

Worcester, R. 1994. Societal values, behaviour and attitudes in relation to the human dimensions of global environmental change. Paper presented to the xvith International Political Studies Association World Congress, Berlin, August.

Wynne, B. 1982a. *Rationality and ritual: the Windscale inquiry and nuclear decisions in Britain*. Chalfont, St Giles: British Society for the History of Science.

Wynne, B. 1982b. Institutional mythologies and dual societies in the management of risk. In *The risk analysis controversy: an institutional perspective*, H. C. Kunrether & E. V. Ley (eds), 127–43. Berlin: Springer-Verlag.

Wynne, B. 1996. May the sheep safely graze? A reflexive view of the expert–lay knowledge divide. In *Risk, environment and modernity: towards a new ecology*, S. Lash, B. Szerszynski, B. Wynne (eds), 44–83. London: Sage.

Yearley, S. 1991. *The green case: a sociology of environmental issues, arguments and politics*. London: HarperCollins.

Yearley, S. 1992. Green ambivalence about science: legal-rational authority and the scientific legitimacy of a social movement. *British Journal of Sociology*

43(4), 511–32.

Yearley, S. 1994. Social movements and environmental change. In *Social theory and the global environment*, M. Redclift & T. Benton (eds), 150–68. London: Routledge.

Index

231